A STRONG DELUSION

Fallen Angels & Demons Revealed

TO MELITA
THERE IS MUCH MORE TO THIS WORLD
THAN WHAT MEETS THE EYE!
LORD BLESS!

MARK G. TOOP

A STRONG DELUSION
Copyright © 2018 by Mark G. Toop

The views and opinions expressed in this publication belong solely to the author, and do not reflect those of Word Alive Press or any of its employees.

All Bible Scriptures quoted from the Authorized King James Version.

All passages quoted from I Book of Enoch, Ethiopic Text, Richard Lawrence, published 1821.

All Hebrew and Greek word translations are quoted from the Strong's Exhaustive Concordance.

Printed in Canada

ISBN: 978-1-4866-1487-5

Word Alive Press
131 Cordite Road, Winnipeg, MB R3W 1S1
www.wordalivepress.ca

Cataloguing in Publication may be obtained through Library and Archives Canada

TABLE OF CONTENTS

SECTION THREE: Relevance in a Modern Society

ACKNOWLEDGEMENTS

This work, brought forth, is the culmination of 13,000 hours of study and research over a period of thirty years. This has been a journey of understanding of spiritual matters and discernment, primarily led by the Holy Spirit, mostly through the inspiration of the research of others led on the same journey of understanding by the Holy Spirit yet, at times, through the direct impartation of knowledge by the Holy Spirit. On this basis, I fully acknowledge the working of the Holy Spirit in my life. Without and apart from that, none of this would have come to fruition.

I fully acknowledge and declare Jesus Christ as Lord and Saviour over my life: "Jesus saith unto him, I am the way, the truth, and the life: no man cometh unto the Father, but by me" (John 14:6).

I fully acknowledge God Almighty as creator and sovereign above all things. Through His love and grace, He gave me the abilities and ignited the desire within me to diligently work towards developing this book. On this basis, I fully dedicate this book for His will, His purpose, and His plan for the knowledge of the truth to be fully realized for others to grasp in a lost and perishing world.

SPECIAL THANKS

Special thanks to my wife Jacquie and my daughter Lindsey, who have been blessings of support and stability in my life and who are a constant reminder of the purpose of this ministry.

Special thanks to Roger Oakland, Larry McLean, and the late Dr. Glen McLean, whose early video series *The Bible: The Key to Understanding* (1988) was a turning point in my life. I have come to realize there are no random 'chance' events—there is a reason for everything.

Special thanks to the late Grace Jacobson, who lovingly gave me my first copy of the Authorized King James Bible—the very same Bible I have quoted from and used to formulate this book. Grace was the daughter of the late Elwood McLean (a local pastor) who baptized me at Living Faith Pentecostal Church. Elwood was the brother of Dr. Glen McLean, who was a pioneer of Creation Science during the 1950s. Again, there is a reason for everything.

Special thanks to Gene Aven, whose diligent research into ancient cultures, comparative religions, and the Occult, in relation to the truth of God's Word, presented in his highly informative series *Oranges and Onions*, Volumes I, II, and III, was also a turning point in my life which brought me to a clear understanding of spiritual matters, clearly pointing out the only path to salvation is through Jesus Christ, alone.

Special thanks to Glen Dow, who graciously provided me with my first computer system and taught me MS Word and MS Windows in the early 1990s to get me started in the writing process. This has progressed to the formulation of (17) three-hour seminar presentations on various topics that are biblically based, all of which have been presented to live audiences.

Special thanks to Clement Tannouri, who sent me a copy of his personal photo of Mount Hermon all the way from Lebanon! This sparked the realization of the relationship between the ancient site of Mount Hermon and the Sun Pyramid at Teotihuacan, Mexico.

Special thanks to Nick Sperounes for his work on my personal photographs.

Special thanks to the staff of Lakeland College for their support and for use of the Main Lecture Theatre.

Special thanks to the management and staff of the local Coles Book Store (Chapters-Indigo) for their huge support of my published books.

Special thanks to the management and staff of the local Christian bookstore, Verses, for their huge support of my published books.

Special thanks to McKenzie Spies for her gracious support of proofing the original manuscript.

Special thanks to Ryan Bowd for his gracious support of proofing the original manuscript.

Special thanks to Reverend Tim Acey of Living Faith Pentecostal Church for his gracious support and review of the original manuscript regarding the overall content—and for his words of encouragement!

Special thanks for Colin and Crystal Campbell, Micah Newman, Ryan Bowd, and Garnet Powers for each of their support and prayers towards this ministry. For many others, near and far, who have also prayed for this ministry, God is in control and God has a plan. Thank you all!

The purpose of this book is to set out to truthfully reveal the facts, and by this, where the facts lead—that is where we need to go, to bring a greater and clearer understanding of the issues discussed herein.
—Mark G. Toop

2 Thessalonians 2:11–12

And for this cause God shall send them strong delusion,
that they should believe a lie:
That they all might be damned who believed not the truth,
but had pleasure in unrighteousness.

PREFACE

During the initial steps of becoming a believer in Christ, and for a period there-
after, I believed the generally accepted idea that the angels, who had rebelled with
Lucifer in the Kingdom of Heaven (Third Heaven) and were subsequently cast
out, not only became the fallen angels, but also became the demons here on earth.

Along with this generally accepted idea, two other concepts proclaimed as
truth were also commonly taught: (1) that fallen angels have no power, because
they are *all* currently bound in chains, usually citing Jude 1:7 and 2 Peter 2:4
and, (2) that angels are 'sexless' when it comes to procreation, usually citing Matthew 22:30 and Mark 12:25.

I had accepted these teachings, quite naively, as absolute truth. After extensive research and carefully considering the Word, and through much prayer and
leading of the Holy Spirit, I have discovered the teachings described above are,
at best, very simplistic explanations for a very complex subject—and really, are
in error. Through the Holy Spirit I have discovered (and continue to discover)
subtle yet profound revelations within the Scriptures as well as in other research
supported and confirmed in the Word. In addition, I'm becoming more and
more convinced that *some*, not all, explanations and definitions found in various
dictionaries and other research texts are also in error.

I am not presenting this foundational viewpoint out of arrogance or pride.
Instead, I am absolutely convinced this information is vitally important to the
body of Christ, to those who consider themselves to be disciples and prayer warriors. Like a military general engaged in warfare, one must be fully aware of the
positions of the enemy, the number of enemy soldiers deployed, their types of

weaponry, and the various tactics utilized in order to be *fully* successful in defeating the enemy.

We are told in God's Word that *"my people are destroyed for a lack of knowledge"* (Hosea 4:6). In considering this, it needs to be stated that knowledge in itself is not the complete or final answer. Our personal relationship and faith in Christ is paramount; however, God *does* place a high value on knowledge—especially Spiritual knowledge.

Satan is the great deceiver. I believe vital spiritual information has been generally overlooked due to a lack of spiritual maturity—outright discounted, selectively considered, or even purposely withheld as a result of deception from within the historical church leadership and authority. Satan does not like to be exposed. When the Light of truth is shown into the darkness, the darkness must scatter.

The time has come; the truth needs to come out. Time is precious. We are indeed living in the last days. Just like the angel had spoken to Daniel regarding his revelations within his vision:

Daniel 12:9–10
And he said, Go thy way, Daniel: for the words are closed up and sealed till the time of the end. Many shall be purified, and made white, and tried; but the wicked shall do wickedly: and none of the wicked shall understand; but the wise shall understand.

There will come a time where these sealed truths and revelations of God will be 'opened' in the last days. They were not meant for the understanding of past generations—they are pertinent to the end times. They are pertinent to us, now.

IMPORTANT
FOUNDATIONAL POINTS

2 Timothy 3:16–17

All scripture is given by inspiration of God, and is profitable for
doctrine, for reproof, for correction, for instruction in righteousness:
That the man of God may be perfect, throughly
furnished unto all good works.

1.

FOUNDATIONAL POINT ONE: THE SONS OF GOD

Jesus made this emphatic warning:

Matthew 24:37
But as the days of Noah were, so shall also the coming of the Son of man be.

Jesus went on to say that they were *"eating and drinking, marrying and given in marriage"* right up to the very day Noah entered the Ark (Matthew 24:38).

On one level, the people of Noah's time seemed to be carrying on with life as though things were normal. The truth is that life throughout this ancient society was anything but normal. Jesus states that, as the days of Noah were, this *abnormal* state of society will reoccur just before His return. Throughout this book we will examine this abnormal state of society. What most people today and, surprisingly, many people within various church circles fail to fully recognize is how bad it actually had to get for God to say "enough" and finally step in to destroy a possible 1.5 billion people *and* roughly 95 percent of all other life forms on the planet by way of a global flood.[1]

This is a very serious question—which makes this warning by Jesus, much more alarming and profound.

Essentially, God found it necessary to purge the world of *something*. It becomes absolutely imperative to fully understand what that something was—and as Jesus stated, what it *could* be once again repeating itself just before the Second Coming.

We can conclude with absolute certainly it was not sin in itself. Although sin did increase exponentially before the Great Flood from the fall in Eden, sin also carried on and continued to increase exponentially after the flood. It would be Jesus, God in the flesh (John 1:14), who would be sent to earth as a final sacrifice for all the sins of mankind, past, present, and future. The Great Flood did not purge the world of sin, nor did it correct the fallen nature of man. No, God found it necessary to purge the world of something else.

We know that the 'sons of God' came unto the daughters of men and took wives in Genesis 6:1–4:

> And it came to pass, when men began to multiply on the face of the earth, and daughters were born unto them, That the sons of God saw the daughters of men that they were fair; and they took them wives of all which they chose. And the LORD said, My spirit shall not always strive with man, for that he also is flesh: yet his days shall be an hundred and twenty years. There were giants in the earth in those days; and also after that, when the sons of God came in unto the daughters of men, and they bare children to them, the same became mighty men which were of old, men of renown.

The "sons of God" is absolutely a reference to the fallen angels. It cannot be a reference to the human line of Seth (as taught in some church circles). This foundational premise is addressed by the following points:

- ▸ The connotation of "sons of God" has radically changed from the Old Testament to the New Testament. In the New Testament it is a reference to the believers in Christ (John 1:12). In the Old Testament it is clearly a reference to angels, and more specifically fallen angels (Job 1:6).

- ▸ As cited in Job 1:6, there came a day when the "sons of God" presented themselves before God (in His throne room), and Satan (already banished as the fallen angel Lucifer) came also among them. Clearly, this is *not* the human line of Seth spoken about here, as we are told in God's Word that no man shall see the face of God and live (Exodus 33:20). Therefore, the "sons of God" are clearly the other fallen angels.

▶ We need to understand that, despite their banishment from the Kingdom of Heaven, Satan and the fallen angels can still present themselves in Third Heaven before God. This is echoed in Revelation 12:10, where Satan accuses the brethren before God, day and night. Another example of this is found in Zechariah 3:1.

▶ Revelation 12:8 also clearly states that, after the initial heavenly war, the fallen angels had lost this conflict—but also that their "place" was no longer found in Third Heaven. This refers to losing their *permanent* residence in Third Heaven—since obviously they can still present themselves before God in Third Heaven on occasion (on a temporary basis).

▶ Job 38:7 also describes that the "morning stars" *and* the "sons of God" were together when God laid the foundations of the earth. Again, it is impossible (and absurd to think) that any of the line of Seth were present at this event. Man was not yet created.

▶ Job 38:7 also demonstrates that the loyal angels of God (those who continue to be loyal) and the soon to be disloyal angels (those that subsequently decided to rebel) were all together in unity at one point. All angels are essentially morning stars. God is making a point here to differentiate between the *loyal* morning stars and the *disloyal*—calling the latter the sons of God.

▶ The previous point is also supported in Job 38:7; this differentiation between the morning stars and the sons of God is demonstrated by their unique response to the unveiling of the foundations of the earth. God describes the morning stars' response as *singing*, something that carries a connotation of vocal, yet serene praise. This also conveys unity by vocalization as a group. Conversely, God describes the response of the sons of God as *shouting*, something that is also vocal yet can be disruptive, belligerent, and offensive. This also conveys individual vocalization that is disjointed, not in unity. This reveals that while the morning stars and the sons of God were obviously unified in presence, they were not necessarily unified in their vocalization.

5

- Besides the New Testament believers, Adam was the only pre-flood human to be called a son of God in the New Testament (Luke 3:38). This is stated because, like the original angels, Adam was created *directly* by the hand of God. Adam was not a result of human procreation.

- The term sons of God was (and is) intended to be a title in a positive light. So God has stripped this title from the fallen angels and bestowed it over the believers in Christ—reborn of the Spirit (born again—John 1:12).

- As a final point, Genesis 6:2 does not state that the sons of *men* chose the daughters of *men* as wives. Rather, it clearly states that the sons of *God* chose the daughters of *men*. Understand clearly that *three* separate groups are spoken of in this reference: daughters, men, and fallen angels.

From this point forward, I'm going to introduce various passages from the non-canonical Book of Enoch (an overview on the Book of Enoch is found at the end of this book). Many have proclaimed Enoch as "uninspired" text. However, Enoch was in fact considered part of Scripture between second century B.C. and fourth century A.D. right up until the Council of Laodicea in 363 A.D. (where it was banned by the early Church of Rome). The Book of Jude (Jude 14–15) in the Bible quotes Enoch (1 Enoch 2:1), almost word for word. Why is so-called "uninspired text" somehow found within the inspired Word? Jesus Himself quoted Enoch several times (examples of this are also included at the end of the book). I am absolutely convinced this text has been withheld (besides other vital information) until now, the time of the end. Similarly, as Daniel tells us the Lord instructed him that his recorded revelation was to be "closed" and "sealed" until the time of the end (Daniel 12:8–9), 1 Enoch 1:2 states:

From them I heard all things, and understood what I saw, that which will not take place in this generation, but in a generation which is to succeed at a distant period, on account of the elect.

We must first recognize that this text is really meant for a distant generation. It is certainly within this current generation, taking into consideration the advent of the worldwide internet bringing us all into the information age (the age of knowledge), that the text of 1 Enoch is now opening up with its revelations, as does the book of Daniel in these current times.

1 Enoch 7:1–2
It happened after the sons of men had multiplied in those days, that the daughters were born unto them, elegant and beautiful. And when the angels, the sons of heaven, beheld them, they became enamoured of them...

Here it is clearly stated that the *angels* are the "sons of heaven," synonymous for the "sons of God" (Genesis 6:2). It is further understood that these particular angels are the fallen angels, as described throughout the rest of the Book of Enoch.

First point established: the 'sons of God' are in fact the fallen angels. Which begs the question, if the fallen angels took wives from out of the lineage of the daughters of men, how could they procreate—especially when it is widely accepted that angels are sexless?

2.
FOUNDATIONAL POINT TWO: UNHOLY PROCREATION

THE PREMISE THAT ANGELS ARE SEXLESS, WIDELY ACCEPTED IN MANY CHURCH circles, has primarily been based on the Scriptures found in Matthew 22:30 and Mark 12:25. It is here that the disciples asked Jesus about marriage in heaven after the resurrection. As a note here, this is not a *specific* reference to life in heaven immediately following the event of the Rapture. This is a reference to life in heaven after the First Resurrection (at the Second Coming) and after the *final* Second Resurrection (at the Great White Throne Judgment)—when everything is said and done (the end of the Thousand-Year Reign of Christ on earth).[2] The event of the Rapture precedes the two end-time main Resurrections.

> Matthew 22:30
> For in the resurrection they neither marry, nor are given in marriage,
> but are as the angels of God in heaven.

The overall point here is that many fail to recognize the *full* significance of this answer Jesus gave the disciples. Jesus states there is no marrying, nor being given in marriage, in heaven. However, Jesus goes on to say that this absence of marriage is like the "angels of God" that currently reside in heaven. This is *not* referring to the fallen angels. This is directly referring to the loyal morning stars who, by their very obedience to God, abstain from marriage. That is, they willingly abstain from marriage in the earthly sense. This will become clearer as we continue.

So now, regarding the aspect of procreation, applying to both humans and angels, we will first look at God's intention for his created angels.

Enoch 15:6–7
But you from the beginning were made spiritual, possessing a life which is eternal, and not subject to death for ever. Therefore I made not wives for you, because, being spiritual, your dwelling is in heaven.

The angels were created to live for an eternity. Therefore God did not create wives for these spiritual beings. According to this text, there are no female angels. In the Bible, angels are always referred to in the masculine context (sons of God are obviously males). Three of these angels are named in the Bible: Michael, Gabriel, and Lucifer (who fell). Other angels named are found in 1 Enoch: Raphael, Uriel, Raguel, Sarakiel, Zateel, and Phanuel, who have remained loyal to God. We will look at other angels named, who were fallen, later on in chapter Foundational Point Four. All of these angels cited are male. As a subtle yet revealing observation, nowhere in the Bible or Enoch states (or suggests) there were daughters of God choosing any sons of men. In other words, there are no references of fallen *female* angels taking earthly sons (males) as husbands. In addition, the Greek word *angelos* only appears in the masculine form.

I have also listened to some individuals who take Galatians 3:26–28 completely out of context:

Galatians 3:28
For ye are all the children of God by faith in Christ Jesus. For as many of you as have been baptized into Christ have put on Christ. There is neither Jew nor Greek, there is neither bond nor free, there is neither male nor female: for ye are all one in Christ Jesus.

Here, God is making the distinct point that the unifying factor of all children of God is not ethnic background, social status, or gender, but rather our faith in Christ. Bottom line, we are truly unified through the Spirit of God. To be born again, one must be born of the Spirit (John 3:5–8) and that Spirit is of one accord through God under Christ.

Some have taken this Scripture and applied it to the so-called 'neutral' gender of angels. Again, in error, rendering them sexless.

Conversely, comparing the spiritual angels (that became fallen) to the flesh and blood humans, we read:

Enoch 15:3–5

You being spiritual, holy, and possessing a life which is eternal have polluted yourselves with women, have begotten in carnal blood, have lusted in the blood of men; and have done as those *who are* flesh and blood do. These however die and perish. Therefore have I given to them wives, that they might cohabit with them; that sons might be born of them; and that this might be transacted upon the earth.

Human men were given wives to procreate since, being of flesh and blood, humans do not live forever. It was God's intention that human men perpetuate human existence through procreation with the God-given human women. It was *not* God's intention that the spiritual angels do the same. However, as stated, some of the spiritual angels had "polluted" themselves with earthly women (namely, human women already in a fallen state of sin since Adam). The spiritual angels had crossed a line.

It has been speculated that the sons of God spiritually possessed human men to procreate with earthly women. Spiritual oppression and possession of a human host can happen through the invasion of a demonic spirit—as well as through the invasion of a fallen angel. This is *not* in question here. What is in question is that fallen angels are *not* demons. While they are closely related, they are separate entities. This foundational premise will become absolutely clear as we proceed.

Pertaining to this point that fallen angels themselves have the ability to procreate with earthly women, we read in Jude 6:

And the angels which kept not their first estate, but left their own habitation, he hath reserved in everlasting chains under darkness unto the judgment of the great day.

The word "habitation" in the Greek Language is *oiketerion*. It also means residence and is associated with *cohabiting* with the *earth*, or *world*. In addition, it refers to the body as a dwelling place for the spirit. Therefore, the sons of God, who left the "first estate of heaven," began to cohabit with the earth and because of this action will face severe judgment in the eternal fire (we will examine this judgment later).

2 Corinthians 5:2
For in this we groan, earnestly desiring to be clothed upon with our house which is in heaven.

The word "house" in this Scripture comes from the *same* Greek word, *oiketerion*. These two Scriptures are the only times the Hebrew word *oiketerion* appears in the Bible.

In this passage we read that the believer in Christ is earnestly awaiting the day to be clothed with the exact same thing the fallen angels apparently disrobed from as they exited the Kingdom of Heaven. So the fallen angels did the exact opposite to what believers aspire to become. The opposite of being clothed is disrobed. This is referring to 'spiritual' or 'heavenly' clothing within a heavenly residence.[3]

We can now see clearly that God's angels in heaven remain true to God's will; they do not marry, nor are they given unto marriage in heaven. Especially since they are *all* male. They also have free will. They choose to be celibate and remain in the heavenly estate according to God's will. Whereas the fallen angels, by their own choice (by their free will), not only gave up heaven but also gave up their heavenly state of being (or spiritual clothing) and cohabited with earthly women on earth—against the will of God.

1 Enoch 7:1–3
It happened after the sons of men had multiplied in those days, that the daughters were born unto them, elegant and beautiful. And when the angels, the sons of heaven, beheld them, they became enamoured of them, saying to each other, Come, let us select for ourselves wives from the progeny of men, and let us beget children.

This passage is a direct confirmation of Genesis 6:1–2:

And it came to pass, when men began to multiply on the face of the earth, and daughters were born unto them, That the sons of God saw the daughters of men that they were fair; and they took them wives of all which they chose.

Clearly stated, the fallen angels selected human wives and directly had offspring with them. It does not even suggest they spiritually possessed men before they procreated. In fact, Genesis 6:4 plainly states that "… the sons of God *came in unto* the daughters of men…" (emphasis added).

Also, clearly stated, the "sons of God" cited in Genesis 6:2 are directly referred to as *"angels, the sons of heaven"* in 1 Enoch 7:2–3 (emphasis added).

1 Enoch 15:2
Wherefore have you forsaken the lofty and holy heaven, which endures forever, and you have lain with women; have defiled yourselves with the daughters of men; have taken to yourselves wives; have acted like the sons of the earth, and have begotten an impious offspring.

In this passage we have confirmation of the following:

▸ The fallen angels had left their normal, spiritual habitation

▸ The fallen angels directly procreated with earthly women (physically lain with women after disrobing from their normal spiritual clothing)

▸ The fallen angels had defiled *themselves* by doing this (defile means corrupt, spoil, desecrate, or lose purity)

▸ The fallen angels have acted in the same manner as human men— they procreated in the same fashion as human men (not *through* men)

▸ The result of this unholy, sexual union was the appearance of an impious offspring (meaning ungodly, sinful, sacrilegious and blasphemous)

As a note here, angels can take on many different forms. Satan has been known to take on the form of a dragon, a serpent, a human, a goat, etc.[4] The angels of the Lord took on the form of men when they visited Lot to warn him of the impending destruction of Sodom and Gomorrah (Genesis 19:1–5). They *physically* walked through the gate of the city and sat down and ate with Lot. The immoral people of the city recognized these angels as foreign *men* not from the city. However, this does not conclude or suggest that angels need to inhabit another *existing* human to procreate.

As a second note, the Antichrist will appear as a result of an unholy sexual union between Satan (the father) and a willing human woman.[5] God knew each and every one of us before he laid the foundations of the earth and before we were each conceived in the womb (Jeremiah 1:5). I am quite confident that God, the Father, would not sacrifice one of His own created to become the Antichrist. This would be contrary to John 3:16:

> For God so loved the world, that he gave his only begotten Son, that whosoever believeth in him should not perish, but have everlasting life.

Second point established: fallen angels entered an unholy sexual relationship with earthly women. This leads to the next question: what about the offspring of this unholy union?

3.

FOUNDATIONAL POINT THREE: UNHOLY OFFSPRING

Genesis 6:4

There were giants in the earth in those days; and also after that, when the sons of God came in unto the daughters of men, and they bare *children* to them. The same *became* mighty men which *were* of old, men of renown.

Consider the following points:

- ► The result of this unholy union was the presence of giants "in those days" (pre-flood) and "also after that" (post-flood).

- ► It is clearly stated that the presence of the giants occurred as a direct result of when the sons of God "came in unto" (had sex with) the daughters of men.

- ► The "same became *mighty* men." The word mighty comes from the Hebrew word *Gibbor,* which means powerful, tyrant, champion, strong man, and also giant.

- ► Post-flood we are told of the continued presence of giants, such as King Og of Bashan, considered to have been at least twelve feet tall, one of the last of the Rephaites (Deuteronomy 3:11).

- To this day the Rujm el-Hiri monument (located in northern Israel) is also known as Gilgal Rephaim, referring to the Temple of the Giants (we will look at this in more detail in Chapter 16 of Section Two).

- King David, as a boy, fought the giant Goliath (at least 9.5 feet tall). David had gathered five stones, ready to take on the other four brothers of Goliath, also giants (1 Samuel 17:40; 2 Samuel 21:18-22).

- Goliath was referred to as a champion, which is derived from *Gibbor* (1 Samuel 17:51).

- Giants were reported throughout the land of Canaan when Moses sent the twelve spies into the ancient Promised Land (Numbers 13).

- Three giants are named in Joshua 15:14: Sheshai, Ahiman, and Talmai. They were initially chased out by Caleb and finally killed (Judges 1:10).

- It was God's intent to have all regions and valleys exterminated of these giants and other abominations—including all humans involved in the worship and interaction of false gods that initiated this progressive stage of genetic altering in the first place.

- The land of Canaan (ancient Israel) was God's promised land to His People, but it needed to be purged and cleansed of all false worship and defilement first (genetic contamination).

Another example of the purging and cleansing of temples and altars of false worship, the centres of satanic-inspired worship that caused direct interference, interaction, and manipulation by the fallen angels amongst humans is found in two passages of Scripture:

2 Chronicles 14:2–4
And Asa did *that which was* good and right in the eyes of the LORD his God: For he took away the altars of the strange *gods*, and the high places, and brake down the images, and cut down the groves: And

commanded Judah to seek the LORD God of their fathers, and to do the law and the commandment.

1 Kings 15:11–13
And Asa did *that which was* right in the eyes of the LORD, as *did* David his father. And he took away the sodomites out of the land, and removed all the idols that his fathers had made. And also Maachah his mother, even her he removed from *being* queen, because she had made an idol in a grove; and Asa destroyed her idol, and burnt *it* by the brook Kidron.

Asa, great grandson of Solomon and fifth king of the house of David, found it compelling to rid the region of any worship and subsequent physical link to the false gods (fallen angels) which brought forth the defilement and progression of genetic alterations and abominations, such as the Nephilim and the Raphaim.

The word giant is translated from a few main parts of the ancient Hebrew language:

1. Rapha—Raphaite—Rephaim: meaning giant or giants
2. Nephil—Nephiyl—Nephilim: meaning giant or fallen one, tyrant
3. Naphal: meaning to fall, cast out, fugitive

Other Hebrew references are:

1. Beyth Rapha: meaning house of the giant
2. Gibbowr—Gibbor: meaning giant man, mighty man, or strong man

The word giant(s) is mentioned twenty-one times in Scripture; Rephaim is mentioned eight times, for a total of twenty-nine. There are various tribes mentioned in the Scriptures that were either comprised of giants entirely, or were partially comprised of giants—or in some way were associated with the giants:

- Canaanites   mentioned (14) times
- Hittites   mentioned (48) times
- Hivites   mentioned (25) times
- Amorites   mentioned (89) times
- Moabites   mentioned (29) times

- Edomites   mentioned (18) times
- Ammonites   mentioned (35) times
- Jebusites   mentioned (39) times
- Girgashites   mentioned (7) times
- Amalekites   mentioned (27) times
- Perizzites   mentioned (23) times
- Philistines   mentioned (281) times
- Anakims   mentioned (11) times

Looking at all the references to giants, or to the tribes consisting of giants, these are mentioned at least six hundred seventy-five times in the Bible. And this does not include any other indirect references.

In addition, the name Anak is mentioned nine times in Scripture. Anak was the forefather of the Anakims, who were known to be a mixed race of giants and were the descendants of the Nephilim.[6]

In Aramaic, Niyphelah or Nephila refers to the star constellation Orion, and thus the Nephilim were also called the offspring of Orion. The Egyptians believed that the god Osiris came from Orion. The three main pyramids at Giza are purposely aligned in the exact same configuration of Orion's Belt (with a 19.5-degree offset of the third pyramid representing the third star).

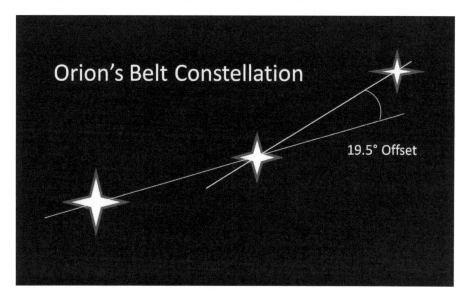

Interesting that the god Osiris was considered by the Egyptians to be the god of the dead and of the underworld. This is the same association given to Lucifer as Satan after his fall from the Kingdom of Heaven (from out of Third Heaven into Second and First Heavens).[7] Coincidentally, on the other side of the world (from Giza), the Sun and Moon pyramids at Teotihuacan, Mexico, combined with the Temple of the Feathered Serpent (Quetzalcoatl), form the exact same configuration replicating Orion's Belt. In addition, the main thoroughfare between these structures is called The Avenue of the Dead. Not a coincidence.

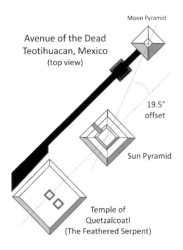

Two other important points pertain to both pre-flood ("in those days") and post-flood ("also after that") situations as cited in Genesis 6:4.

Regarding pre-flood, we find that Noah was cited in Scripture (Genesis 6:9) as displaying three important qualities: (1) he was a *just* man, (2) he was *perfect* in his generations and, (3) he *walked* with God. Point one describes a man with wisdom and moral character, qualities lacking throughout the ancient society around him. Point three describes a man who held to godly values and had great faith in God—but who also had a deep spiritual relationship with the Father. It is the second point that is the least understood and has been grossly misinterpreted in many church circles. The term "perfect" is *not* describing someone who was "without sin" (I've heard this idea that Noah was without sin on more than one occasion). The word perfect is derived from the Hebrew word *Tamiym,* which means "without blemish" or "undefiled." This is referring to the *physical* body being genetically perfect. In fact, it is specifically stated that Noah was "*perfect* in his *generations*"—in his genetic lineage. Noah, his wife, his sons, and their wives kept themselves separate and apart from the genetic altering and defilement that was so rampant throughout the land. Satan and the fallen angels were altering the creation "his way" (Genesis 6:12), so much that God found it necessary to purge and cleanse the *entire* world.

Genesis 6:12
And God looked upon the earth, and, behold, it was corrupt; for all flesh had corrupted his way upon the earth.

We need to fully understand that the phrase "his way" in fact refers to Satan's way. Obviously this was not God's way, since He was grieved and lamented at what had happened to His beloved creation (Genesis 6:6, 13). We must also conclude that it was not man's way. While man had definitely fallen into progressive sin, violence, and genetic decay, man did not conceive the *idea* of genetic alteration by his own volition (through rebellion). However, some could understand this passage in the context that it was "God's way" that was corrupted, especially if one were to remove the word "had" from the Scripture (reinforcing that it was "God's way" that was corrupted). Yet, the Scripture specifically cites that "all flesh" became corrupt, and it is clear that this is result of Satan's direct influence on "all flesh" (inferring *by* "his way"). This was conceived, orchestrated, and implemented by Satan. Satan manipulated God's creation. Satan cannot create. He can only attempt to alter what is *already* created.

Regarding post-flood, we find that the same influence, manipulation, and genetic altering by the fallen angels began once again, but only on a limited and regional basis (not quite on the same encompassing, global scale as during pre-flood times). However, one example of the boundaries of limitations exceeded was the eventual destruction and annihilation of Sodom and Gomorrah. We read:

Jude 7
Even as Sodom and Gomorrha, and the cities about them in like manner, giving themselves over to fornication, and going after strange flesh, are set forth for an example, suffering the vengeance of eternal fire.

What was happening at Sodom and Gomorrah, and other similar cities in the region, was actually something beyond immorality. Most people understand that "giving themselves over to fornication" refers to sexual immorality. This is echoed in the previously cited Scripture of 1 Kings 15:12 where Asa drives out the *sodomites* before he destroys the altars of false worship.

What most people don't understand is that the second term, "going after strange flesh," refers to something beyond sexual perversion. The word strange used here is derived from the Greek word *heteros*, which means altered, different, or something other. In other words the people of these fallen cities were also going after *altered flesh*, or going after something *other than* normal flesh. This is a clear indication that genetic altering and abominations were occurring during this time (at this specific isolated region) when sexual immorality was peaking. And once again (post-flood), God found it necessary to destroy and annihilate any trace of their existence, with the exception of Lot and his remaining family. Similar to Noah, Lot was also warned before the judgment to come; subsequently, he and his family were spared (with the exception of Lot's wife, Genesis 19:25–26).

Third point established: The offspring of the unholy union between fallen angels and earthly women resulted in the appearance of genetically altered life forms. These were considered abominations in God's eyes, a total defilement of His intended creation.

4.

FOUNDATIONAL POINT FOUR: THE ORIGIN OF DEMON SPIRITS

CONSIDERING GOD'S INTENDED PURPOSE FOR THE CREATION OF MAN, AND MAN'S subsequent procreation, humans were created with three main components: (1) a body (flesh and bone), (2) a spirit, and (3) a soul. Based on the introduction of sin to the world, through Satan's temptation appearing in the form of a serpent and man's subsequent transgression, God provided a way of redemption through His Son, Jesus Christ—the final sacrifice.

Considering the previous foundational point, the terms Nephil, Nephiyl, Nephilim, and Naphal are not only references to the giants, they also carry the connotation of being fallen—to fall, fallen ones—along with referring to being cast out and being a fugitive. Lucifer was essentially cast out of the Kingdom of Heaven, becoming a fugitive—a fallen angel. We are told in Scripture that corruption cannot inherit incorruption when it comes to entering into a residence within the Kingdom of Heaven (I Corinthians 15:50). This is a direct reference to the human condition of the body, spirit, and soul in a fallen state. However, this premise can also be applied to the genetic corruption of altered life forms. The Raphaim and Nephilim (the giants) will never enter, nor will they ever see, the Kingdom of Heaven. This is because they were bred in an unholy fashion, in a way that completely defied the sanctity of life the almighty Creator intended. The Raphaim and Nephilim were missing a very important component. When they were brought into the world they had a body (flesh and bone) and they had a spirit—but they didn't have a soul.

The giants were not only a genetic (physical) abomination; they were also a *spiritual* abomination. Salvation or redemption for them is simply impossible. Without the essential soul, and upon death, the spirit released from the physical body of an ancient giant has no place to go—except to roam the land, seeking some other human host for a temporary embodiment. Temporary, because the spirit continues to live indefinitely, while the physical body does not. Consider the following Scripture:

Matthew 12:43
When the unclean spirit is gone out of a man, he walketh through dry places, seeking rest, and findeth none.

The spirits of the deceased giants are what we now refer to as demons. They are *not* the fallen angels (or fallen angels becoming demons), although their very presence is an indirect result of the interference of fallen humankind and cross-breeding by the fallen angels. This foundational premise is clearly stated in the following passage:

1 Enoch 15:8–9
Now the giants, who have been born of spirit and of flesh, shall be called upon the earth evil spirits, and on earth shall be their habitation. Evil spirits shall proceed from their flesh, because they were created from above; from the holy Watchers was their beginning and primary foundation. Evil spirits shall they be upon the earth, and the spirits of the wicked shall they be called. The habitation of the spirits of heaven shall be in heaven; but upon earth shall the inhabitation of the terrestrial spirits, who are born on earth. The spirits of the giants shall be like clouds, which shall oppress, corrupt, fall, content, and bruise upon the earth.

By this passage we learn the following:

▸ The giants were "born of the spirit and flesh"—the important soul is not mentioned, and therefore we conclude it is absent.[8]

▸ Evil spirits (demons) proceed from their flesh (upon death).

▸ Their habitation is on earth and they originated on earth—not in heaven.

- ▶ They were "born on earth," therefore, they are also known as "terrestrial spirits."

- ▶ They were created by the holy Watchers (another term for angels). It is understood that these particular holy Watchers became *unholy*— hence the fallen angels (confirmed in other passages such as 1 Enoch 6:4, 10).

- ▶ These "spirits of the giants" are numerous (described like clouds) and in many ways they shall be a great affliction towards humankind.

So the question on the minds of many is this: Are fallen angels and demons *really* separate entities? And if so, is this confirmed in the Scriptures of the Bible?

I have read the following Scripture many times over, until one day the Holy Spirit revealed something to me:

1 Timothy 4:1
Now the Spirit speaketh expressly, that in the latter times some shall depart from the faith, giving heed to seducing spirits, and doctrines of devils;

It is stated here, by the Apostle Paul, that the Holy Spirit has revealed that in the latter days (during the end times) some individuals will depart from Christianity (the faith). They will do this on account of being swayed by *two* distinct influences, "giving heed" to *both* "seducing spirits" and "doctrines of devils."

A very important point needs to be raised here. Only a handful of Bible versions clearly state "…and doctrines of devils" within 1 Timothy 4:1. These include the authorized King James Bible (KJV), the American King James Bible (AKJV), and the English Revised Version (ERV). Most other Bible versions cite "…and doctrines of *demons*" or "…and teachings of *demons*" (emphasis added). As we continue, I will demonstrate that the latter references (the majority of versions) are actually in error.

The term "seducing spirits" that proceeds the phrase "…and doctrines of devils" is a direct reference to demons. As we have established, demons are the disembodied spirits of the deceased giants. They are seducing because they seek embodiment in other human hosts (including some who profess to be Christians) who can be adversely influenced (giving heed) by their invasive presence.

These spirits are also known as wandering spirits because they wander the earth seeking physical embodiment. They will never enter into the Kingdom of Heaven. As we saw in Matthew 12:43, the demon spirit that invaded a human man and was driven out of his body is referred to as "unclean." The word unclean used in this Scripture is derived from the Greek word *akathartos,* which means foul and unclean when referring specifically to demons.

Demon spirits are also known as familiar spirits because, while the physical body has a relatively short, finite existence, the spirit itself continues to live on indefinitely, primarily within the spiritual realm. Conversely, a human spirit returns to God upon the finality of death (Ecclesiastes 12:7). Due to this, these demonic spirits are very familiar with the personal histories of their human hosts throughout history. They can deceive and influence mankind through this accumulated familiar knowledge.

However, the term "doctrines of devils" is referring to another, separate aspect of negative influence. Take note that 1 Timothy 4:1 does not say "giving heed to seducing *devils,* and doctrines of *spirits*" (emphasis added). As we have demonstrated, demons and fallen angels are related but separate entities. Fallen angels are also referred to as devils. Satan is known as the Devil. Throughout God's Word, Satan is never referred to as a demon. We'll look at this in greater detail in a moment, after we examine another important, related point.

Fully understand that demons and fallen angels can both oppress and possess, but fallen angels can also teach (demons are *not* the teachers). Demons can influence man through familiar knowledge, but the fallen angels actually introduced *new* knowledge to humankind. Fallen angels hold much (not all) of the ancient knowledge of the creator God. This represents far more knowledge than humankind understands. The word doctrine is defined as "a set of ideas or beliefs that are taught." This is in addition to the false teaching that can occur through man himself. We need to understand that our entire history has been influenced and altered on a grand scale by the introduction of specific knowledge given to man by the fallen angels.

So, to reaffirm, most versions of the Bible that cite 1 Timothy 4:1 as "doctrines of *demons*" or "teachings of *demons*" are in error. In a nutshell, we are clearly informed in Timothy 4:1 that it is the *spirits* that *seduce,* while it is the *devils* that *teach*—false doctrine. This important point will intersect with various chapters in Section Three dealing with the modern phenomenon of UFOs and *extraterrestrials.*

This is confirmed in 1 Enoch:

1 Enoch 8:1–9

Moreover Azazyel taught men to make swords, knives, shields, breast-plates, the fabrication of mirrors, and the workmanship of bracelets and ornaments, the use of paint, the beautifying of the eyebrows, the use of stones of every valuable and select kind, and all sorts of dyes, so that the world became altered. Impiety increased, fornication multiplied; and they transgressed and corrupted all their ways. Amazarak taught all the sorcerers, and dividers of roots: Armers taught the solution of sorcery; Barkayal taught the observers of the stars, Akibeel taught signs; Tamiel taught astronomy; And Asaradel taught the motion of the moon, and men destroyed, cried out; and their voice reached to heaven.

For the very first time, humans learned knowledge of warfare and weaponry, the development of cosmetics and jewelry to enhance natural beauty, the application of paints and dyes, and stonework construction. They were also taught the disciplines of astrology and astronomy and, even more alarmingly, the disciplines of sorcery, witchcraft, and mind-altering drugs (known as Pharmakeia in the New Testament—also referred as "incantations" and the "dividing of roots and trees" in 1 Enoch 7:10). In fact, the Greek word *Pharmakeia* is where we also derive the modern word pharmacy. We're going to take a closer look at the connection between mind-altering drugs and witchcraft in Chapter 25, The 'Man' From the North Pole.

Due to this overwhelming influence, impiety increased, which is a lack of reverence for God and sacred things. Transgression and corruption increased, due to the accelerated increase of sin. Sexual immorality also increased, and through all of this, "the world became altered…and men destroyed, cried out; and their voice reached unto heaven." It is worthwhile to emphasize the phrase "the world became *altered*…" Satan's direct influence and manipulation has drastically changed the course of our history. As we saw earlier, the world was corrupted "his way."

Also in this passage, we now discover that some of the fallen angels are named. We're told in the Scriptures that the total number of all angels (loyal and disloyal) is innumerable (Hebrews 12:22). However, we are given a hint as to the actual number as being at least 200 million (20 thousand x 10 thousand: Psalm 68:17). Based on this estimate, there are at least 67 million fallen angels (representing one third—Revelation 12:3–4).

This warning about falling away from God's will, purpose, and design by being led astray is clearly stated by the Apostle Paul once again:

Galatians 1:8
But though we, or an angel from heaven, preach any other gospel unto you than that which we have preached unto you, let him be accursed.

Besides the possible false teaching by men, here we need to also recognize that Paul is *not* talking about the angels who remain loyal to God. They, in their obedience to God, would *not* preach some other gospel—some other false message. All angels, fallen or loyal, originated from the Kingdom of Heaven. So, Paul really means possible false teaching by a *fallen* angel. Again, this is another confirmation of what we just covered in 1 Timothy 4:1. Also interesting is that Paul was writing during the time of the Roman Empire. Even though much time had passed since the time of the Great Flood and of Sodom and Gomorrah, the negative influence on man by fallen angels was obviously still a great concern. We'll address this renewed concern pertaining to our time within a current, modern society throughout Section Three.

Getting back to the previous point that demonic spirits and devils are separate entities, I will restate that Satan is never referred to as a demon—he is always referred to as a devil and, more specifically, the Devil. When we look at the Hebrew terminology, some interesting aspects begin to emerge.

Satan has many different names or titles. One of those titles is *Baalzebub* in the Hebrew language. When we take a close look at the definitions and consider the root words of this title, we discover the following:

Baalzebub: "lord of the flies," "lord of the heavenly dwelling"
Baal: "owner," "lord," universal "god of fertility," "prince, lord of the earth," "lord of the rain and dew," epithet: "he who rides on the clouds" (god of storms)
Zebub: to flit, to fly

The two definitions of the title Baalzebub are consistent with the reference to Satan as the "prince and power of the air" (Ephesians 2:2), and this particular Scripture goes on to describe the "prince and power of the air" as "the *spirit* that now worketh in the children of disobedience" (emphasis added). We must recognize that God can present Himself as a Spirit (Holy Spirit)[9] and that Lucifer as an angel (in his purest form) was created as a *spiritual* being. However, this does not conclude that the "prince and power of the air" (the Devil), as a *spirit*, is in any way the same as the evil *spirits* that have proceeded from the flesh of the deceased giants losing their embodiment (i.e. a fallen angel becoming a demon).

More specifically, Baalzebub is also "the lord of the flies" (1176 Hebrew—*Strong's Exhaustive Concordance*)—he is the *lord* (the leader) over all the *flies* (I would submit that the flies symbolically represent the other fallen angels—a significant group under Satan's lordship). This title also means "lord of the heavenly dwelling." Again, this is consistent with the title "prince and power of the air" (referring to First Heaven—the earth's atmosphere or skyline), with Satan's current reign over the fallen angels within Second Heaven (their ability to continue to travel throughout the known universe) and with Satan's desire to elevate his throne above the throne of God in Third Heaven (Isaiah 14:12–14), not to mention the association with his former reign over all the angels within Third Heaven before the rebellion (the heavenly angel, Lucifer, holding a pinnacle position of presence, intellect, and musical worship, Ezekiel 28:12–15).

Very interesting are the two root words that comprise the title Baalzebub. The first root word, *Baal,* was a false god worshipped in ancient times, most commonly in the land of Canaan. One central place of Baal worship was the Philistine town of Ekron (2 Kings 1:2), the most northern of five towns in the region, eleven miles north of Gath (home of the giant Goliath—1 Samuel 17:4).[10] Canaan was the general region where the giants and other genetic abominations flourished during the post-flood era. So, it is no surprise that Baal was commonly worshipped as the universal god of fertility. Also the connotations "lord of the rain and dew" and "he who rides on the clouds" again is consistent with the "prince and power of the air." The other connotations—lord, owner, and prince, lord of the earth—are consistent with references to Satan as the "god of this world" (II Corinthians 4:4).

The second root word, *zebub,* means to fly or to flit. The word flit in modern language can be expressed as a verb, meaning to skip or dart to and fro, and from place to place. This is consistent with the fact that angels can travel at the speed of light. This is described in Ezekiel 1:14. Lucifer is the "angel of light" (2 Corinthians 11:14) and his name translated means "light bringer" or "light bearer." However, angels can also travel *faster* than the speed of light—which is at the speed of thought. God's angels, when dispatched, are not limited to the speed of light which, as an example, would take an angel one million years to travel one million light years. Angels are not bound by physical space and time.

Having said that, the angels are not omnipresent as God is, but they certainly can flit or zip from place to place in extremely quick fashion. Also, the word flit can be expressed as a noun, meaning: "in an act of leaving one's home or moving, typically secretly so as to escape creditors or obligations" (British connotation, thefreedictionary.com). This is also reminiscent of being a fugitive.

Another title we're going to look at is *Beelzebub* [954 Greek—*Strong's Exhaustive Concordance*] where the root word *Baal* is now replaced with *Beel*.

Beelzebub: "chief of the devils" (Luke 11:15)
Beel: "commander"
Zebub: to flit, to fly

Satan is the commander and chief of the devils—over the other fallen angels (devils). Here, it does *not* say "chief of the demons." However, an amazing revelation is brought forth when we consider this next title called, *Beelzebul* [also 954 Greek—*Strong's Exhaustive Concordance*] where *Zebub* is now replaced with *Zebul*.

Beelzebul: "prince of the evil spirits," "prince of demons"
Beel: "commander"
Zebul: dwell in, habitation

This is a distinct and defined title referring to both "prince of the *evil spirits*" and "prince of *demons*." The word devil does not appear in this title. As we saw, confirmed in 1 Enoch 15:8, evil spirits are that which have proceeded from the flesh of the deceased giants. Satan is simply the "prince of demons" (Beelzebul); he is also the "chief of the devils" (Beelzebub). Satan has two separate and distinct titles in regard to both demons and devils. Again, looking at the two root words, we see the reappearance of *Beel* as referring to the commander, Satan. The other root word has now changed from *Zebub* (referring to the quick and extensive travel of the fallen angels) to *Zebul* (referring to the confined and limited *habitation* of the demons on *earth*). Obviously so, as *Beel* refers to the commander being the prince and *Zebul* is referring to the evil spirits and, simply, demons—and what 1 Enoch 15:8 also confirms: "...shall be called upon the earth *evil spirits*, and on *earth* shall be their *habitation*" (emphasis added). Also related is the term "dwell in" which has also been a reference to demonic possession of a human host as well as referring to an earthly habitation.

It should be stressed that demons have significant limitations in terms of physical actions and extensive travel (as compared to fallen angels) unless, of course, they reside within a physical host. Demon spirits (ghosts impersonating the deceased) tend to inhabit specific locations—hence the term haunted houses.

Job 1:6
Now there was a day when the sons of God came to present themselves before the LORD, and Satan came also among them.

In this Scripture we see that the sons of God (fallen angels) had present-ed themselves before the Lord. As we've established, the sons of God are not demons. Demons do not present themselves before the throne room of God. Demons are limited to movement and travel on Earth. We also know by this Scripture that the sons of God presented themselves at some point after their initial banishment from the Kingdom of Heaven, since Satan (the fallen angel Lucifer) came with them. It does not state that it was Lucifer, the heavenly angel, who came with them, which would have put this event sometime before the rebellion. Obviously, this event occurred after the rebellion. This is reinforced by the fact that Satan had a conversation with God discussing the created human, Job (after the rebellion, Job 1:8).

We must understand that Satan and the fallen angels continue to present themselves before the Lord as demonstrated by this next Scripture—the key word being "again."

Job 2:1
AGAIN there was a day when the sons of God came to present them-selves before the LORD, and Satan came also among them to present himself before the LORD.

Taking this further in understanding, it is Satan himself who goes before the throne room of God, day and night, and brings accusations against the brethren (the believers) on earth.

Revelation 12:10
And I heard a loud voice saying in heaven, Now is come salvation, and strength, and the kingdom of our God, and the power of his Christ:

for the accuser of our brethren is cast down, which accused them before our God day and night.

Satan's accusations and petitions before the throne room of God will end at the second stage of Satan's banishment—the first stage being his loss of permanent residence in heaven at the rebellion. It was after this first stage when Satan disguised himself as a serpent and deceived Adam and Eve at the Garden of Eden.

As a few more detailed notes to this point, when we consider the definition of the word demon in a modern dictionary, such as the Merriam Webster's Dictionary, we commonly find this:

1. a: an evil spirit
   b: a source or agent of evil, harm, distress, or ruin
2. an attendant power or spirit
3. a supernatural being of Greek mythology intermediate between gods and men

Almost all dictionaries state the first definition as "an evil spirit." Some dictionaries go on to state "an evil spirit—a devil." I firmly believe the latter is done in error due to a lack of understanding of the information we've covered thus far. (www.merriam-webster.com/dictionary/demon)

Some of the words, or names, associated with the word demon are: evil spirit, familiar spirit, wandering spirit, seducing spirit, apparitions, phantom, poltergeist, ghoul, ghost, banshee, spectre. These all have the connotation of disembodied spirits, or apparitions—they simply do not have the full presence or capabilities of angels (fallen or not) such as the angel Michael, or the angel Gabriel.

According to the same Merriam Webster's Dictionary, even the antonym (or opposite) of a demon is considered to be an angel. While a demon is certainly considered bad, and an angel is certainly considered good, this does not completely address the reality that demons originally came into existence indirectly through the manipulation of *fallen* angels (once considered loyal or good angels before the rebellion). However, at least the third definition above does recognize demons as a "supernatural being...*intermediate* between gods and men" (emphasis added; false gods = fallen angels)—even though this understanding was obviously widely accepted within (and somehow confined to) Greek mythology. Understand that myths usually have some basis in fact, which we will cover in more detail in Section Two.

Even in the New Testament, according to *Strong's Exhaustive Concordance*, the word devils is found in many Scriptures describing demonic possession and is derived primarily from two words in the Greek language:

(1142) "daimon"—a demon or supernatural spirit (of bad nature):— devil

(1140) "daimonion"—a demonic being; by extension a deity—devil, god

The second word "daimonion" is the more prevalent of the two Greek words throughout the New Testament. However, note again that in both cases the *primary* definition is the word demon, and the *secondary* definition, devil, is simply tagged on. Also note that, in the definition of the second Greek word *daimonion*, it states "a demonic being; *by extension a deity*" (emphasis added). Then we see the words devil and god (lowercase 'g') are again tagged on. In other words, it is stated that a demonic being *came out of something* (by extension). Again the question is raised, did demons *directly* come out of fallen angels (angels becoming demons) or did they *indirectly* come out of the sexual union between fallen angels and earthly women?

This is a real concern because, as in the case of I Timothy 4:1, the term "doctrines of devils" (in reference to the teachers—the fallen angels) is definitely stated as a second and separate aspect in relation to the aforementioned "seducing spirits." The term spirit in itself (based on the Hebrew *pneuma*) can apply to a human spirit, an angelic spirit, and demon spirit or a divine Spirit (the Holy Spirit). The combined term seducing spirit, however, is definitely referring to a demon spirit. The separation between the "seducing spirits" and the "doctrines of devils" is amplified by the very fact that they are presented in the plural, indicating *many* seducing spirits and, in addition, "doctrines of [*many*] devils" (emphasis added).

Despite this clear statement of these two separate powers of darkness within the same fallen kingdom, the word devils used in this Scripture is also derived from the same Greek word *daimonion* (with its primary definition, demon)— which begs the question, are there some errors within the original language translation, and/or within the original language definitions? Based on what we've covered thus far, this appears to be the case.

Again, I Timothy 4:1 (KJV) does not say "seducing devils, and doctrines of spirits," "seducing spirits, and doctrines of spirits," nor "seducing spirits, and doctrines of demons," etc. In this case, why would the translators choose the *secondary* definition, devils (demonstrating a distinct difference from a seducing spirit), instead of the *primary* definition, demon—if it is commonly thought that they are the same?

Additionally, in the Old Testament, there are Scriptures describing the all-out worship of devils (not demons). Bear in mind that the fallen angels (devils) had presented themselves as gods to ancient man. Prior to this, Lucifer had totally rejected God's plan for humankind where the angels were to serve man. Satan's interference with God's creation has been (and is) driven with the focused intention that man, instead, serve (and worship) him and his fallen kingdom.

The very first Scripture where the word "devils" appears is in the Old Testament Book of Leviticus.

Leviticus 17:7
And they shall no more offer their sacrifices unto devils, after whom they have gone a whoring. This shall be a statute for ever unto them throughout their generations.

Devils used here is derived from the Hebrew word:

[8163] *saiyr*—a devil, a goat, hairy

Notice that the word demon does *not* appear here—*saiyr* is clearly defined as a devil alone. The important point here: it is the fallen angels who encourage both worship and sacrifice. While demons may be revered in false worship (by extension as a *deity*), they are not the main, or pinnacle, false deity.

In two other versions of the Bible, the New International Version (NIV) and the New Living Translation (NLT), the reference to "…sacrifices unto devils" is stated as "…sacrifices unto goat idols." However, this tends to shift the clear understanding of the influence and the actual presence of real devils and relegates this particular phrase to sacrifices unto mere idols (lifeless statues). Clearly, the Hebrew word *saiyr* does not infer, in any way, an idol or statue.

Again, considering two more versions of the Bible, the English Standard Version (ESV) and the New American Standard Bible (NASB), the same reference is stated as "…sacrifices to (the) goat demons." However, once again, the Hebrew word *saiyr* is *not* defined as a demon.

This is echoed in 2 Chronicles where the same Hebrew word *saiyr* is found:

2 Chronicles 11:15
And he ordained him priests for the high places, and for the devils, and for the calves which he had made.

There are two other Scriptures where the word "devils" is found in the Old Testament:

Deuteronomy 32:17
They sacrificed unto devils, not to God; to gods whom they knew not, to new *gods that* came newly up, whom your fathers feared not.

Psalm 106:37–38
Yea, they sacrificed their sons and their daughters unto devils, and shed innocent blood, *even* the blood of their sons and of their daughters, whom they sacrificed unto the idols of Canaan: and the land was polluted with blood.

In these two Scriptures, devils is derived from the Hebrew word *shed*:

(7700) *shed*—a demon (as malignant)—a devil

Very interesting here that the primary definition of the Hebrew word *shed* refers to a demon, and the secondary definition is devil. Here again, the translators have chosen the secondary definition. However, as a note, the primary definition "a demon (as malignant)" is interesting, since malignant can refer to a disease, or to being malevolent—and that in turn refers to being spiteful, malicious, vindictive, vengeful, nasty, cruel, mischievous. This is reminiscent of the "clouds" of the evil, terrestrial spirits spoken of in 1 Enoch 15:9 becoming a great affliction (a disease) and malevolent towards humankind.

However, putting all this into perspective, the plain text of Deuteronomy 32:17 directly associates the devils with false gods (the main object of ancient human worship—again, fallen angels presenting themselves as false gods). Also, Psalm 106:37–38 indicates human sacrifice unto "devils," in addition, specifically citing "even" (also) sacrificing sons and daughters unto the "idols of Canaan"—where Baal worship was most prevalent. As we covered previously, Baal was known as the prince, lord of the earth and the god of this world—Satan himself (not a demon). Therefore, between verses 37 and 38 in Psalm 106, the sacrifice was before *actual* devils and began to extend to idols in their absence.

A couple of interesting final points, the first pertaining to Judges 9:23:

Judges 9:23
Then God sent an evil spirit between Abimelech and the men of Shechem; and the men of Shechem dealt treacherously with Abimelech:

Despite the pervasive influence of demonic spirits on humanity, God is in control. This is clear here, as it is God who sends an evil spirit (a demon) between Abimelech and the men of Shechem to do His will and rectify the evil slaying of seventy of his brothers (born to several mothers through polygamy) as described in Judges 9.

Secondly, Jesus, being God in the flesh, recognized the difference between a demonic spirit and a devil, despite the fact that aspects of the two can be similar and can cross over, such as oppression and possession:

John 6:68–70
Then Simon Peter answered him, Lord, to whom shall we go? thou hast the words of eternal life. And we believe and are sure that thou art that Christ, the Son of the living God. Jesus answered them, Have not I chosen you twelve, and one of you is a devil?

The word devil here is derived from the Greek word *diabolos* [1228], which means "false accuser, devil and slanderer." This term specifically refers to Satan (Matthew 4:1, Ephesians 6:11, Hebrews 2:14, 1 Peter 5:8, Revelation 12:9), who we've already determined is never referred to as a demon. Here again, the term demon is not applied to the Greek word *diabolos*. Referring to Judas Iscariot, the one disciple who would betray Jesus, it is the fallen angel, Satan, who enters into Judas and possesses him to follow through with the betrayal. The previous points mentioned are then confirmed in the following passage:

John 13:25–27
He then lying on Jesus' breast saith unto him, Lord, who is it? Jesus answered, He it is, to whom I shall give a sop, when I have dipped it. And when he had dipped the sop, he gave it to Judas Iscariot, the son

of Simon. And after the sop Satan entered into him. Then said Jesus unto him, That thou doest, do quickly.

In conclusion, there seems to be various discrepancies regarding some ancient language translations and the definitions of important words.

Fourth point established: While fallen angels and demons are related by close association and can certainly share many attributes, such as oppression and possession, they are actually separate entities. The term devil refers specifically to a fallen angel, and the chief devil is Satan himself. Fallen angels originated in heaven, while demons originated on earth.

5.
FOUNDATIONAL POINT FIVE:
THE ARRIVAL

We're now going to examine when and where the fallen angels began to interfere with man.

It is generally known that the first interference of the first man and woman, Adam and Eve, was orchestrated by Satan himself (transformed into a serpent) at the Garden of Eden (Genesis 3:1–8). This is the point of human history when both sin and death entered into the world (Romans 5:12). As a result, Adam and Eve were removed from Eden to prevent them from eating the Tree of Life and possibly remaining in a state of sin for eternity (Genesis 3:22–24). God's plan of redemption provided Jesus Christ as the last sacrificial Lamb to the world (Revelation 13:8) and manifested salvation, as a free gift, to all who would receive (John 3:16). Although the Garden of Eden does not exist today in its original state, we do know the general region of its original location.

Four rivers flowed into one main river through the Garden of Eden (Genesis 2:10–14). Three of those river sources still exist today: the Tigris (ancient Hebrew name Hiddekel), the Karun (ancient Hebrew name Gihon), and the Euphrates. The Pison is currently a dry riverbed. All four of these rivers once merged exactly at the location of ancient Sumeria (post-flood) and at the same original location of the Garden of Eden (pre-flood). It is interesting that modern historians refer to this ancient region as the Fertile Crescent, but it is also known as the Cradle of Civilization—the beginning of *recognized* human history (albeit post-flood only). Today, this is a region in southern Iraq, just north of the Red Sea.

However, this initial interference at the Garden of Eden didn't end there. Subsequent arrival of other fallen angels to earth (after the fall of man) began an escalating progression of manipulation and deliberate genetic altering.

Based on the fallen angels' decision to select human women as wives, we read in 1 Enoch 7:3–8:

Then their leader Samyaza said to them; I fear that you may perhaps be indisposed to the performance of this enterprise. And that I alone suffer for so grievous a crime. But they answered him and said, We all swear; And bind ourselves by mutual execrations, that we will not change our intention, but execute our projected undertaking. Then they swore all together, and all bound themselves by mutual sexecrations. Their whole number was two hundred, who descended upon Ardis, which is the top of mount Armon. That mountain therefore was called Armon, because they had sworn upon it, and bound themselves by mutual execrations.

In these passages we learn the following:

- A specific number of two hundred fallen angels had descended to earth.

- The leader of this particular group was a fallen angel named Samyaza.

- Samyaza declared he alone was going to take full responsibility of the decision to procreate with earthly women.

- The other fallen angels decided to follow Samyaza's lead and swore an oath (a covenant) to one another that they would be all united in this endeavor.

- The location of this covenant was a place called Ardis on top of Mount Armon.

Some of these fallen angels who participated in this covenant are specifically named in the following passage (bear in mind that, again, these angels are *all* male):

1 Enoch 7:9
These are the names of their chiefs: Samyaza, who was their leader, Urakabarameel, Akibeel, Yamiel, Ramuel, Danel, Azkeel, Saraknyal,

Asael, Armers, Batraal, Anane, Zavebe, Samsavell, Ertael, Turel, Yo-myael, Arazyal. These were the prefects of the two hundred angels, and the remainder were all with them.

The location of this initial covenant is cited as Mount Armon, also known as Mount Hermon in the Bible (Deuteronomy 3:8–9; Psalm 133:3). Today, this region is a cluster of mountain peaks straddling Lebanon and Syria, just north of Israel, and extending into the Golan Heights. The summit of Mount Hermon is the highest point in both Israel and Syria (photo on page 40). It is also known as Ba'al Hermon and Sirion.[11] Interesting fact: the name *Sirion* was used by J.R.R. Tolkien in the fantasy series *The Lord of the Rings* as the main river that flows through Middle Earth.[12]

Mount Hermon is *Jabal al-Shaykh* in Arabic and *Jabal Haramun* in Hebrew, both meaning Mountain of the Chief. This is very interesting, since the worship of Baal had flourished in this area, extending throughout Canaan (post-flood) which was instrumental in the reappearance of giants in these regions. In fact, the military campaigns by Joshua to exterminate the giants had extended north right up to Baal-gad, an ancient Canaanite town in the valley of Lebanon at the base of Mount Hermon (Joshua 13:5).

The title Mountain of the Chief is no doubt in reference to Satan as the chief (god of this world), Baal (prince, lord of the earth), and Beel (commander)—root of Beelzebub (chief of the devils). So it seems we have a glimpse of the chain of command with Satan (chief devil), Samyazal (the chief leader of the 200) and the other fallen angels named in 1 Enoch 7:9 (the *prefects* of the remaining 200—prefect meaning chief officer).

A subtle example of this chain of command between angels is found in the Book of Zachariah.

Zachariah 2:1–4
I lifted up mine eyes again, and looked, and behold a man with a measuring line in his hand. Then said I, Whither goest thou? And he said unto me, To measure Jerusalem, to see what is the breadth thereof, and what is the length thereof. And, behold, the angel that talked with me went forth, and another angel went out to meet him, And said unto him, Run, speak to this young man, saying, Jerusalem shall be inhabited as towns without walls for the multitude of men and cattle therein:

Besides the fact that one angel is giving orders to another, two other confirmations are demonstrated here as well: (1) the angel is described as a "man" taking on a human form, and (2) the angel is male (not female).

Another example of angel hierarchy is found in the Book of Joshua:

Joshua 5:13–14
And it came to pass, when Joshua was by Jericho, that he lifted up his eyes and looked, and, behold, there stood a man over against him with his sword drawn in his hand: and Joshua went unto him, and said unto him, Art thou for us, or for our adversaries? And he said, Nay; but as captain of the host of the LORD am I now come. And Joshua fell on his face to the earth, and did worship, and said unto him, What saith my LORD unto his servant?

The term "Lord of hosts" refers to the armies of the loyal angels of God. Hosts is derived from the Hebrew *tsabaah,* which means "army" and "organized for battle." This particular angel of the Lord presents himself as a "captain," demonstrating rank within an army. Once again, this angel comes in the form of a human man.

Another Scripture that sheds light on this is found in the Book of Ephesians:

Ephesians 6:12
For we wrestle not against flesh and blood, but against principalities, against powers, against the rulers of the darkness of this world, against spiritual wickedness in high places.

This Scripture is both interesting and revealing. It is cited often in church circles that fully recognize that spirit-filled, born-again believers in Christ are continually engaged in a *real* spiritual battle, with a *real* enemy. Only, this battle is primarily fought against the unseen, not against "flesh and blood"—not against *physical* adversaries. Although we have seen that angels can present themselves in physical form, such as appearing as men, angels (both loyal and fallen) operate primarily within the unseen, spiritual realm.

However, generally overlooked within this Scripture is the clear presentation of a hierarchy within the spiritual realm (in this case, the fallen spiritual realm). We see the introduction of at least four distinct levels: (1) "principalities," (2) "powers," (3) "rulers of darkness," and (4) "spiritual wickedness in high places." These are not exactly four descriptions referring to a single entity. They are four distinct aspects, uniquely described, within the fallen spiritual realm. This is reinforced by the word "against" that precedes each of the four aspects. Our battle, our fight ("we wrestle") is against each of these aspects.

Mount Hermon, Golan Heights

Sun Pyramid, Teotihuacan, Mexico

Contemplating the photograph of Mount Hermon, the exact location of the fallen angels' descent to earth, the Lord showed me something profound.

The first realization was that, upon comparing the photograph of Mount Hermon with the photograph of the Sun Pyramid (in central Mexico, halfway around the world from the Land of Canaan), I suddenly noticed the similarity between the two. It is as if the Sun Pyramid was constructed to replicate the original site of Mount Hermon. This makes even more sense if you consider that after God destroyed and purged the world through a catastrophic global flood, the people began to re-establish contact with the fallen angels ("reach unto heaven"—Genesis 11).

Genesis 11:4
And they said, Go to, let us build us a city and a tower, whose top *may reach* unto heaven; and let us make us a name, lest we be scattered abroad upon the face of the whole earth. (Emphasis added)

They intended to re-establish this contact by building a massive structure, the Tower of Babel, which God had no other choice but to destroy; then, as a second measure, He confounded their language and dispersed them throughout the world (Genesis 11:5–9). However, despite God's preventative measures, the people migrated to various parts of the earth, retaining this ancient knowledge of the interaction between fallen angels and humans. In fact, before the dispersion, the people knew what they were doing was in violation of God's will, so they made a secret pact just before God's judgment ("…and let us make us a name, lest we be scattered…").[13]

Wherever the people migrated throughout the world, massive temples were built, such as the Sun Pyramid in Mexico, dedicated in worship of the fallen angels (the false gods). So obviously this "reaching unto heaven" was not directed to God Himself (it was an intended *reaching* unto First and Second Heaven—not specifically to the Kingdom of Heaven, Third Heaven).

The second insight God showed me was that after contemplating the photograph of the Sun Pyramid, and looking more closely at all the details, the Lord drew my attention to the woman in the lower-left of the picture. Based on her height, in relation to the constructed platform in the foreground, I estimated the height of this platform to be around fourteen feet high. There are twelve steps that lead up to the top of this front platform. Based on the overall height, each step would have to be roughly fourteen inches tall.[14] The average height of a step for humans is between six to eight inches. Then the Lord revealed something to me. This structure was not designed and built for humans to climb and *ascend* to the top. This structure was actually designed and built for *something else* to *descend* from the top level down to the bottom platform. Certain orders of angels have been known to be very tall (twelve feet—double that of a human).[15] Essentially, the top level of the pyramid is where the fallen angels descended to from out of Second and First Heaven. The steps leading from the top landing level to the lower, frontal platform were built on a scale for taller beings. This makes the lower, frontal platform essentially a podium where they presented themselves to the people.

We previously covered that Satan transformed himself into the form of a serpent at the Garden of Eden. The Aztecs worshipped the Feathered Serpent god Quetzalcoatl. The Mayans worshipped the Feathered Snake god Qu'qu'matz, and the Incas in South America worshipped the Feathered Serpent god Virococha (who was known to shapeshift between serpent and human form). The Temple of the Feathered Serpent is an integral structure at Teotihuacan and part of the long Avenue of the Dead (illustration on page 18).

As a note, the worship of the serpent (or dragon) is recognized within many other cultures throughout the world. One of the main symbols of China is the dragon. Both the serpent and the dragon are direct biblical references to Satan:

Revelation 12:9
And the great dragon was cast out, that old serpent, called the Devil, and Satan, which deceiveth the whole world: he was cast out into the earth, and his angels were cast out with him.

Although the Sun Pyramid is not the tallest in the world (third-highest), it is certainly one of the highest places in the general region at 7,448 feet above sea level between various mountain peaks at Teotihuacan. This is again reminiscent of Mount Hermon being one of the highest points in its region at 9,232 feet above sea level.

Another "high place" is the structure complex found at Machu Picchu, South America.

Machu Picchu, Peru

The local tribe's people claim this complex was constructed in medieval times under the direction of Satan himself.[16] It is considered a very mystical place and the last great city of the Inca civilization. And it is certainly a very high place, resting within the Andes mountain range (closer to First and Second Heaven) at 7,972 feet above sea level.

There are specific references to high places throughout Scripture. The almighty God summoned Moses to Mount Sinai (a high place) to meet God and to receive His instructions. Some of the altars prepared by Abraham (Genesis 12:6–8), Joshua (Joshua 4:20), and Samuel (1 Samuel 7:16) were built on "high places."

Satan, in his quest to stand in the place of God, has often attempted to duplicate the things of God. This includes the construction of various temples in high places, and these were often associated with Baal (Judges 3:7; II Kings 22–23; 2 Chronicles 11:15; Jeremiah 32:35) and "strange gods." Pursuing His will to prevent another global catastrophe during the post-flood era, God encouraged various men of God to destroy these evil altars in the high places.

2 Chronicles 14:2–3
And Asa did that which was good and right in the eyes of the Lord his God: For he took away the altars of the strange gods, and the *high places*, and brake down the images, and cut down the groves: And commanded Judah to seek the Lord God of their fathers, and to do the law and the commandment. (Emphasis added)

Obviously, halfway around the earth from the ancient Middle Eastern region, the false worship of strange gods continued for some time, even right up to the fifteenth century A.D. What is very interesting is the fact that, while Jesus was leading the disciples to the true gospel of salvation throughout Judea and Samaria, at the very same time on the other side of the world, the Teotihuacan tribes (ancestors of the Aztecs and Mayans) were constructing the Avenue of the Dead which includes the Sun Pyramid in Central Mexico. It seems Satan's third attempt of manipulation and genetic alteration was in full thrust—essentially far removed and hidden from sight by the inhabitants of the Roman Empire, oblivious to its presence. We will look in more detail at some of these evil altars, including circular altars such as Stonehenge, in Section Two.

The term "strange gods" can be found multiple times throughout Scripture. In this particular Scripture, strange is derived from the Hebrew *nekar,* which means foreign, heathendom or alien.

Fifth point established: Many ancient cultures had multiple-god systems of worship. The remnant of this focused worship is clearly evident with the presence of remaining great structures (temples and altars) built throughout the earth.

It is interesting to note that Satan's inspired global system of false worship began to crumble with the arrival of the Son of God, Jesus Christ, and by the presentation of His Gospel to our world. This progressive decline of the dominant false worship systems began within the far-reaching expanse of the Roman Empire itself. The subsequent decline of the Aztec, Mayan, and Inca cultures followed after the Gospel had reached their lands, centuries later. The majority of these sacrilegious temples are now abandoned, as most are visited as curious sites for tourists and a few are still considered relevant by fledgling sects and cults (such as Stonehenge by the modern cult remnant of the Druid priesthood).

However, while these once-dominant false worship systems have faded from the public's sight, we need to fully recognize that these false worship systems are still fully engaged behind closed doors. Hence, the advent of secret societies hidden within the general population. Secret societies are basically an extension of the dispersion of people from the Tower of Babel who pledged to "...and let us make us a name, lest we be scattered..." before God confounded their single language and scattered them throughout the earth (Genesis 11:1–9). It's interesting to consider that, in modern times, when one is considered to be speaking nonsensical language or gibberish, this is often described as speaking "babble" (Babel) or "babbling on" (Babylon). We will continue to touch on this important aspect, an unbroken thread throughout human history, throughout the rest of this book.

6.

FOUNDATIONAL POINT SIX: STAGES OF BANISHMENT

At this juncture, the question can be raised, what happened to the fallen angels? Are all the fallen angels in hiding? Are they *all* bound?

There is a perception in some church circles that the fallen angels are now powerless, all bound in chains. This notion has its basis from the Book of Jude:

Jude 6
And the angels which kept not their first estate, but left their own habitation, he hath reserved in everlasting chains under darkness unto the judgment of the great day.

As we covered previously, 1 Enoch 7:3–8 tells us a group of two hundred fallen angels had initially proceeded (by a mutual oath) to engage in procreation with earthly women. We know that one-third of the heavenly angels had rebelled, with Lucifer as their leader, representing at least sixty-seven million fallen angels. Although it is possible that other fallen angels participated in the systematic genetic contamination of God's creation, we cannot conclude that all the fallen angels were involved in the unholy procreation during ancient times.

Jesus Himself made this statement in Matthew:

Matthew 25:41
Then shall he say also unto them on the left hand, Depart from me, ye cursed, into everlasting fire, *prepared for the devil and his angels...* (Emphasis added)

Jesus says the everlasting fire (the lake of fire—the final judgment) is *prepared* for the devil and his angels. This suggests a future event yet to come, which is confirmed and fulfilled in Revelation 20:10–15. This event is the Great White Throne Judgment, where those who are not written in the book of life will be cast into the eternal lake of fire. Understand that hell is also cast into the lake of fire at that time; therefore hell is actually a *temporary* location (Revelation 20:14). Also note that Jesus did not say the devil and his *demons*; He clearly states that this future, final judgment is prepared for the "devil and his *angels.*" This stands to reason since, as stated, fallen angels can be bound by some form of chains—not referring to demon spirits. It should be noted, through engaging in spiritual warfare, demon spirits can be cast out of a human host. They can also be commanded to be sent into the pit of hell. Both of these scenarios require calling on the name, power, and authority of Jesus Christ.

John 5:22
For the Father judgeth no man, but hath committed all judgment unto the Son:

John 5:26–27
For as the Father hath life in himself; so hath he given to the Son to have life in himself; And hath given him authority to execute judgment also, because he is the Son of man.

Taking both of the previous Scriptures (Jude 6 and Matthew 25:41) in context, we must conclude that only a select group of fallen angels are currently bound in chains awaiting the final judgment and the remaining fallen angels are *not* bound at this time. This select group is specifically referred to as the "Watchers" in the Book of Enoch (angels—whose intended role was to oversee the creation and the well-being of humankind). Also taking the last two Scriptures in context, it is Jesus Christ who will execute the final judgment upon the world at His Second Coming (Revelation 19:11–21). No doubt, this will include a final judgment on the remaining fallen angels as well. However, despite the fall of some, there are Watchers still to this day who have remained loyal to God.

Enoch 20:1–7
These are the names of the angels who watch. Uriel, one of the holy angels, who *presides* over clamor and terror. Raphael, one of the holy

angels, who *presides* over the spirits of men. Raguel, one of the holy angels, who inflicts punishment on the world and the luminaries. Michael, one of the holy angels, who, *presides* over human virtue, commands the nations. Sarakiel, one of the holy angels, who presides over the spirits of the children of men that transgress. Gabriel, one of the holy angels, who presides over Ikisat, over paradise, and over cherubim.

Also, we must note that Satan himself is not bound in chains until the time of his *future* defeat at Armageddon (Revelation 20:1–3) at the closing of this current world age. He is subsequently released at the end of the Thousand-Year Reign (Revelation 20:7) until the Great White Throne Judgment (Revelation 20:10–12) to deceive the nations of the remnant (the repopulation of the earth after the Second Coming, Revelation 20:7–8) at the closing of the future world age.[17]

God instructed some of his loyal and steadfast angels, such as the archangel Michael, to deal directly with the fallen Watchers and arrest them in the bondage of chains until they will be finally cast into the lake of fire.

Enoch 10:15–16
To Michael likewise the Lord said, Go and announce *his crime* to Samyaza, and to the others who are with him, who have associated with women, that they might be polluted with all their impurity. And when all their sons shall be slain, when they shall see the perdition of their beloved, bind them for seventy generations underneath the earth, even to the day of judgment, and of consummation, until the judgment, *the effect of* which will last forever, be completed. Then shall they be taken to the lowest depths of the fire in torments, and confinement shall they be shut up for ever.

It is the archangel Michael who is called to do battle against Satan (the dragon) at this particular stage of Satan's overall banishment (Revelation 12:7–9).

As a note here, there are actually four separate stages to the overall banishment of Satan: (1) his banishment from a permanent residence in the Kingdom of Heaven, (2) his banishment to Earth, the confines of First Heaven exclusively. This occurs at the same time as the coming Rapture, where the remaining (alive) "church bride" is removed (raised) from the Earth (1 Thessalonians 4:17) at which point, simultaneously, the fallen realm is cast down to the Earth (the complete separation of the righteous from the unrighteous). This second stage is described in Revelation 12:12:

> Therefore rejoice, ye heavens, and ye that dwell in them. Woe to the inhabiters of the earth and of the sea! for the devil is come down unto you, having great wrath, because he knoweth that he hath but a short time.

It's clear that two separate groups are described here: (a) those "that dwell in heaven" (the now raptured) and (b) "the inhabiters of the earth" (those left behind during the seven-year Tribulation period). This Scripture also describes Satan as quite agitated (as a hornet trapped inside a glass jar—confined to First Heaven) and having "but a short time" (less than seven years until the Second Coming where, (3) he is banished and confined in chains to the bottomless pit for one thousand years (Revelation 20:1–2), and finally (4) banished to the Lake of Fire for eternity at the end of the Thousand-Year Reign of Christ (Revelation 20:7–10).

A good example demonstrating the fact that not all fallen angels are currently bound in chains is found in the Book of Daniel. Daniel has a vision and is visited by an angel (Daniel 10:5–12) who explains that he was held up for twenty-one days before he was able to make his way to Daniel.

Daniel 10:13–14
But the prince of the kingdom of Persia withstood me one and twenty days: but, lo, Michael, one of the chief princes, came to help me; and I remained there with the kings of Persia. Now I am come to make thee understand what shall befall thy people in the latter days: for yet the vision *is* for *many* days.

This particular angel tells Daniel he was in a battle with the "prince of Persia." Not until the archangel Michael came and assisted this angel in the fight was the prince finally overcome and defeated. Interestingly, Michael is referred to as "one of the chief princes." In the spiritual realm, God's angels are entrusted with the care of various aspects and territories of His creation (as we saw concerning the Watchers). This is also true within the fallen kingdom(s) on earth under the enemy's control and influence (known as spiritual strongholds). However, this passage is not referring to a demon but a fallen angel. In fact, it refers to a fallen angel who is also a "prince" over the territory known as Persia. This stands to reason that this fallen angel was so pervasive that it required the combined effort of an angel of the Lord and the archangel Michael over twenty-one days to defeat! Obviously, this was not a mere "prince" in the sense of a normal, physical human. This is a major lesson that the spiritual fight against demonic spirits may be great, but the spiritual battle against fallen angels is even greater. Hence, the bottom line here is that not all fallen angels are bound in chains.

Another example is the future event of four angels, most likely four of the original two hundred in chains, who are to be loosed (unchained) during the Tribulation period as described in the Book of Revelation.

Revelation 9:13–15
And the sixth angel sounded, and I heard a voice from the four horns of the golden altar which is before God, saying to the sixth angel which had the trumpet, Loose the four angels which are bound in the great river Euphrates. And the four angels were loosed, which were prepared for an hour, and a day, and a month, and a year, for to slay the third part of men.

The overwhelming majority of Bible versions state "four angels" in this passage. This is very important, as this unequivocally dispels the notion that fallen angels have become (transformed into) demons after being banished from the Kingdom of Heaven. Again, this also demonstrates the pervasive ability of fallen angels. It takes only four of them to slay one-third of the earth's population over one year, one month, one day, and an hour.

As a confirmation to the binding of *specific* angels, we read:

1 Enoch 10:6–9
Again the lord said to Raphael, Bind Azazyel hand and foot; cast him into darkness; and opening the desert which is in Dudael, cast him in there. Throw upon him hurled and pointed stones, covering him with darkness; There shall he remain for ever, cover his face, that he may not see the light. And in the great day of judgment let him be cast into the fire.

Concerning the other fallen angels and their eternal punishment, they confide in Enoch to petition the Almighty God for forgiveness of their devastating transgressions, but God rejects their plea:

1 Enoch 12:1–7

Before all these things Enoch was concealed; nor did any one of the sons of men know where he was concealed, where he had been, and what had happened. He was wholly engaged with the holy ones, and with the Watchers in his days. I, Enoch, was blessing the great lord and King of peace. And behold the Watchers called me Enoch the scribe. Then *the Lord* said to me: Enoch, scribe of righteousness, go tell the Watchers of heaven, *who* have deserted the lofty sky, and their holy everlasting station, *who* have been polluted with women. And have done as the sons of men do, by taking to themselves wives, and who have been greatly corrupted on the earth; That on the earth they shall they shall never obtain peace and remission of sin. For they shall not rejoice in their offspring; they shall behold the slaughter of their beloved; shall lament for the destruction of their sons; and shall petition for ever; but shall not obtain mercy and peace.

Finally, as a reminder concerning Job 1:6 and 2:1, Satan and the other fallen angels do present themselves before God, on occasion—and they do so *not* as demons.

Sixth point established: Not all fallen angels are currently bound in chains. In fact, it seems that only a limited, select group is currently prevented from interacting with humanity—which leaves the inevitable, distinct possibility that millions of fallen angels are still able to influence and interact with humanity. We will look at this in more detail throughout Section Three.

Based on what we've just covered, where are all the other fallen angels (those not bound) now? Along with Satan, are they simply hiding in the shadows? We will address this question in the seventh foundational point, after we first examine a few more related foundational premises.

7.

FOUNDATIONAL POINT SEVEN: SATAN'S INFLUENCE – PRE-FLOOD AND POST-FLOOD

As asked near the beginning of this book, how bad did it have to get for God to find it absolutely necessary to destroy all of humanity (except eight humans) and destroy nearly all other life on the planet?

Essentially, God found it necessary to purge the world of *something*. It becomes absolutely imperative to fully understand what that something was—and what it could be, once again repeating itself just before the Second Coming.

Most people understand the concept that when Adam and Eve fell from grace at the Garden of Eden, through the temptation and manipulation of Satan, both sin and death were introduced to the world. A perfect world became a fallen world. As mankind went forth and multiplied on the earth, sin not only continued to be present, sin also grew exponentially—especially when humankind continued to fall further and further away from God.

It is a well-known fact that each and every one of us is born into the world of sin. We did not actually *choose* for ourselves to be born into a world of sin. Each of us came into the world by the decisions directly made by our parents. The fact that we are all born as sinners is directly related to the initial decision (the first sin) made by Adam and Eve from the very beginning. There are three things man (by his own power) cannot do: (1) change history, (2) eliminate sin, and (3) save himself spiritually. The presence of sin in the world continues to escalate, generation to generation, as it is passed down through the bloodline. We are all part of the initial bloodline of Adam and Eve.

Based on this premise, when God decided it was necessary to destroy much of the initial creation by way of a catastrophic, global flood, God made a provision to spare many species of living creatures that were not corrupt (not genetically altered). He also spared eight humans who were also not corrupted of the flesh. However, these eight individuals were still part of the generational bloodline of Adam. Therefore, these eight individuals were still sinners—just like everyone else who is subsequently born into the world of sin (1 John 1:8–10).

When God saved these eight individuals and destroyed all remaining trace of humankind, He did not yet eliminate the presence of sin. God, in His almighty power, could have wiped the slate entirely clean and started all over again. He didn't. Instead, sin carried on through the post-flood generations as it had through the pre-flood generations. God's plan was to deal with sin by having the Saviour (Jesus Christ), born into the world of sin, but separate and without sin (Immaculate Conception),[18] offered as a final sacrifice (the Lamb slain from the foundation of the world—death and resurrection at the cross) to provide the *only* way to salvation (belief, faith, confession, and repentance) so that we can be saved (John 3:16).

We need to understand that God did not destroy sin by way of the global flood. God found it necessary to destroy the majority of the world to eliminate *something else*—something that had gone beyond the presence of sin. While we need to acknowledge the presence of sin as an extremely detrimental aspect within society, we also need to understand that sin is actually the primary foundation that leads to something much larger—sin leads to destruction and finally death (Romans 6:23). However, even this statement, in itself, does not describe the full picture. With sin as the foundation, there are a series of gradual steps that can lead to eventual destruction and death. These are the gradual steps that have been commonly overlooked.

THE PROGRESSION OF SIN

- ▸ The fall of Adam & Eve introduces sin to the world

- ▸ Sin is passed through the generations (bloodline). We are all born into the world of sin.

- ▸ As the population grows exponentially, sin has been shown to grow in step when that population continues to turn away from God's purpose and will.

- ▸ If sin continues to grow exponentially, wickedness and evil begin to envelop society (clearly stated in Genesis 6:5)

- In an ever-increasingly sinful environment, apart from God, satanic influence begins to take hold

- Satanic strongholds begin to shift all worship from God to full-out worship of false gods (fallen angels) resulting in a deeper spiritual decay

- Once full worship is achieved, unrestricted advancement and manipulation begin to occur (manifestations and appearances begin with no opposition)

- Once unrestricted advancement and manipulation take hold, genetic contamination begins (a society completely apart from God). This is now an extreme level of physical decay emerging from spiritual decay. Remember, Satan cannot create, he can only *attempt* to alter what is already created.

- If Satan cannot alter the creation "his way," he is just as happy to see it destroyed. Satan absolutely *hates* the things of God.

- Destruction inevitably becomes the end result of this progression anyway; as wickedness, evil, and violence propel discord and chaos, there is a continual shift away from God's intended structure of balance and order.

- The final result becomes a physical death (first death) and a spiritual death (second death).

We must understand the full significance of what Jesus declared just before His death on the Cross: *"it is finished"* (John 19:30). While Satan, as god of this world, continues to have great influence within a fallen and deceived world, God ultimately is in control. Satan knows this. He also knows that eventually all things will come to an end. Based on this, Satan is relentlessly attempting (and in many cases successfully) to bring down as many souls to eternal destruction as possible.

Satan was well aware of God's plan and has tried (and continues to try) to intervene and prevent Christ's finished work on the Cross, individual by individual.

1 Peter 5:8
Be sober, be vigilant; because your adversary the devil, as a roaring lion, walketh about, seeking whom he may devour…

Well aware of God's plan from the very beginning, Satan even tried to sway Christ Himself:

Matthew 4:8–10
Again, the devil taketh him up into an exceeding high mountain, and sheweth him all the kingdoms of the world, and the glory of them; And saith unto him, All these things will I give thee, if thou wilt fall down and worship me. Then saith Jesus unto him, Get thee hence, Satan: for it is written, Thou shalt worship the Lord thy God, and him only shalt thou serve.

Satan appealed to Jesus' humanity with his offer to hand over the kingdoms of the world in exchange for Christ's allegiance. Note that Satan took Jesus to a high mountain (a high place). However, it was the divine side of Jesus (as God in the flesh) who rejected this offer, quoting the Word of God to qualify his rejection.

Here's a question: where is our current society in this progression of sin? While considering this very important question, also consider these other important points that pertain specifically to our society (the current fallen kingdoms).

While some cultures still ascribe to religious belief systems with multiple gods (such as Hinduism), the majority of the population, within our modern technological and information-driven world, does not view the presence of gods as being anything close to the realm of reality. Satan is well aware of this. While his multiple-god platform may not be working as well today as it once did in ancient times, Satan still has two other main methods of achieving a strong degree of control over humanity.

The first method has its roots within the initial fall at the Garden of Eden. Talking to Eve, the serpent stated:

Genesis 3:5
For God doth know that in the day ye eat thereof, then your eyes shall be opened, and ye shall be as gods, knowing good and evil.

Although Satan has made great strides to have man (especially naïve ancient man) worship him and his fallen angels as gods, Satan has also encouraged and enticed humans to become their own god—effectively suggesting and persuading a personal decision to cast away the need for any close relationship with the almighty God. This is precisely what many have done in a modern society. Many have squeezed God out of their busy schedules and relegated any hint of a relationship with God to empty aphorisms like "In God we trust" or "God will get you for that." Even atheists, who claim they do not believe in God or any other religion, are in fact actively participating in a false religion—the religion of self. Atheists believe they are completely in control of their own destiny (actually their own *fate*). They essentially *believe* they are their own god—precisely the same lie Satan fed to Adam and Eve at the Garden of Eden.

An interesting aspect about the term atheism is that, in its original connotation, it was meant as a derogatory comment towards someone who held to a single-God theology. Atheism is actually two words: "a" (meaning one or single) and "theism" (meaning the belief in a god or gods—the prefix root word "a" cancelling out the plural). This was especially true during the Roman Empire. Christians and Jews were often ridiculed for proclaiming the one, true, and almighty God of Scripture—Jehovah. However, after much conquering and expansion of the empire, the Romans had embraced *all* gods, even to the point of generally tolerating the Synagogues and Jewish temples. The Roman Emperor Hadrian built the Pantheon between 118 and 125 A.D. It was a temple dedicated to all gods ("pan"—all and "theon"—divinity).

Ironically, this single-God connotation has shifted to "no God" in modern times. Yet, as mentioned, atheism is truly a religious belief system focused on the singular self, also described as *me*. In recent times the me generation has transcended into the "I am" generation (I AM, in all uppercase, being the definitive bold statement reserved for the almighty God Himself—Exodus 3:14). One of the sign posts of the modern "I am" generation was the book *Out on a Limb* released in 1983 (TV mini-series in 1987) that presented the New Age spiritual journey of actress Shirley Mclean. She documented her involvement and promotion of reincarnation (the recycling of souls), channeling (demonic possession), astral travel (human spirit leaving the body) and seeking out *extraterrestrials* and UFOs while on a trip throughout the Andes Mountains, including the ancient site of Machu Picchu. In both the book and the TV mini-series, Shirley Mclean stands on a beachfront, outstretches her arms, and then arrogantly proclaims, "I am God."

Jesus stated that one of the prerequisites required to be born again, to be saved, one must die to self, *not* exalt self (Matthew 10:38; Mark 8:35; Luke 9:23; Galatians 2:20).

The second method Satan uses to gain control over modern society is through man's pride and intellect. Tied to this, Satan is a master of logic. What might seem logical to man may in fact be in complete error, and what may seem illogical to man may in fact be God's perfect will.

In today's world, the following scenario would seem absolutely illogical. Picture a military general engaged in battle. He suddenly commands his troops to lay down their weapons, and instead pick up trumpets and horns. Then he orders them to march in a circle around the enemy's position seven times while blowing their horns, with the promise of delivering complete victory over the enemy. That is precisely how God commanded Joshua to take down the fortress of Jericho (one of many fortified cities throughout the ancient land of Canaan—Joshua 5:13, 6:27).

During a time when it did not rain on the earth (Genesis 2:5–6), Noah spent an estimated fifty to seventy-five years building the Ark.[19] He also built this massive ship hundreds of miles inland from any access to a common body of water. Again, to most people, this would seem completely illogical. Yet, Noah remained obedient to God and kept his family separated from the rest of the world. It is hard enough to live a Christian life in these modern times of political correctness, and in the face of an all-out assault on Christian values, but just imagine for a moment being one of only eight individuals (one family) pitted against the entire world!

Proverbs 14:12
There is a way which seemeth right unto a man, but the end thereof *are* the ways of death.

Apart from God, man's pride can essentially become a cloak to hide the fact that one is really running away from God. Apart from God, exceptionally brilliant people can be rendered as absolute fools not knowing (oblivious), not understanding (ignorant indifference), or not recognizing (spiritually blind) even the simplest things of God.

The Scribes and Pharisees studied the Word of God the majority of their lives, yet failed to recognize the actual Son of God, Jesus Christ. This even when all the prophesies found in the same Word were being fulfilled right before their very eyes, signifying that this man was indeed their awaited Messiah.

Satan uses man's pride, intellect, and logic to deceive. This brings us to our current dilemma—the *logic* of the Theory of Transitional Evolution.

It seems logical to man that all life, the earth, and the entire universe developed and evolved over some thirteen billion years. It seems illogical to man that everything we know came into existence less than ten thousand years ago (a chart of the biblical history of the earth is found at the back of this book). Yet, that is what God's Word clearly indicates. Man uses his own intellect, fueled by his pride, to attempt to validate the notion that everything we know of came out of "nothing" (physical matter suddenly, *miraculously*, appearing after an explosion)—the so-called Big Bang. Conversely, it seems illogical to man that *something* had to bring something out of "nothing"—that being a creator, God. Ironically, man refers to everything as the universe, which actually means "the single, spoken sentence" (uni/verse). It is clearly stated in Scripture that God "spoke" everything into existence (Genesis 1:3–29). The very word universe itself suggests that God (Intelligent Design) was present before its inception.

The evidence clearly shows that explosions bring about destruction, as well as chaos, discord, and subsequent decay. Explosions do not bring about perfect order and symmetry. An example of this was the large-scale destruction of the city of Hiroshima by a nuclear bomb on August 6, 1945. The direct result was major chaos and discord and, if left on its own, the city would have continued to decay and crumble. It took the *creative* force of human beings using resolve, fortitude, compassion, strength, love, determination, and intelligence to rebuild (recreate) the city. Hiroshima did not rebuild itself.

Man insists that it is logical to believe life began as the simplest form, the single cell, when it is now known that the single cell is the most complex form of life we know of (everything we are as living, individual human beings was first encoded within a single cell).

Man insists it is logical to believe all life evolved from a single cell to modern man over 2.5 billion years (912.5 billion days). There would need to have been *at least* one trillion to the trillionth power of microscopic transitional changes over this period to achieve that overall progression—millions of changes per day, every day—to achieve this overall progression. This has never been observed. 912.5 billion days is short at least one trillion days. The single cell alone has one thousand million components to its structure![20] Secular scientists insist that this complex lifeform somehow appeared *miraculously*, out of water and minerals (non-living material) without the presence of a Creator God. For more information on the structure of a single cell, I would highly recommend *The Design and Complexity of the Cell* by Dr. Jeffrey Tomkins.

Man also insists it is logical to believe the next stage of the progression of Transitional Evolution is the probability of the presence of higher advanced life-forms originating somewhere in the universe—the speculation of the existence of *extraterrestrial* life.

But it doesn't end there; the next and final stage in the progression of Transitional Evolution is the *transcendence stage*, from an advanced intelligence to a higher state of "consciousness." In other words, the idea that intelligent life will eventually become one with the universe, essentially attaining the same level as God Himself, becoming omnipresent and all-knowing.

So it seems that it is illogical for man to think he was created by God, but by his own intellect and pride, man deems it absolutely logical that he can *evolve* to become a god. Again, this is the exact same lie, repackaged, that Satan used at the Garden of Eden.

As mentioned previously, the term "strange gods" can be found multiple times throughout Scripture. As we saw in the Scripture passages of 2 Chronicles 14:2–3, strange is derived from the Hebrew word *nekar,* which means foreign, heathendom, or alien.

The idea of higher, advanced forms of life *somewhere* within the known universe is referred to as being alien or extraterrestrial. These terms are defined:

Alien: foreign, differing in nature or character typically to the point of incompatibility

Extraterrestrial: of or from outside the earth or its atmosphere

The term alien is clearly describing something different than the native residents. In the case of the human race, *alien life* would be foreign to earth. Evolutionists propose that *alien life* would have originated on other planets—other worlds.

The term extraterrestrial describes something originating beyond earth. The root word *extra* means "in addition to" and the root word *terrestrial* refers to "of earth; relating to earth; or an inhabitant of earth"—basically stating *in addition to life on earth.*

However, it needs to be pointed out that neither of these two terms definitively states, nor refers to, foreign or other life *directly* originating on other planets. Scientists have determined the existence of some two thousand other planets (termed *exoplanets*) within our own galaxy (as of January 2016). None of these discovered planets is capable of supporting life as we know it. It has *not* been officially stated that some form of *alien life* actually exists beyond our earth. Yet ironically, at the same time, reported sightings of UFOs and *alien* abduction cases are at a record high. Obviously, something is not adding up.

What if the invasion of *extraterrestrial* UFOs through our atmosphere and the invasion and violation of a person's normal life through sudden, abduction experiences has not originated from other planets beyond our earth? What if this is not necessarily just a physical invasion by advanced beings that, supposedly, are higher on the evolutionary scale? What if this is actually a spiritual invasion (with physical aspects) orchestrated by Satan and the fallen angels—*spiritual beings* who actually do originate from Second Heaven (the known universe) upon being banished from Third Heaven (the Kingdom of Heaven) and subsequently entering our world through First Heaven (the earth's atmosphere)?

It's really interesting when one stops to think that the idea of advanced beings (aliens/extraterrestrials) is a lifeform right in between the level of existence of modern man and the *desired* level of existence of a higher state of consciousness—godhood. Similarly, the fallen angels (false gods) placed themselves right in between the level of existence of ancient man and of God Himself.

Since God's Word tells us all the morning stars were present at the time of the creation of the universe and everything in it (including humankind, Job 38:4–7), it is not difficult to understand that all the angels know a great deal about the cosmos. They know about every galaxy, every star system, and every planet that was brought into existence. Based on the fact that angels were entrusted with the stewardship of the cosmos, they have travelled the universe and have visited these heavenly bodies. Therefore, it should come as no surprise that these fallen angels, presenting themselves as *extraterrestrials,* come with advanced knowledge of other star systems and planets.

Regarding the progression of sin, I posed the question earlier, at what point is our current society along in the progression of sin? What if we are currently somewhere in, or near, the following stages?

- ▸ Satanic strongholds begin to shift all worship from God to full-out worship of false gods (fallen angels), resulting in a spiritual decay

Based on this, what if Satan and the other fallen angels have simply changed their overall presentation from appearing as replacement gods (as they did in ancient times), to gradually appearing and falsely representing themselves as *extra-terrestrials* (as they are now doing in modern times). In the first statement above, let's replace the term false gods with the word extraterrestrials:

> ▸ Satanic strongholds begin to shift all worship from God to full-out worship of *extraterrestrials* (fallen angels), resulting in a spiritual decay

Then, of course, the following statement would be the obvious next step in the overall progression:

> ▸ Once full worship is achieved, unrestricted advancement and manipulation begin to occur (manifestations and appearances begin with no opposition)

Hence, a direct increase in UFO sightings and *alien* encounters.

What if this is all simply a grand, deceptive ploy to influence and manipulate man's pride, intellect, and logic—all designed to perpetuate the underlining lie of *transitional* evolution. What if this is all part of a malevolent master plan to effectively turn modern man away from the almighty creator God? Satan's manipulation of man through deceptive logic—the inevitable "reality" that there are advanced life forms beyond earth, causing one to conclude (falsely) that *transitional* evolution is now a fact (not a theory), and therefore humankind was not created by God; therefore there is no God, and man now concludes that he alone is in the driver's seat, only accountable to himself. Sounds logical, but it is not actually a fact. It is actually a lie.

Regarding the unbelievers of God's Word, representing the majority of the world, we read:

John 8:44
Ye are of your father the devil, and the lusts of your father ye will do. He was a murderer from the beginning, and abode not in the truth, because there is no truth in him. When he speaketh a lie, he speaketh of his own: for he is a liar, and the father of it.

Once again, the Hebrew word *nekar* means foreign, heathendom, or alien. Pertaining to the definition heathendom, this means Godless or non-Christian.

There is a direct correlation that can be measured over the past fifty years or so. The more society continues to decay (greed, indifference, pride, immorality, wickedness, false religion, etc.) moving towards a Godless foundation, the more the UFO phenomenon increases. As stated previously, the progression of sin continues with "manifestations and appearances begin with no opposition."

In Canada, 2012 had the highest level of reported UFO sightings in twenty-five years, and 2013 was the second-highest (CBC News report, March 11, 2014).

Some claim that the increasing presence of extraterrestrials and UFO phenomena is based on the foundational reason and purpose that "they" are here to help us. While the evidence continues to mount that *something* continues to invade our skies and is indeed present amongst us, there is absolutely no evidence that they are actively involved in helping us. If their presence was good news to our world, it would not be kept a secret.

If man continues to decide, of his free will, to leave God out of his day-to-day living—to the point of totally discarding any chance of a personal relationship with his Creator, God will simply withdraw. This creates a spiritual vacuum. It is at this stage of the progression that the enemy rushes in to fill this spiritual void, usually with little or no opposition. We are currently in an era of God's grace. The judgment of the nations does not occur until the Second Coming of Christ. Currently, only the presence of God's people and the working of the Holy Spirit is limiting and holding back a full-scale take over.

This brings us full circle to Jesus' warning in Matthew 24:37:

> But as the days of Noah were, so shall also the coming of the Son of man be.

In Noah's time, there was a full-scale takeover. This led God to the unavoidable and regrettable decision to destroy the majority of life on earth (Genesis 6:6–7). The very fact that countless life forms were trapped and most of them buried alive between various sedimentary strata is absolute proof that a catastrophic event occurred at some point in our history. We are all walking, daily, on top of a massive *graveyard* all over the earth. Only a minute fraction of our earth has ever been excavated to reveal these deceased life forms. The earth was once teaming with life—far more diverse species existed in our past than now. It needs to be stated that the many sedimentary layers could not have been formed without water—tremendous amounts of water. The very word *sediment* means "minerals or organic matter deposited by water" (www.merriam-webster.com/ dictionary/sediment).

In our time, the full-scale takeover is not yet complete—but it is definitely underway. The systematic attack and ridicule of Christian values is at an all-time high and continues to intensify exponentially. This is the thrust of the gospel of the Antichrist (delivered through political correctness ushering in a false world peace and false religious unity) which precedes his eventual arrival and his mandated seat of power and authority (Revelation 13:5; 13:11–12).

Daniel 7:25
And he shall speak great words against the most High, and shall wear out the saints of the most High, and think to change times and laws: and they shall be given into his hand until a time and times and the dividing of time.

Two things will happen simultaneously during the end times: (1) God will pour out His Spirit upon His people (Joel 2:28; Acts 2:17) and (2) there will be a great falling away from the gospel and Christianity (Acts 20:29–31; I Timothy 4:1; II Timothy 3:13–17; II Thessalonians 2:1–3). The dividing line between born-again (spirit-filled) believers and non-believers (including the deceived) will become clearer towards the end of this age as the Second Coming of Christ approaches.

The Lord showed me a vision many years ago when I was embarking on this journey of research. He impressed on my spirit that as we draw closer to the time of the end, the last days, the dividing lines between the righteous and the unrighteous would continue to become clearer. Ironically, God illustrated this progression by showing me a single cell dividing under a microscope. As the cell begins to divide, the central nucleus, with its chromosomes, begin separating first. There is a flurry of activity as DNA proteins "run" back and forth from one side to the other, interchanging. Finally, after the central chromosomes have separated, the cell actually separates into two when its cell walls open and then close around the newly formed cells.

Similarly, as we draw closer to the end, multitudes of people "run" back and forth with their convictions of personal beliefs, until finally there is a definite division between those who are with God (the righteous "cell" on one side) and those who are against God (the unrighteous "cell" on the other side). Even still, there will be the undecided left within the space between the two well-defined sides (the undecided left behind with the unrighteous after the Rapture).

Other signs that precede Christ's return are as follows:

- False teachers, false prophets and false Christs will arise (Matthew 24:5; 24:11; 2 Timothy 4:3–4)

- Many wars and rumours of wars (Matthew 24:6)

- Increased famine and diseases (Mathew 24:7)

- Increased earthquakes in diverse places (Matthew 24:7)

- The seas and oceans will be raging, producing severe storms (Luke 21:25)

- Many will be offended, hatred and betrayal will increase (Matthew 24:10)

- Children will rise up against their parents (Mark 13:12)

- Nations will be in a state of perplexity (Luke 21:25)

- There will be profound signs in the sun, moon, and stars (Luke 21:25)

- Hearts of many will fail from intense fear (Luke 21:26)

This short list does not take into consideration the full effect of the (21) judgments during the final seven years known as the Tribulation Period, of which the final three-and-a-half-year period is known as the Great Tribulation.

Yet, despite all of this bad news, the good news of the gospel will be preached to all four corners of the world—and then the end will come (Matthew 24:14).

Intertwined in all of these signs of both increase and intensity, knowledge will abound along with increased global transit (Daniel 12:4).

The comparison Jesus made between the days of Noah and the time of His return is not only a repetition of increased sin; it is also a repetition of manipulated genetics. Modern man, through secular science, is genetically altering living things (known as Genetically Modified Organisms) such as various kinds of food, as well as engaging in cloning and the genetic altering of certain animal and fish species. We will take a closer look at this in the chapter entitled Genetic Manipulation.

In addition to these recent developments, *alien* abductions of humans have progressively increased since the 1950s. Many individuals claim to have been suddenly kidnapped against their will, brought aboard supposed UFO craft, and then become unwilling participants in bizarre medical procedures and experiments. Many of these individual victims suffer from post-traumatic stress and many have visible scars; some have tiny implants embedded in their bodies, and others have unnatural markings on their bodies as ongoing reminders of their living nightmare. With most of these *alien* procedures concentrated on the reproductive systems of their hostages—genetic manipulation is at the central core of the *alien* abduction scenario. Considering where we're at in the overall progression of sin within our society, this could hardly be coincidence.

We are living in the last days. The intention of a full-scale takeover is currently underway.

Seventh point established: The fallen angels, who presented themselves as replacement gods to ancient man, are the same fallen angels now presenting themselves as extraterrestrial *aliens* to modern man. Both instances are concentrated efforts to focus man's full attention on false entities and/or the heavenly bodies (planets and stars) of the cosmos to distract man's attention away from a true relationship with the almighty, creator God.

How bad did it have to get for God found it necessary to destroy all of humanity (except eight humans) and destroy roughly ninety-five percent of all other life forms on the planet?

As previously stated, God found it necessary to purge the world of *something*. It becomes absolutely imperative to fully understand what that something was—and what it could be, once again repeating itself just before the Second Coming. Based on what we have just covered, we now know what that something was (and is).

As we continue through the next chapters of Sections Two and Three, startling evidence and revelations of understanding will be presented that document these foundational points. There is definitely more to this world than what meets the eye.

SECTION I ENDNOTES

1   My father received his PhD and graduated as the top student in the world, out of a class of 44 (hand-picked students globally), in the field of Metallurgy at the University of London, England, in 1962. Based on his mathematical genius, I asked him to calculate the pre-flood population on earth by using a set of parameters. These parameters applied to a world within pristine, pre-flood conditions (healthier nutrients, richer atmosphere, calm weather, less UV rays, etc.). Such a perfect environment included:

    a)   Exactly 1,656 years of time between Adam and Eve and the Great Flood

    b)   Average lifespan of 900 years and a half-life of 450 years (as indicated in the lineage of men in Genesis Chapter 5)

    c)   A minimum of 15 children per family, ranging to 50 children (each ancient man cited having many "sons and daughters" other than those specifically cited by name)

    d)   It is clearly demonstrated that some post-flood, modern families (having lesser lifespans of 75 years) had as many as 10 to 20 offspring. Some post-flood, ancient dynasties saw nobility having 50 to 100 offspring through multiple wives.

    Based on my father's mathematical equation, the earth's population would have been a minimum of 200 million to a maximum range of 2.5 billion people, with a likely range of 1.5 billion people.

2   For those who hold to the doctrine of a future event of the Rapture, the general teaching of the church is that the latter day church, metaphorically referred to as the "church bride" (Isaiah 62:5; Joel 2:16; Revelation 19:7–9; 21:2; 21:9-11) will be taken up (raptured up) from the Earth when Christ appears in the clouds (1 Thessalonians 4:17), just before the twenty-one judgments are initiated during the subsequent Seven Year Tribulation period as described throughout the Book of Revelation. The point of contention here is that it is generally taught that deceased believers will resurrect

from their graves first, and then the living would be raptured up secondly. After extensive research into the Word, I have discovered this teaching is actually in error. The deceased believers are not lying in their graves to await the Rapture. Rather, they are the "dead in Christ" who are "asleep in Christ" (1 Thessalonians 4:13–15), literally asleep in the body of Christ, who are then awakened (rise first) at the sound of the trump of God. We are created in the image of God, in three parts: (1) body), (2) Spirit, and (3) soul. The corrupted body returns to the ground as dust (Genesis 3:19); the spirit returns to God (Ecclesiastes 12:7); and the remaining soul is held in the body of Christ, not in the grave, until awakened at the Rapture as stated in Thessalonians 4. After much consideration of many Scriptures, it becomes clear that the event of the Rapture and the First and Second Resurrections (the main resurrections) are separate and distinct events. In addition, there are other examples of singular rapture events, as well as examples of singular resurrection events throughout the Bible, which further demonstrate that a rapture event is not the same as a resurrection event. For more in-depth analysis on this I will refer you to my first publication, *What Happens at the Rapture: What Happens When We Die?*

3   For an in-depth overview on this, I would recommend the video *Return of the Nephilim* by Dr. Chuck Missler.

4   Satan is directly referred as a dragon, a serpent, and called the Devil (capital D) in God's Word (Revelation 12:9). This is repeated throughout the Bible in various Scriptures. In addition, ancient cultures such as the Incas, Mayans, and Aztecs worshipped the "feathered serpent god" or "feathered snake god." In the case of the Incas, the "feathered serpent god" was known as Viracocha, who was able to transform between serpent form and human form before the people. Hollywood films have often depicted Satan in human form, such as *Angel Heart* (1987) and *End of Days* (1999). Often, Hollywood movies portray elements of a spiritual nature as reflection of either cultural folklore or actual elements of the fabric of human history. Satan's ability to shapeshift between different forms, including animals, has been described by the personal testimonies of various individuals, most notably those who are active within the Occult/Satanism. These testimonies have been published in books, magazines, journals, newspapers, and news programs, recorded in criminal court transcripts and at times shared person to person.

5   The Bible describes the coming Antichrist as a *second beast* in the form of a man (Revelation 13:11) who is given the authority of the *first beast* (the composite conglomeration of end time nations of the 1st, 2nd and 3rd world dominating kingdoms described in Daniel 7). Thus, the *first beast* actually represents the 4th and final world kingdom just before the Second Coming of Christ. This *second beast*, this "man"—the Antichrist, appears to be the messiah (still awaited by the Jewish Orthodox priests preparing the 3rd Temple) as he displays "two horns like a lamb," which is the opposite, mirror image of Christ described as the "Lamb slain from the foundation of the world." (Capital L—Revelation 13:8). He also "speaks like a dragon," having the attributes of his father, Satan himself. Exercising "all the power of the first beast" (Revelation 13:12), he directly receives his power and authority, over the *first beast* from his father, Satan (Revelation 13:2). The Antichrist is clearly the son of Satan, referred to as the "son of perdition" which is defined as absolute destruction, eternal damnation, doom, and the prevailer of hell (2 Thessalonians 2:3). This is also the mirror image to Christ, the Son of God, also presented to the world in the form of a man. Based on all of the preceding points, it is clear that a son is born to Satan as a father. Satan cannot create. He can only attempt to alter what is already created. The only possible way Satan can father a son in the form of a man is through the sexual union between himself and a human woman, most likely a woman who has given herself over to this unholy union with Satan. It is interesting that the Hollywood film series *The Omen* (1976, 1978 and 1981) and the film *Rosemary's Baby* (1968) present this very premise. However, unlike the sanctified procreation of a normal human being comprising body, spirit, and soul, the Antichrist is actual a spiritual abomination in the form of a human, comprised of body and spirit only—missing the important component of the soul (as with the Nephilim giant offspring described in this book). Therefore, the birth of the Antichrist is a life form doomed to eternal damnation—never able to receive salvation through the provision of Christ. Having no soul equates to not being able to receive salvation. The Occult speaks of male demons having sexual relations with women while they are sleeping, known as an *incubus*. The female counterpart of this is known as a *succubus*. However, it needs to be clarified that demon spirits cannot procreate, producing offspring—only fallen angels (all male) can procreate with earthly women, producing spiritually corrupt offspring. Satan is not a demon, he is a fallen angel.

6   Article, *Anak Meaning*, Abarim Publications: http://www.abarim-publications.com/Meaning/Anak.html#.WMV-j4WcGUk

7   We are told in God's Word that the last statement of Christ before his death on the Cross was, "It is finished" (John 19:30). Based on this, upon His subsequent resurrection, Christ would officially become the "Lord of the dead and of the living" (Romans 14:9). This is only one title of many attributed to Jesus Christ. Likewise, Satan has many titles and many names. As such, these titles often reflect the opposite mirror image to Jesus Christ directly, or of the things of God. Satan is definitely not original. Examples of this are "angel of light" versus "Light of the world"; Satan the "adversary" versus Jesus the "advocate," "prince of darkness" versus "Prince of peace," etc. Based on this, a common title for Satan throughout many ancient cultures, using different names, has been the "lord of the dead." This is contrary and in opposition to the title of Christ found in Romans 14:9. Examples of this are Orion (Egyptian) and Samhain (Celtic Druids) as the "lord of the dead." However, based on the death and resurrection of Christ, this particular title will be reduced exclusively to "lord of the dead" in hell and subsequently the lake of fire, never more in application to the remaining living and redeemed in a new heaven and a new earth for the rest of eternity.

8   In the configuration of the human form, the soul contains the aspects of the mind (including intellect and personality), will, and emotions (Job 38:25; Psalm 43:5; Jeremiah 13:17). The human soul is currently in a state of corruption, due to the presence of sin in a fallen world. Upon receiving Christ as Lord and Saviour, the human spirit becomes regenerated (born again—John 35:8); the body is re-created as a born-again believer at the event of the Rapture, or as a resurrected Tribulation Saint at the end of the seven-year Tribulation period, or as a judged righteous resurrected (found in the Book of Life) at the Great White Throne Judgment at the end of the Thousand-Year Reign. However, until such time, the soul remains in a constant struggle with the regenerated spirit, yet can be brought into a conformed alignment with the regenerated spirit through the "renewing of the mind" by prayer, studying God's Word and fasting (Psalm 51:10; 119:11; Mark 12:30; Romans 10:10, 12:2; 1 Thessalonians 5:16–18; Titus 3:4–7; 1 Peter 1:22–23). However, in the case of a Nephilim or Raphaim giant, the soul is a missing component. Obviously, these life forms still had a brain within a body and still had a spirit (essential essence of the living entity).

Furthermore, as a corrupted genetic abomination, these life forms would have a corrupted or disconnected mind, will, and emotions. They would not act or react like normal human beings. They would also have a lack of conscience. This is evident in 1 Enoch, which describes these genetic abominations as "impious" meaning "ungodly, sinful, wicked, immoral, lack of respect, unremorseful," especially by the fact that they resorted to eating humans (cannibalism) when food became scarce.

9   Some churches have different doctrinal views regarding the teaching of the Trinity, one God in three persons: Father, Son, and the Holy Spirit. While the word *Trinity* is not found in the Bible, the description of the three main components of God is absolutely found in the Scriptures. First thing we see is that God speaks about Himself in the plural, "And God said, Let *us* make man in *our* image, after *our* likeness…" (Genesis 1:26—emphasis added). God the Father is stated throughout the Scriptures (e.g. Ephesians 1:3, 4:6). Jesus is actually God in the flesh and dwelt on Earth (John 1:1–14; 14:9–11). As for the Holy Spirit, we are told not to grieve the Holy Spirit (Ephesians 4:30). Jesus physically breathed upon the disciples to receive the Holy Spirit (John 20:21–23). The Holy Spirit moved upon the face of the waters as one of the initial steps to the creation of the Earth (Genesis 1:2). While many still grapple with this concept of "three, yet one," the easiest way to understand this concept is to think of water. Water is a substance that can be found in three forms—as liquid (water), as gas (water vapour or mist) and as a solid (frozen water or ice). These are three, yet they are one. Yet, despite these few of many examples in Scripture, various church denominations and other comparative religions, such as Islam, still refuse to acknowledge the Holy Trinity. What is truly amazing, and something that would make the naysayers' jaws drop to the floor, is the fact that God, Himself, is further described as being comprised of the seven Spirits of God (Revelation 1:4, 3:1, 4:5, 5:6; Isaiah 11:2).

10   Article, *Ekron*, King James Bible Dictionary, Easton's Bible Dictionary: http://www.kingjamesbibledictionary.com/Dictionary/Ekronites

11   Article, *Sirion*, Bible Study Tools: http://www.biblestudytools.com/dictionary/sirion/

12   Article, *Sirion*, One Wiki to Rule Them All, The Lord of the Rings Wiki: http://lotr.wikia.com/wiki/Sirion

13   The 'name' cited in Scripture is not mentioned, but was clearly intended to be secret. I firmly believe that name is the modern name known as Freemasonry, which is comprised of two words *free*, meaning "freedom" and *masonry*, meaning "to build with stone or brick." In other words Freemasonry represents the "freedom to build with stone or brick" and more specifically it represents "freedom from God, to build with stone or brick." Freemasonry, in today's world, is a *secret society*. It is a *secret* organization that continues to build the *invisible pyramid* of structural influence within society. Freemasonry is comprised of craft Masons (various construction trades) and speculative masons (various career disciplines involving high learning, university degrees). There are thirty-three levels within Freemasonry, with the top level expressed as 33º (Scottish Rite) and thirty-two levels expressed as 32º (York Rite). What is truly amazing is that the longitude and latitude lines of the earth are also displayed in degrees. The ancient site of Babylon, where the Tower of Babel was located, lies exactly between 32º and 33º latitudes in a region of what is now known as southern Iraq!

14   While this is a close and reasonable estimate of the actual height of each step of the Sun Pyramid, I have had discussions with various individuals who, after visiting this site in person, describe these steps as being abnormal in height in relation to the normal height of steps commonly used by humans. Many further commented that the ascent to the top of the Pyramid is an arduous and difficult climb. One such person, a close friend, who spent time at this site as part of his wedding anniversary trip to Mexico, stated that the steps are indeed 14 inches high by 7 inches deep. He also reported that the Mexican tourist authorities have recently closed these stairways to tourist climbing due to the increase of serious injuries resulting from falling. The following reference confirms this:

    Article, *Teotihuacan Pyramid of the Sun*, Mexico Archeology, 2017: http://www.mexicoarcheology.com/teotihuacan-pyramid-of-the-sun/

15   There are many examples of angels taking on male human form that are the same height as normal human beings. We are not given detailed descriptions of all the various types of angels; however, one of the most detailed descriptions is contained in Ezekiel 1. Indications of this particular description are that this type of angel is quite large. Over the years, I have heard personal testimonies of some individuals who claim to have seen angels on the order of twelve feet tall. Certainly, the Nephilim giants were quite tall,

which should bring pause for deeper consideration when contemplating various ancient structures built on a scale for much taller beings.

16 Human sacrifice was performed at the site of Machu Picchu. Time and time again, this is a direct result of satanic influence that can be traced back to ancient roots.Video overview: https://www.youtube.com/watch?v=ga3Eyo-bU7vQ Article overview: http://www.enjoy-machu-picchu.org/architecture/funerary-rock.php

17 Many assume that the future event of Armageddon is the grand finale to the end of the world. This is not biblically correct, as Armageddon concludes the end of the current world age, at which time the Thousand-Year Reign of Christ ushers in a subsequent world age. Pertaining to the reference to the "end of the world" in Matthew 24:3, world is translated from the Greek word *Aion* which actually means an age.

18 The placenta is the link between a pregnant mother and a developing fetus within the womb. It is also a barrier that separates the blood of the fetus from the blood of the host mother. The placenta also acts as a barrier to stop immune system attacks from the host mother. The fetus can be viewed as a foreign life form by the mother's own immune system. Such aggressive attacks can actually trigger a natural, spontaneous abortion. During the 1990s, Immunologist, Dr. Andrew L. Mellor (Medical College of Georgia) determined that an enzyme (IDO) was produced within the placenta to ward off such immune system attacks. On this basis the developing fetus is considered to be a distinct, physical entity separate from its host, maternal mother. The historical bloodline, stemming from Adam (fallen man), is passed on through the union of the male sperm and the female egg. As this physical union did not occur with Mary and Joseph, Jesus remained in the womb, separate and distinct—and without the fallen nature through sin.

19 Noah had three sons: Japheth, Shem, and Ham. His first son Japheth was born when Noah was 500 years old (Genesis 5:32). Noah's second son, Shem, was 100 when he had his first son, Arphaxad, who was born two years after the flood (Genesis 10:10). Noah was 600 at the time of the flood (Genesis 7:11), which would make him 502 years old when Shem was born. Noah's third son, Ham, was born and married by the time the Ark was built (Genesis 7:13). It stands to reason all three sons were old enough to help their father build the Ark, which would put the start of construction when

Japheth was at least 25, allowing for Shem to be 23 and Ham to be around 20. Hence, the construction phase of the Ark would take a maximum of 75 years to complete before the first rain on earth.

20   Article, *Cell Structure—The Complexity of the "Simple" Cell,* All About the Journey, 2002: http://www.allaboutthejourney.org/cell-structure.htm

ANCIENT CIVILIZATIONS & ALTERED LIFE FORMS

Job 8:8–13

For enquire, I pray thee, of the former age, and prepare thyself to the search of their fathers: (For we are but of yesterday, and know nothing, because our days upon earth are a shadow:) Shall not they teach thee, and tell thee, and utter words out of their heart? Can the rush grow up without mire? can the flag grow without water? Whilst it is yet in his greenness, and not cut down, it withereth before any other herb. So are the paths of all that forget God; and the hypocrite's hope shall perish:

8.
TALES OF GIANTS

IN THIS CHAPTER WE'RE GOING TO HAVE A CLOSER LOOK AT SOME OF THE examples of genetically altered life forms throughout our ancient history. Many of these historical events in our past seem far removed from the day-to-day bustle of current modern living. This is especially true the further back in time any given historical event occurred. Today, many people simply cannot relate to such events, let alone come to terms with some of the outlandish, shocking, and "stranger than fiction" aspects that arise through these stories. The easiest way a modern society can come to terms with these problematic aspects is to relegate these stories to the realm of fantasy and myth. However, more often than not, myths have some sense, if not a considerable basis, in fact.

Perhaps one of the most well-known historical accounts of an altered life form, as described in the Bible, is the story of David and Goliath. For the record, many recount this biblical story as nothing more than fable or myth. Yet, modern archeology continues to uncover factual evidence that document these biblical accounts as historical fact. This is highlighted in the recent excavation (2016) of the actual site where this historic battle between young David and Goliath took place.[21]

In 1 Samuel 17, we read about David as a young boy before becoming king. While the Philistine Army begins to assemble in preparation to attack, a challenge is presented by King Saul (the very first king of the United Kingdom of Israel and Judea), that if any man is able to kill the Philistine's champion soldier, that same man would receive riches and be granted to marry Saul's daughter.

1 Samuel 17:2–4

And Saul and the men of Israel were gathered together, and pitched by the valley of Elah, and set the battle in array against the Philistines. And the Philistines stood on a mountain on one side, and Israel stood on a mountain on the other side: there was a valley between them. And there went out a champion out of the camp of the Philistines, named Goliath, of Gath, whose height was six cubits and a span.

A cubit is the equivalent of eighteen inches. So, including a "span" (the distance between a fully outstretched thumb and little finger, roughly eight to ten inches), Goliath stood roughly nine foot, nine inches tall—almost ten feet in height!

1 Samuel 17:5–7

And he had a helmet of brass upon his head, and he was armed with a coat of mail; and the weight of the coat was five thousand shekels of brass. And he had greaves of brass upon his legs, and a target of brass between his shoulders. And the staff of his spear was like a weaver's beam; and his spear's head weighed six hundred shekels of iron: and one bearing a shield went before him.

Goliath's coat of mail weighed 5000 shekels alone, equaling 153 lbs. (the weight of an average young man). The spear head of iron was 600 shekels, roughly 18.5 pounds, not including the spear shaft itself described as a "beam" rather than a pole. Although the weight of the helmet of brass is not stated, brass is a very dense and heavy metal. Based on the overall size of Goliath, this particular helmet would be much beyond the comfortable weight for the average human.

Take note that this account is a very detailed description. In fact, the Bible is full of detailed accounts throughout our past; for example, since that showdown between David and Goliath, David goes on to have taken part in other battles involving other giants (other genetically altered life forms). Also take note that one of these altered life forms had six fingers and six toes.

2 Samuel 21:15–22

Moreover the Philistines had yet war again with Israel; and David went down, and his servants with him, and fought against the Philistines: and David waxed faint. And Ishbibenob, which was of the sons of the giant, the weight of whose spear weighed three hundred shekels of brass in weight, he being girded with a new sword, thought to have slain David. But Abishai the son of Zeruiah succoured him, and smote the Philistine, and killed him. Then the men of David sware unto him, saying, Thou shalt go no more out with us to battle, that thou quench not the light of Israel. And it came to pass after this, that there was again a battle with the Philistines at Gob: then Sibbechai the Hushathite slew Saph, which was of the sons of the giant. And there was again a battle in Gob with the Philistines, where Elhanan the son of Jaareoregim, a Bethlehemite, slew the brother of Goliath the Gittite, the staff of whose spear was like a weaver's beam. And there was yet a battle in Gath, where was a man of great stature, that had on every hand six fingers, and on every foot six toes, four and twenty in number; and he also was born to the giant. And when he defied Israel, Jonathan the son of Shimeah the brother of David slew him. These four were born to the giant in Gath, and fell by the hand of David, and by the hand of his servants.

A lesser known story in the Bible is the story of Joshua and the twelve spies. While the popular 1956 film *The Ten Commandments* by director Cecil B. Demile is readily recognized by the general public, the events depicted in this movie only represent part of the story. In fact, the film ends before another interesting chapter in the saga begins.

As the movie recounts, this was a time when the Israelites (the lineage of the Hebrew people) were enslaved by the Egyptians. Note that a detailed account is found throughout the Book of Exodus. It was declared that the increasing population of the Israelites was becoming a possible future threat to Pharaoh's kingdom. Moses is adopted by the Pharaoh's daughter after being found floating in a wicker basket on the Nile river. This was an effort by his birth mother, Yoshebel, to hide and avert the killing of her baby amongst all the other firstborn male Israelites in the land. Moses subsequently grows up and is nurtured as a prince of Egyptian royalty. Upon discovering his true Hebrew heritage, and upon killing an Egyptian slave master who was attacking a fellow Hebrew, Moses flees Egypt. It is at this point Moses receives a revelation from God at the "burning bush," at a high place (Mount Horeb). Moses returns to Egypt to confront Pharaoh and demand the release of his people, the Israelites. After many events of divine intervention through God's will (ten plagues), Pharaoh reluctantly grants the release of the enslaved

Israelites. Moses leads the people out of Egypt (the exodus) and averts the pursuit of Pharaoh's army by the spectacular event of the parting of the Red Sea.

The Israelites first settle at the base of Mount Sinai, where Moses climbs the mount to meet God and receive the Ten Commandments. Upon the extended absence of Moses, and despite their newfound freedom, a large number of the Israelites begin to question Moses' leadership and their continued journey into an unknown land. They decide to take matters into their own hands and revert to the ways of their past Egyptian enslavers (traditions they had lived for generations). They make a golden calf as an idol of false worship. God intervenes and destroys this rebellious group. This is just one example of God's chosen people turning away from His purpose and will, and amazingly doing so despite everything God had provided and promised for them.

Upon his return, and presenting the remaining people with the guideline laws of the Ten Commandments, Moses proceeds to enter into the foreign land. However, the Israelites endure forty years of wandering in the desolate wilderness before Moses appoints his successor, Joshua, to lead the people into the Land of Canaan (ancient Israel—the Promised Land). Moses leaves to go off in exile to follow his own divine appointment. It is at this point the movie ends before the amazing next part of the story begins. This detailed continuation is described in the Book of Numbers.

Before Moses' solitary departure, he sends out twelve spies into the Land of Canaan.

Numbers 13:17
And Moses sent them to spy out the land of Canaan, and said unto them, Get you up this *way* southward, and go up into the mountain:

Numbers 13:23–24
And they came unto the brook of Eshcol, and cut down from thence a branch with one cluster of grapes, and they bare it between two upon a staff; and *they brought* of the pomegranates, and of the figs. The place was called the brook of Eshcol, because of the cluster of grapes which the children of Israel cut down from hence.

The first thing the men discover is a land rich with vegetation and fruit-bearing trees. The grapes are so large it takes two men to carry only one cluster lifted by a pole in tandem between their shoulders. Obviously, grapes don't grow that large in today's world. After searching out the land for forty days, the spies also report the following:

Numbers 13:28–30
Nevertheless the people *be* strong that dwell in the land, and the cities *are* walled, *and* very great: and moreover we saw the children of Anak there. The Amalekites dwell in the land of the south: and the Hittites, and the Jebusites, and the Amorites, dwell in the mountains: and the Canaanites dwell by the sea, and by the coast of Jordan. And Caleb stilled the people before Moses, and said, Let us go up at once, and possess it; for we are well able to overcome it. (Emphasis added)

Numbers 13:31–33
But the men that went up with him said, We be not able to go up against the people; for they are stronger than we. And they brought up an evil report of the land which they had searched unto the children of Israel, saying, The land, through which we have gone to search it, *is* a land that eateth up the inhabitants thereof; and all the people that we saw in it are men of a great stature. And there we saw the giants, the sons of Anak, *which come* of the giants: and we were in our own sight as grasshoppers, and so we were in their sight. (Emphasis added)

As we saw in Section One of this book, the Amalekites, Hittites, Jebusites, Amorites, and Canaanites were all ancient tribes settled in the Land of Canaan either including giants or directly associated with them in some way. The "children of Anak" were the direct descendants of the giants.

The twelve spies observe established cities with well-fortified walls. As the Israelite people gather to hear this report, there is obviously a rush of murmurs of apprehension and fear, since Caleb has to motion for silence. Caleb bravely announces a motion to enter the land and attack, to subdue its occupants. It is the rest of the spies (with the exception of Joshua) who plead to Moses and Caleb to reconsider this proposal, since they argue the people of the land are "men of great stature" (men of great height)—giants. They explain they witnessed various races of giants and their offspring, referred as the "sons of Anak." They go on to explain that they, as normal average men, were relatively the size of grasshoppers to these formidable giants. It is also stated that the region "*is* a land that eateth up the inhabitants thereof." In other words, it was a region where normal humans were being eaten by abnormal, genetically altered life forms—the overwhelming presence of giants. This is confirmed in the Book of Enoch:

Enoch 7:11–14
And the woman conceiving brought forth giants…These devoured all which the labor of men produced; until it became impossible to feed them. When they turned themselves against men, in order to devour them, And began to injure beasts, reptiles, and fishes, to eat their flesh one another, and to drink their blood.

The practice of eating human flesh is known as cannibalism. When I first began to study this area of the Scriptures and subsequently began to piece these references together with the confirming passages of Enoch, the Lord gave me a spiritual revelation regarding this word. Cannibalism is actually comprised of three root words: (1) canni, (2) bal, and (3) ism. This was an amazing discovery for me, as the root word canni actually refers to the Land of Canaan; the root word bal is Baal (as covered in Section One, Baal is one of many alternate names for Satan); and the third root word, ism, is actually a suffix referring to "the act, practice, or process of doing something."

After this spiritual revelation, I learned that the ancient Chaldean word Cahna-bal means Priest of Baal. Cahna is the emphatic form of Cahn, a priest. These sacrilegious priests would eat their human sacrifices. Putting this all into perspective, cannibalism actually refers to the act, or practice of the worship of Baal originating in the Land of Canaan. It is through the worship of Baal that genetically altered life forms came into existence in Canaan, and through this manipulation, the practice of eating human flesh resulted and became widespread.

According to Bernal Diaz del Castillo, under the leadership of the Spanish explorer Hernán Cortés during the Mexican conquests of the early 1500s, the Aztecs performed fifty-thousand human sacrifices per year and were heavily engaged in cannibalism.[22] However, take note that the Land of Canaan is the actual origin of the word cannibalism, not the *perceived* origin stemming from various indigenous tribes from regions such as Africa, Indonesia, Mexico, and the Caribbean. As a reminder, Mount Hermon, where the fallen angels *first* began their campaign of genetic manipulation, is located in the northernmost part of the Land of Canaan.

Back to our twelve spies. Of the twelve spies Moses initially sent into Canaan, only Joshua and Caleb respond with conviction, bravery, and obedience to return and proceed to seize the land. Due to the murmurs of fear, sowing seeds of disobedience, brought on by the other ten spies report of certain death and doom awaiting in the land, God punishes the Israelites, sentencing them to forty years of wandering the desert (one year for every day of searching out the land). As for the other ten spies who resisted God's will:

Numbers 14:36–37
And the men, which Moses sent to search the land, who returned, and made all the congregation to murmur against him, by bringing up a slander upon the land, Even those men that did bring up the evil report upon the land, died by the plague before the LORD.

As the story continues, the Israelites go forth from the south into the Land of Canaan led by Joshua and Caleb and fiercely take, seize, and possess city after city and valley after valley. This included the well-known story of the city of Jericho. Through these military campaigns, God's people were spiritually protected—provided they remained fully obedient to God's purpose and will. God made it very clear that nothing was to be spared. Not only were the giants to be annihilated, but all men, women, and children were to be eliminated.

Today, many critics accusingly refer to this as unjustified genocide by an "unloving God." This is misguided reasoning and total ignorance of the facts. It was through the falling away from God's Word, replaced with the expanded practice of Baal worship, that the inhabitants succumbed to the direct manipulation of the fallen angels. God had previously destroyed the *entire* world with a global flood based on this very same progression. It was God's will and purpose that the Land of Canaan (the Promised Land) be completely eradicated of any trace of this spiritual and physical cancer. This was a necessary and righteous cleansing.

However, as we have seen, time and time again God's people have fallen short of His purpose and will. This is the result of the fallen nature of mankind, within a fallen world. While God commanded the systematic removal of the giants and the inhabitants, He also warned that no food or possessions were to be taken by the Israelites. An example of this warning is stated in Joshua 6:17–18 regarding Jericho. Unfortunately, the faith and the obedience of God's people began to falter as the continued weight of military campaigns took its toll. Not only did the enemy's food and possessions start to become the "spoils of victory," various regions of Canaan did not completely fall into the hands of the Israelites. Cities that were initially taken did not become fully possessed. Some Canaanite tribes had worshipped Baal as the sun god and Ashtoreth as the moon goddess. After the fractured and incomplete possessing of the Land of Canaan by the armies of Joshua, the worship of Baal and Ashtoreth began to creep into some of the settlements of the ancient Israelites—particularly after Joshua's death (Judges 2:8–13).

This ongoing struggle lasted generations. This whole progression is accounted throughout the Book of Numbers, Deuteronomy, Joshua, Judges, Samuel, Kings, and Chronicles. In fact, it is still playing out in today's world. Three of the main regions where Israelites failed to eradicate the giants and its inhabitants are now known as the Gaza Strip (where Goliath originated), the West Bank (multiple military campaigns occurred here) and the Golan Heights (as we covered previously, the military campaigns by Joshua had extended north right up to Baal-gad, an ancient Canaanite town located in the valley of Lebanon at the base of Mount Hermon—Joshua 13:5). These are three regions within the Promised Land of Israel that are still in contention—still under a curse of insurrection.

In yet another story of the Bible, Deuteronomy 3, we read about King Og of Bashan, a region in northern Canaan (the Golan Heights):

Deuteronomy 3:11
For only Og king of Bashan remained of the remnant of the giants; behold, his bedstead was a bedstead of iron; is it not Rabbath of the children of Ammon? Nine cubits was the length thereof, and four cubits the breadth of it, after the cubit of a man.

King Og's bed was nine cubits long (13.5 feet) by four cubits wide (6 feet). A modern king-sized bed is roughly 6.7 feet long by 6.3 feet wide. This would suggest King Og's bed was made for a someone twelve feet tall! Over two feet taller than the giant Goliath!

Prior to the days of Goliath and King Og, the oldest known civilization (post-flood) was the Sumerian culture. This civilization arose within the Fertile Crescent, also known as Mesopotamia, beginning around 4,500 B.C. Historians also refer to this region as the Cradle of Civilization. However, the same historians do not recognize the pre-flood civilization that arose from this exact same location whose beginning stemmed from the Garden of Eden some 1,656 years prior to the flood.[23] It is here, now southern Iraq, where the ancient cities of Babylon and Ur were once located (post-flood). There are many artifacts still intact in these regions today, including elaborate statues depicting giants with twelve fingers and twelve toes.

At the time of early Babylon, as described in Genesis 11, God looked down upon the people and saw that they were uniting to build a *"tower whose top would reach unto heaven"* (Genesis 11:4). God knew this would result in repeated contact with the realm of the fallen angels. Hence, the term "heaven" in Genesis 11:4 is actually referring to Second Heaven (the cosmos), not Third Heaven. Had this intended contact been solely directed to Third Heaven, to God Himself, God would not have been upset and concerned enough to destroy the Tower of Babel. He also confounded their single language and dispersed this single race of people throughout the earth. In a moment, a single language became multiple languages. God did this to dissuade communication of the knowledge of tower building from reoccurring.

A single race subsequently became multiple races, as environmental changes influenced nominal changes in the human DNA through basic adaptation (not through *transitional* evolution).[24] Although different races occurred, the fact does remain that humans are still humans. Humans did not continue to *transition* into some other life form. Hence, initially fair skin and lighter hair became prevalent in the tribes that migrated to the northern regions (less sun and cooler); and darker skin and darker hair became prevalent in the tribes that migrated to the regions nearer to the equator (more sun and hotter). Of course, over time, subsequent migrations of tribes and races resulted in ongoing mixtures of various races in different regions of the earth.[25]

It should be known that the term tower is an old-world term for a structure, not necessarily a tall building higher than its width. Tower is also defined as "to reach or to rise to a great height." The towers built in ancient times were pyramid structures. In order to "reach to a *great* height" (emphasis added) the base of the structure must be as wide (or wider) than its height. Besides the smooth-faced pyramids located at Giza, Egypt, the majority of these pyramid structures where built with central staircases leading to the top, known as stepped ziggurats. There are more than one hundred thousand pyramids discovered worldwide.[26] Pyramids have been discovered at the bottom of various oceans and seas, such as off the coast of Japan, a site known as the Yonaguni Monument discovered in 1987 near the southern part of the Ryukyu Islands. Despite God's direct intervention at the Tower of Babel to prevent further contact of the fallen angels in Second Heaven, the people defiantly carried on the "secret name" and the knowledge of pyramid building throughout the world. Wherever the people went, pyramid structures and various altars followed; wherever these are found, stories of giants are an integral part of the culture's folklore.

The worldwide dispersion resulted in the migrant occupation and subsequent construction of pyramids in Central Mexico (Aztecs), Central America (Mayans), and South America (Incas). The indigenous races of North and South American Indians, now referred to as First Nations in Canada, were certainly the first tribes to settle within these parts of the world. However, from the beginning (post-flood society), they were not always here. The current First Nations are actually the descendants of the original ancient tribes of Babylon. Over time, ancient Chinese cultures (also from the dispersion) from the East visited and mixed with the West Coast and mid-Southern Indian tribes as early as 1,200 B.C., including evidence of direct influence of one of the oldest cultures, the Olmec civilization in southern Mexico (who also worshipped the feathered serpent god).[27] There are many pyramid sites throughout China; as of 2008, that number was estimated at four hundred.[28]

There is strong evidence that Egyptians came to the Americas in the past as well. Ancient artifacts and common language hieroglyphs have been discovered to support these migrations. Even the Vikings landed in North America as early as the tenth century A.D., long before the touted "official" discovery of America by Christopher Columbus in 1492. I highly recommend reading *America B.C.* by Barry Fell and *Mysteries of the Mexican Pyramids* by Peter Tompkins to learn deeper revelations of our history (not taught in our public schools).

The following chart is quite revealing when considering the distant geographic locations between Mexico and ancient Sumeria (the Cradle of Civilization) and considering the millennia separated between them:

SUMERIAN	MEXICAN	BASIC TERMS
Innan	Innan	Mother
Nan-Sin	Nan-Tzin	Reverend mother
Tu-Nan-sin	To-Nan-Tzin	Changeable forms of Reverend Mother (Sumer)
		Resplendent revered mother (Mexico)
Na-Nan-sin	No-Nan-Tzin	Deified revered mother (Sumer)
		Our Revered mother (Mexico)
Malin-Ila	Malin-Ali	Flower bedecked goddess
Tr-Ila	Citalli	Star goddess
Istar/ Ishtar	Ishta/ Ishtak	White princess; moon goddess
Maliya	Maria	Destined to be garlanded with flowers

Regarding First Nations tribes within North America, legendary stories of giants are common. One such example is the Ais Indian tribe that settled in mid-eastern Florida. This particular tribe was regarded as being fierce and very brutal. The following is an excerpt from Jon Hamilton's brief *The Nature of Our Enemy*, which I highly recommend:

THE RIVER OF THE AIS

Soon after Spain discovered the New World, early Spanish explorers began calling our area *Rio de Los Ais*, or River of the Ais. Hence the English called it the Indian River.

Of the Indians that once ruled these coastal waters, little is known. They are shrouded in mystery for a variety of reasons. Contacts with Spaniards were minimal during the years Spain claimed Florida. Available historical data must be translated from old archives located in Spain, and much of this work has only recently been done. Sometimes these historical sources are vague on specific details. Very few archeological surveys have been performed locally. Add to this the fact that, like most archeological areas of study, experts interpret the same finds differently.

Nevertheless, certain evidence is apparent. Man has lived and thrived in our area for thousands of years.

THE "MOTHER" PEOPLE

The fierce Ais ruled the area we call the Indian River for most of this millennium, up until the 1700's. Their lands stretched from present day Cape Canaveral /Titusville to Hobe Sound. The name "Ais" is believed to mean "mother," perhaps a reference to some deity. Some suggest the lagoon may have been worshipped as a "mother." The Ais language was quite different in structure than any other Florida tribe. Some believe the Ais were offshoots of the Mayans or Aztecs of Central America because of similarities in language. There have also been archeological finds that support this hypothesis.

GIANTS IN THE LAND

One discovery that occasionally has been reported, is the finding of the skeletal remains of unusually tall men. Archeological digs in our immediate area have, on at least two occasions, yielded bones described as "unusually large." One archeologist described a people of "considerable stature and massive constitution." Based on the size of the bones recovered, *suggestions of height in excess of eight feet tall have been made.* This would, of course, imply a race of giants when compared to most humans of the same era. It is unclear whether these were Ais, another rival people, or an even earlier unknown race. Other digs find humans of normal heights.

One dig in Micco revealed a burial ground in which all heads faced east. This is indicative of worship of celestial objects (moon, sun, stars, etc.). Numerous recovered artifacts have been identified as religious fetishes of an unknown significance.[29]

Another example is the account of William Cody, widely known as Buffalo Bill. He is etched in American legendary history as a scout, bison hunter, fur trapper, and gold prospector. He enlisted in the Union Army during the American Civil War, later receiving the Medal of Honor. He came to national popularity through his "Buffalo Bill's Wild West" shows that eventually came to Great Britain and mainland Europe. Part of his American legendary mystique was the claim that he had killed as many as four thousand buffalo. Based on this, William Cody had a strong connection with some of the American Indian tribes. However, what is not well known are his entries into his personal diary. Cody writes:

While we were in the sandhills, scouting the Niobrara country, the Pawnee Indians brought into camp some very large bones, one of which the surgeon of the expedition pronounced to be the thigh bone of a human being. The Indians said the bones were those of a race of people who long ago had lived in that country. They said these people were three times the size of a man of the present day, that they were so swift and strong that they could run by the side of a buffalo, and, taking the animal in one arm, could tear off a leg and eat it as they ran.

These giants, said the Indians, denied the existence of a Great Spirit. When they heard the thunder or saw the lightning, they laughed and declared that they were greater than either. This so displeased the Great Spirit that he caused a deluge. The water rose higher and higher till it drove these proud giants from the low grounds to the hills and thence to the mountains. At last even the mountaintops were submerged and the mammoth men were drowned.

After the flood subsided, the Great Spirit came to the conclusion that he had made men too large and powerful. He therefore corrected his mistake by creating a race of the size and strength of the men of the present day. This is the reason, the Indians told us, that the man of modern times is small and not like the giants of old. The story has been handed down among the Pawnees for generations, but what is its origin no man can say.[30]

It's worth noting that the giants "denied the existence of a Great Spirit" (God Himself). This comes as no surprise, as Satan and the fallen angels were bent on humans serving angels and falsely claimed that they alone *controlled* aspects of creation (versus God's *appointed* stewards of the creation). As we've covered, this progressively resulted in the genetic contamination of humankind, to the point of the inception of the giants themselves. However, also interesting is the other statement pertaining to God, "the Great Spirit came to the conclusion that he had made men too large and powerful. He therefore corrected his mistake by creating a race of the size and strength of the men of the present day." This statement is not exactly true. God does not make mistakes. This is nothing more than a shift of the accountability from the fallen angels (the false gods still revered by many Indian cultures), who were fully responsible for this genetic manipulation in the first place, to falsely blaming God Himself for this supposed mistake. The giants were a direct result of fallen angels mating with earthly women. As we've covered, this is fully supported in Scripture. God did not create these abominations, especially altered life forms brought forth without a soul. Satan's lie is simply perpetuated, as in this example, through the Pawnee Indians' mythical story (albeit partly true, with a substantial basis in fact), handed down from generation to generation.

As stated in William Cody's diary, these bones were the remains of a humanoid creature three times the normal size, which would make these altered life forms stand anywhere between fifteen and eighteen feet tall. Imagine, another three to six feet taller than King Og of Deuteronomy!

Also, as stated, when the giants heard and saw the thunder and lightning, "they laughed and declared that they were greater than either." This is a strong indication of the pride and arrogance of the fallen kingdom derived from the pride and arrogance of Satan Himself. In fact, it was through pride and arrogance that Satan fell from the Kingdom of Heaven in the first place (Isaiah 14:11–15; Ezekiel 28:14–17). The proverbial apple doesn't fall far from the tree. In addition, the connection between Satan and *lightning* also refers to the second stage of Satan's overall banishment:

Luke 10:18
And he said unto them, I beheld Satan as lightning fall from heaven.

This connection is also discovered when considering the totem pole idols erected by indigenous people throughout the Pacific Northwest, such as Algonquian, Ojibwe, Bella Coola, and Haida tribes. Totem poles are hand-carved from the large, tall trunks of western red cedar trees and depict various human, part-human/part-animal hybrids and other supernatural beings. These are often carved in a top-to-bottom succession that relay a story or convey a hierarchy. Although it has been often said that these idols are not objects of worship but rather reflect legendary, cultural history, it is quite clear these are instruments fashioned from creation (a cedar tree) that negate the reverence of the Creator, God. We are warned:

Romans 1:25
Who changed the truth of God into a lie, and worshipped and served the creature more than the Creator, who is blessed for ever. Amen.

God goes on to state an even sterner warning to those who should know better:

Romans 1:32
Who knowing the judgment of God, that they which commit such things are worthy of death, not only do the same, but have pleasure in them that do them.

We are also warned in the Ten Commandments about "graven images," which is something carved by hand, usually in stone or wood:

Exodus 20:4
Thou shalt not make unto thee any graven image, or any likeness *of any thing* that *is* in heaven above, or that *is* in the earth beneath, or that *is* in the water under the earth...

Considering the hierarchal aspect of totem poles, the top pinnacle position is usually reserved for the supernatural being known as the Thunderbird. This legendary creature is associated with power. It was thought the flapping of its enormous feathered wings caused the wind and thunder, therefore it was known as "the creator of storms." Sheet lightning resonated from its sharp eyes and lightning bolts were dispatched from glowing snakes held in its talons. The Thunderbird is often depicted with razor-sharp teeth exposed in a grimace within its beak, often with two curled *horns* upon its head. Once again the attributes of Baal continue through the historical unbroken thread.[31]

Thunderbird Totem Poles Displaying 'Horns'

The Nuu-chah-nulth indigenous tribe of Vancouver Island describes the Thunderbird as a supernatural being that resides on the top of a mountain. It controlled the rain. This, again, is very reminiscent of Baal worship in the Land of Canaan, where Baal was the god of rain, storms, and fertility.

Apparently, this creature was the servant of the Great Spirit. This is interesting, since it is *not* the Great Spirit that takes the pinnacle position on the totem pole, but rather the Thunderbird. It was said this creature could shapeshift between feathered bird form and human form (remember Viracocha worshipped by the Incas). There are legendary stories of various thunderbirds (obviously plural form for the other fallen angels) marrying into human families.

Stories of Thunderbirds are also prevalent within other indigenous peoples who settled in the Great Lakes, Great Plains, and American Southwest regions such as the Anishinaabe, Menominee, and Sioux tribes.

Hollywood's depiction of American Indians in many old western movies shows chief leaders greeting other chiefs (at times greeting cavalry or cowboys) by raising their right hand with the fingers spread and saying, "How." This has often been portrayed as a gesture demonstrating that one "comes in peace." However, more accurately, some modern indigenous people recount how this was done in ancient times to determine the number of fingers one had on their hand. Obviously, six fingers was an indication of the genetic lineage of the giants, something to be avoided by many peaceful, nomadic tribes. Again, this genetic deviation is specifically mentioned in both 2 Samuel 21:20 and 1 Chronicles 20:6.

The Pueblo Indians of Central Midwest America (known as the Four Corners region where the borders of Colorado, Utah, Arizona, and New Mexico meet) referred to these altered life forms as the Anasazi. They believe the Anasazi were the Ancient Ones, also thought to be the ancient ancestors of their tribe. However, the name Anasazi actually comes from the Navajo language and means "enemy ancestors" (*aana*—enemy and *sazi*—ancestor). The Navajo tribe had settled in Southwestern America and they bordered and crossed over into the southern and western regions of the Pueblo tribes.

Today, the Navajo are regarded as the largest group of indigenous peoples of America. As we saw in William Cody's memoirs with the mention of the Pawnee Indians, they were also one of the largest tribes settled in the Central America plains. Other tribes worth mentioning that speak of ancient legends involving giants are Apache, Algonquian, Cherokee, Cree, Iroquois, Hopi, Wabanaki, Micmac, Wampanoag, and Chickasaw. So there appears to have been a tremendous influence and interaction between early American Indian tribes and the giants of ancient times (obviously post-flood) especially in the southern parts of the nation closer to northern Mexico. Clearly, the giants had migrated northward from the Central and Southern Americas region, stemming from the Olmec, Aztec, Mayan, and Inca false god worship bringing about fallen angel interaction and genetic contamination (essentially a second, mirror image of the original Land of Canaan).

9.

GREEK AND ROMAN MYTHS

Back on the other side of the world, prior to the arrival of Jesus Christ, the once great Greek Empire thrived. This was a society based on a multiple-god platform of worship, as were most of the dominant cultures prior to the arrival of Jesus Christ and the advent of the Church Age, a return to a monotheistic system of worship. As mentioned in Section One, the multiple-god system is actually Satan's false system of worship intended to negate and replace mankind's worship and relationship with the one true, almighty God. This false system continued with the Roman Empire, but eventually faded with its decline. Therefore, as we just covered, Satan simply shifted his focus to the other side of the world. Hence, the multiple-god systems of the Olmec, Mayan, Aztec, and Inca cultures began to flourish in those regions.

The multiple-god system is based on a hierarchy ranging from lesser gods to higher gods, up to the pinnacle god at the top of the invisible pyramid (the capstone of the hierarchy). In almost all of these hierarchal structures, the name of the pinnacle god can be referenced in some way, or traced back, to Satan. The other higher and lesser gods represent the hierarchy of the other fallen angels. We previously covered this chain of command as the chief, the chief officers, and the remaining band of fallen angels representing one third of all the angels created by God.

Based on this premise, we can determine that the basic framework of the hierarchal structure remains intact (often identical) from culture to culture. This can be observed throughout human history, although the actual names of each god may change. However, while the names may change, the actual personalities and attributes are either very similar or identical. As the following chart (en.

wikipedia.org/wiki/List_of_Greek_mythological_figures) reveals, this similarity can be easily observed within the historical transition of the Greek Empire to the Roman Empire:

GREEK	ROMAN	ATTRIBUTES
Zeus	Jupiter	king of the gods; god of sky, rain, thunder, and lightning
Poseidon	Neptune	god of sea, horses, carried the trident spear
Ares	Mars	god of war
Aphrodite	Venus	goddess of love and fertility
Hermes	Mercury	god of travelers, messenger of the gods
Apollo	Apollo	god of sun and prophecy, music and medicine
Artemis	Diana	goddess of hunting and wild animals
Hades	Pluto	god of the underworld

We previously covered that the angels (fallen or not) are all of male, yet here we see the inclusion of goddesses (female) amongst the many gods. However, when you review the complete list of Greek and Roman gods, the male gods definitely outnumber the female. In addition, the female gods somehow appear after the introduction of male gods.

The lineage of all the Greek and Roman gods derives from the point of origin known as Chaos, a primeval state of darkness and void space that somehow (1) brings forth four elements of air, water, earth, and fire and (2) brings forth male and female; while Chaos itself is neither established as male or female (although some references indicate Chaos as male with Arche being the female counterpart). Conversely, the Creator God of Scripture is clearly male, existing apart from the formless void of the Universe before it began (Genesis 1:1–2). However, after the point of the Greek mythical inception, from out of Chaos various goddesses are introduced and some are somehow formed out of a male god. One example of this is Aphrodite, who is claimed to have arisen from the castrated genitals of Uranus that were discarded into the ocean by Cronos. She *miraculously* arose from out of the resulting sea foam (sea foam is *Aphros* in Greek, also applied as the name of a male, centaurine sea-god). Interesting is the term hermaphrodite, referring to an individual abnormally having both male and female genitalia. This term is a splice between the names Hermes (male) and Aphrodite (female).

The bottom line here is that we live in a fallen world (that includes genetic abnormalities) and Satan does not have the ability to create. It is God who created both male and female (the female brought forth secondly, stemming from the removed rib, the actual DNA of the first man, Adam—Genesis 2:21–25). So, pertaining to the female goddesses, it appears (1) the female gender was brought forth out of nothing, concocted to conform to the created human cycle of procreation between man and woman (something the fallen angels had desired and considered worthy of giving up their first estate in heaven), and (2) in some cases the female gender is portrayed to have been derived out of the male form—a blasphemous reinvention of the female, Eve, derived from Adam's rib. Satan is not so original, since almost everything he does is a mirror image of the things of heaven and of God, as in this case a false, quasi and corrupted representation of the process of procreation stemming from the creative hand of God.

Considering the Greek god Zeus, we see the name changes to Jupiter in the Roman deity. However, we also see the overall attributes remain identical. These attributes are described as the "king of the gods" and the "god of sky, rain, thunder, and lightning." The phrase "king of the gods" puts this god at the pinnacle position. Interestingly, the overall list of attributes is strikingly similar to the attributes of Baal, worshipped by the Canaanites and Phoenicians centuries before the rise of the Greek and Roman empires. We covered the attributes of Baal as (i) owner, (ii) lord, (iii) universal god of fertility, (iv) prince, lord of the earth, (v) lord of the rain and dew, and (f) epithet: he who rides on the clouds (god of storms). Further considering the Scripture references *prince and power of the air* (Ephesians 2:2) and *god of this world* (2 Corinthians 4:4), these attributes demonstrate a direct link to Satan.

This is an unbroken thread throughout human history, as we can clearly see when we compare the Sumerian multiple god structure (en.wikipedia.org/wiki/List_of_Mesopotamian_deities), regarded as the earliest beginning of post-flood society:

SUMERIAN	ATTRIBUTES
An (Anu—Annu)	father and king of the gods; god of heaven; god of the sky; ruler of the Annunaki; creator of demons and lord of the spirits
Enhil (Ellil)	god of the air and wind; lord ghost
Enki	god of water
Gibil	god of fire

Ninhursag	goddess of earth
Marduk	snake-dragon god
Ninurta	god of war
Nanna	moon god
Nergal	god of the underworld
Inanna	goddess of love (post lineage: Ishtar, Ashtoreth, and Anath)

Interesting to note that some subsequent Canaanite tribes worshipped Baal as the sun god (Baal having an extension of the attributes of An) and worshipped Ashtoreth as the moon goddess who presided over the temple prostitutes (an extension of the attributes of Inanna).

Not only did the Greeks and Romans worship multiple gods, but they also worshipped demigods. This is a term referring to half-god (*demi* meaning half). Of course, the other half refers to something less than, or not fully, god.

Demigod: 1) a mythical creature that is partly divine and partly human; an inferior deity

              2) a deified mortal

According to this definition (www.thefreedictionary.com/demigod), a demigod is a lifeform that is half *god* and half human (mortal). More accurately, a demigod is a lifeform that is really half *fallen angel* and half human (mortal)—since we have established that fallen angels have falsely represented themselves as gods to ancient cultures. Some of these demigods predate the Greek and Roman empires, such as Gilgamesh stemming from ancient Sumeria.

A partial list (en.wikipedia.org/wiki/List_of_demigods) of notable demigods is as follows:

DEMIGOD	ORIGIN
Achilles	son of King Peleus and Thetis, a sea-goddess
Aeacus	son of Zeus and Aegina, daughter of a river god
Amphion	son of Zeus and Antiope, princess of Thebes
Epaphus	son of Zeus and Lo, priestess of goddess Hera
Gilgamesh	son of Lugalbanda, King of Uruk and goddess Ninsun

Harmonia	daughter of Zeus and Electra (2nd Electra), daughter of King Agamemnon (some account the daughter of Ares and Aphrodite)
Helen of Troy	daughter of Zeus and Leda, Queen of Sparta
Heracles (Hercules Roman)	son of Zeus (Jupiter) and Queen Alcmene
Orpheus	son of Apollo and Calliope
Perseus	son of Zeus and Danae, princess of Argos
Theseus	son of Zeus and Aethra, daughter of King Pittheus of Troezen
Tityos (a giant)	son of Zeus and Elara, daughter of King Orchomenus
Zethes	son of Boreas and Oreithyia, daughter of King Erechtheus of Athens

Considering the partial list above, the majority of these demigods were male, yet some were female—a direct result of the mortal half of the lineage (the introduction of human DNA). However, regarding the male demigods, many of these lifeforms were considered to have extra-human abilities and superhuman strength, as well told in the stories of Hercules. These were regarded as great men of legendary renown.

Amazingly, this is confirmed in God's Word:

Genesis 6:4
There were giants in the earth in those days; and also after that, when the sons of God came in unto the daughters of men, and they bare children to them, *the same became mighty men which were of old, men of renown.* (Emphasis added)

The word *mighty* used in this Scripture is derived from the Hebrew word *gibbowr* or *gibbor,* meaning powerful, warrior, tyrant, champion, chief, giant and strong man. These words imply *greatness* and/or *reverence.* As we previously covered, the word *champion* was applied to the giant Goliath (besides the fact that *gibbowr* also means giant). We also saw the word *chief* as a reference to the chief devil, Satan, and we also covered a reference to the "mountain of the chief" (Mount Hermon). Obviously Genesis 6:4 refers to the Nephilim giants stemming from the sexual interaction by the sons of God with earthly women, but it also refers to the appearance of demigods (powerful, strong men, warriors) such as Hercules. Hercules was considered both a man of renown (a hero) and a tyrant (unleashing fits of rage, leading to the killing of his own children). This duality of good and evil sows deceptive seeds, blurring the lines between morality and immorality. This was also demonstrated in the sexual conquests of Hercules, known to have relations with both women and men.

Considering this point and everything else stated in this book thus far, God has a specific and well-defined plan for human procreation. It is Satan who influences, encourages, and promotes deviation from this plan. The facts bare this truth, as every time society has deviated from God's plan, the fall and subsequent destruction of that society or culture soon follows.

Isaiah 5:20
Woe unto them that call evil good, and good evil; that put darkness for light, and light for darkness; that put bitter for sweet, and sweet for bitter!

This embracing of good and evil, tolerance of morality and immorality, and acceptance of all gods from all belief systems progressed to an all-time peak when the Roman Pantheon was constructed. As we covered earlier, this was a temple dedicated to all gods. Despite the fact that the Romans dominated in their conquests of various nations and regions and were brutal in their system of justice, they generally tolerated everything and anything when it came to belief systems—provided, of course, no person or group would upset the status quo. The arrival of Jesus Christ would do just that.

Another revealing passage of Scripture is found in the Book of Mark, alluding to the spiritual chaos and discord of Satan's fallen kingdom. This also refers to the spiritual battle of recognizing and binding the false spirit of the "strong man" (in this case, Satan himself). The terms "a kingdom divided against itself" and "a house divided against itself" can also be applied to the overall landscape of Christianity (divided into separate denominations), or applied to any specific church congregation (Spirit-filled individuals divided against those devoid of the Spirit), as well as to a family household (believer divided against non-believer). Those who lack Spiritual discernment can actually mistake the workings and "miracles" of Satan as the workings of the Holy Spirit. These deceptions of Satan, having the appearance of miracles, are also referred to as "*lying* signs and wonders" in Scripture (Matthew 24:24; 2 Thessalonians 2:9; Revelation 13:13, 16:14). Likewise, some actually mistake the workings of the Holy Spirit as the workings of Satan, as in the case of the Scribes who accused Jesus of using the authority of the Devil to cast out a demon spirit.

Mark 3:22–27
And the scribes which came down from Jerusalem said, He hath Beelzebub, and by the prince of the devils casteth he out devils. And he called them unto him, and said unto them in parables, How can Satan cast out Satan? And if a kingdom be divided against itself, that kingdom cannot stand. And if a house be divided against itself, that house cannot stand. And if Satan rise up against himself, and be divided, he cannot stand, but hath an end. No man can enter into a strong man's house, and spoil his goods, except he will first bind the strong man; and then he will spoil his house.

As we've seen, the Greek and Roman belief system of worship comprised multiple gods (an established hierarchy) and demigods (genetically altered humans). This is certainly a kingdom divided. However, there was yet one more facet to their system of worship. This was the acknowledgement of other various genetic hybrids such as Centaurs, Minotaurs, Fauns, etc. A partial list and description (en. wikipedia.org/wiki/List_of_hybrid_creatures_in_mythology) follows:

HYBRID	DESCRIPTION
Centaur	upper human body with a lower body of a horse
Dagon	half man and half fish
Echidna	upper half of a woman with lower body of a serpent snake
Faun	upper human body with a lower body of a goat (horns on head)
Harpy	half woman and half bird
Ipotane	upper human body with the hindquarter of a horse
Mermaid	half woman and half fish
Minotaur	head of a bull with a body of a human
Pegasus	full body of horse with wings of an eagle
Siren	woman with fish-like scales (similar to mermaid)
Sphinx	human head with body of a lion

These creatures (and many more not mentioned) are today considered mythological. Modern society does not witness a half-man/half-horse trotting down the avenue or a country road. The mere notion is pure fiction, relegated to the modern wave of fantasy films in our movie theatres.

However, Roger Oakland, a researcher in Creation Science, Ancient Cultures, and biblical Prophecy, made a very interesting observation in his video series, *The Bible: The Key to Understanding*. Highlighting the accomplishments of ancient cultures, he talks about the bronze and marble statues of the Greek and Roman empires. Roger shows how many of these amazing statues have been sculpted with impeccable detail. One statue portrays a governing statesman holding a scroll. Every fine detail is captured in the sculpture: the roll of the scroll, the laps and wrinkles in his robe, the locks of his hair, the features of his face, including the detailed pupils of his eyes, and the fine features of his hands and feet. Another statue portrays a discus thrower in competition. Every single and fine detail is captured, including the muscle tone of the athletic position and the disc in his hand. There are other examples of statues displaying incredible detail such as a maiden holding a platter of fruit, two men in the grip of a wrestling match, and a Roman Centurion complete with shield, spear, and full armour.

Examples of Greek Sculptures Displaying Incredible Detail of Human and Hybrid

After showing many examples of the superior craftsmanship of these statues, Roger points out that a sculptor (or other type of artist) usually has a live subject to pattern their work after. Then Roger presents a bronze statue of a centaur (half-man/half-horse). Again, every single detail is captured in the sculpture. In fact, the joining of the upper body of a human and the lower body of a horse is captured flawlessly.

So, the question must be asked: are these particular sculptured statues the figment of some artist's wild imagination? Or is it possible these statues were fashioned based on the existence of *real* subjects—just like all the other detailed sculptures?

Based on this premise, another question must be raised: if these hybrids actually did exist, what happened to them? Why don't we see any remaining evidence of their existence?

As we've covered, God send a global flood to destroy almost all of humanity and nearly all other lifeforms on planet Earth to exterminate widespread genetic contamination and alteration. Over the past two centuries, paleontologists and archaeologists have unearthed skeletal remains of various lifeforms, such as dinosaurs. What most people don't realize is that, up until the mid-1990s, there were only ten complete skeletons of a Tyrannosaurus Rex on display in various museums throughout the world. A fully complete specimen is very hard to find within the sedimentary layers of the earth. Often, sections of a skeleton are found separated—at times by several metres and in some cases up to a hundred metres apart. Based on this, finding a complete centaur or minotaur would be like finding "a needle in a haystack," especially if the human half and the animal half were separated and strewn over many metres of earth. There is also the possibility of an encompassing and complete burial due to the lava flow of volcanic eruptions. Of course, there is the ultimate end result of God's direct annihilation, preventing any future uncovering of such creatures.[32]

We covered that God found it necessary to destroy Sodom and Gomorrah, including other similar cities in the region. Again, this was to exterminate the *localized* genetic contamination and alteration. Based on this premise, it should not be a stretch to recognize the underlining reason why the Roman city of Pompeii was destroyed by the eruption of a neighbouring volcano, Mount Vesuvius. After all, at the time of Moses, God caused the earth to open up and engulf the dissenting group of Israelites who worshiped the graven idol of a golden calf—intervening in another attempt to return to false god worship, and subsequently preventing yet another possible progression towards genetic contamination.

Pompeii was another ancient city inundated with affluence and immorality. It was a city frequented by the elite of the Roman Empire; one might parallel it to Las Vegas (Sin City) as a popular vacation destination in today's terms. However, Pompeii's destruction parallels God's destruction of Sodom and Gomorrah. In an article on *Bible History Daily*, founded by the biblical Archaeology Society, Hershel Shanks writes:

> After the destruction, the site was subject to looting. And people who had managed to flee came back to see whether they could retrieve some of their possessions.
>
> One such person came back to a house in an area of Pompeii designated today as Region 9, Insula 1, House 26. After having walked through the desolation of the city, he (unlikely to be a "she") looked about and saw nothing but destruction where once there had been buildings and beautifully frescoed walls. Disconsolate and aghast, he picked up a piece of charcoal and scratched on the wall in large black Latin letters:

SODOM GOMOR [RAH]

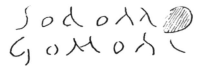

> As he saw it, the divine punishment of these two cursed biblical cities was echoed in the rain of fire on Pompeii.
>
> The inscription was found in a 19th-century excavation at the site. I went to Pompeii to see the place where it was discovered. (The inscription itself is in the stores of the Naples Archaeological Museum; it is nearly illegible at this time). In the center of the insula (a kind of city block) where it was found is a beautifully preserved columned atrium. House 26 is like the others in the insula—dark, destroyed, with vestiges of paintings on the walls, but mostly nothing.[33]

In another parallel to the destruction of Sodom and Gomorrah, there was a second city destroyed by the famous Mount Vesuvius eruption: the city of Herculaneum. This city was named after the man of renown, Hercules (Heracles in the Greek). This city was considered even more affluent than Pompeii. Hercules was exalted above all in this region, as it was considered to be Hercules who founded both Herculaneum and Mount Vesuvius (suggesting a previous Greek historic lineage). This region is known as the Phlegraean Plain, comprising an array of volcanic sites. It is here where the "sons of Earth" once resided. These were known to be giants in Greek and Roman mythology.[34]

This is very interesting, as we saw in Genesis 6, it was the "sons of God" who were the fallen angels that came down and procreated with earthly women, which led to the appearance of giants in those days. Here, we now see a direct confirmation of these Scriptures, albeit through Roman and Greek mythology, that these giants were also known as the "sons of Earth," none other than the offspring of the "sons of God," clearly the false gods/fallen angels.

Pompeii was the location of the House of the Faun. From the previous list of hybrid creatures, we see that Fauns were composed of the upper half of a human and the lower half of a goat, having goat horns on a human head. A life-sized, bronze statue of a dancing faun was one of the hallmarks of this renowned private residence.

There also existed the House of the Centaur in Pompeii. Centaurs were known to be half human and half horse. According to Greek mythology, centaurs came into being through the demi-god Centaurus (himself from a sexual union of the human King Ixion and the goddess Nephele) who, after exile, apparently went on to have sexual union with Magnesian mares (horses) in the region of Mount Pelion, Thessaly. This suggests the acceptance of bestiality, another facet of the downward spiral of Satan's genetic alteration and contamination.

Amongst the centaurs, the most notable was Chiron. Chiron was depicted as having the front legs of a human, not having the full lower body of a horse as with other centaurs. This difference is attributed to his father, Cronus (not Centaurus), who transformed himself into a horse (shapeshifted) before impregnating his mother, Philyra. Chiron was considered knowledgeable and skilled in many disciplines, mentor and teacher to the various "men of renown" such as Achilles, Aeneas, Ajax, Asclepius, Jason, Perseus, Theseus and, at times, Hercules.

Obviously, both ancients cities of Pompeii and Herculaneum were centres of sinful immorality and greatly influenced by both men of renown and hybrid creatures as a result of ongoing genetic contamination as we saw described in Jude 7 "…giving themselves over to fornication, and going after *strange flesh*…" (emphasis added) pertaining to Sodom and Gomorrah. It seems both Pompeii and Herculaneum were destroyed in like manner for the very same reasons.

10.

MYTHICAL CREATURES IN SCRIPTURE

One of the most recognizable mythical creatures known today is the unicorn. *Merriam Webster's Dictionary* provides us with a comprehensive definition:

> Unicorn: a mythical animal generally depicted with the body and head of a horse, the hind legs of a stag, the tail of a lion, and a single horn in the middle of the forehead.

Obviously we don't see this type of creature trotting down an avenue or galloping in an open field today, and yet the description above suggests a well-defined horse-like creature with various hybrid attributes. What we do see today is a sea creature native to the Arctic, known as a narwhal, which is basically a toothy, medium-sized whale with a unicorn-type horn protruding from its upper jaw. This in itself is an interesting creature displaying an interesting combination of physical attributes.

What is somewhat surprising is that the unicorn is mentioned in Scripture nine times: in Numbers 23:22, 24:8; Job 39:9, 39:10; Psalm 22:21, 29:6, 92:10; Deuteronomy 33:17; and Isaiah 34:7.

However, some researchers have concluded that these Scriptures actually refer to a rhinoceros-like creature with a single horn. Most common rhinos (Black, White, and Sumatran) have two horns with the exception of the Indian and Javan rhinos, which do have a single horn. These are powerful, wild, and untamed creatures.

Other researchers believe these Scriptures refer to an extinct bull-like creature known as an *auroch* that was much larger than the two-horned, bovine bulls
we see today. Again, this would be a powerful, wild, and untamed creature.

So it is interesting when we consider the following Scripture in the Book
of Job:

Job 39:10
Canst thou bind the unicorn with his band in the furrow? or will he
harrow the valleys after thee?

To band in the furrows describes the plowing of farmers' fields by animals
such as banded oxen or, in most cases, by horse-drawn plows. Mules, donkeys,
and water buffalo were also used in this way. Often these animals were banded
together using a yoke, a wooden cross beam between the necks and shoulders of
the animals, attached to the plow. Obviously, these particular animals were do-
mesticated (tamed). Some of these animals had two horns—not just a single horn.

While the creatures considered to be the fabled unicorn (rhinos and bulls)
are not tamable, and therefore could not be banded to draw plows for tilling fields,
the horse-like creature most attributed as the unicorn was not a tamable creature
either. It was known that the unicorn was hard to catch, having a very strong
temperament—certainly a wild creature in its own right. As the point alluded to
in Job 39:10, this creature would hardly be appropriate to pull a farmer's plow.

However, despite this, the word unicorn is derived from the Hebrew words
re'em, re'eym, reym and *rem*, suggesting a "wild bull"—yet, for the record, there is
no specific mention of this creature having a single horn.

The reason for this ambiguous confusion may lie in the possible incidental mistranslation of the verse Job 39:9 (preceding 39:10), according to CARM
(Christian Apologetics and Research Ministry):

The LXX—Septuagint
The LXX (the Greek translation of the Old Testament done around
250 B.C.) says of Job 39:9, βουλήσεται δέ σοι μονόκερως δουλεῦσαι ἢ
κοιμηθῆναι ἐπὶ φάτνης σου. The Greek word, μονόκερως *monokeros*, is
what the Hebrews translated the Hebrew word, רְאֵם *reym* into. It is an
unfortunate rendering. It literally means "one horn," and this is why
the KJV rendered it as unicorn since it was using the LXX and not the
original Hebrew here.[35]

Keeping all this in perspective, the nine Scriptural references may not be describing a unicorn in the popular sense after all. However, this in itself does not categorically dismiss the possibility that such a creature existed in our distant past. Some would argue that any acknowledgement of any mythical creature as part of Holy Scripture actually demeans and relegates the rest of God's Word to a non-credible level of myth and fables by association. Still, what we have covered thus far pertaining to the actuality of fallen angels, Nephilim giants, and mighty men of renown clearly demonstrates it is this overall train of thought, aforementioned, which may in fact be narrow-minded, off-base, and out of touch of reality.

This point will come into clear focus as we cover two other mythical creatures mentioned in Scripture.

Job 40:15–22
Behold now behemoth, which I made with thee; he eateth grass as an ox. Lo now, his strength is in his loins, and his force is in the navel of his belly. He moveth his tail like a cedar: the sinews of his stones are wrapped together. His bones are as strong pieces of brass; his bones are like bars of iron. He is the chief of the ways of God: he that made him can make his sword to approach unto him. Surely the mountains bring him forth food, where all the beasts of the field play. He lieth under the shady trees, in the covert of the reed, and fens. The shady trees cover him with their shadow; the willows of the brook compass him about.

Here we see the introduction of a creature called behemoth. The overall description is of a creature of great significance. Its tail is like a cedar, suggesting a very long, thick, and sturdy tail. Its bones are described as having the strength and resilience of both brass and iron, very strong metals used to fashion durable frameworks, tools, and weapons. We are told it has a great appetite, feeding on large amounts of grass vegetation, comparing it to an ox. Also interesting is the phrase "He is the chief of the ways of God..." This suggests the behemoth is at a pinnacle amongst God's other created animals, especially in size, as it is stated that only God can "make his sword to approach unto him." This creature would be unapproachable by a mere man, even with a sword drawn.

Some of the largest creatures to ever roam the earth are known as sauropods. These were massive creatures with huge hind legs to support their enormous bodyweight. They had long necks, similar to the giraffe, and very long tails. They inhabited regions marshy and lush with vegetation, usually near rivers or lakes (exactly as described in the preceding Scripture).

Sauropods were generally docile plant eaters. However, their size would have been quite overbearing for humans as hunters or defenders. Initially, it was determined that these creatures grew to seventy-two feet long and weighed up to thirty-nine tons. These were first discovered (officially) in 1877 by Othniel Charles Marsh and named *Apatosaurus* (meaning "deceptive lizard"). A larger set of bones was discovered at that time and named *Brontosaurus* (meaning "thunder lizard"). This creature was ninety feet long and weighed up to fifty tons. This find was quickly dismissed (perhaps prematurely) as a species of sauropod until 2015 when a call to re-classify the Brontosaurus as a bonafide species was put forth. In fact, an even larger sauropod was discovered in the Patagonian Desert region of Argentina in 2014. This creature grew up to one hundred and thirty feet long and sixty-five feet tall, and weighed up to seventy tons! This sauropod has been named *Titanosaurus* (meaning "titanic lizard" after the Greek gods known as the Titans).

Apparently, this accurate description is found in the Book of Job. This was a time in human history that was certainly ancient, yet humans were definitely present. In other words, according to God's Word, dinosaurs and humans co-existed. The secular notion that dinosaurs and humans existed some sixty-five million years apart is facing serious challenge in an information-driven world. It is currently documented, worldwide, that human footprints have been discovered alongside dinosaur footprints, embedded inside dinosaur footprints, and tread over by dinosaur footprints. In this last example, the human footprint was laid down first and *then* the dinosaur print was laid down overtop, intersecting the preserved human footprint.[36] One of the famous sites of human footprints and dinosaur prints is located along the Paluxy River near Glen Rose, Texas.[37] Other sites include Turkmenistan in Russia.[38]

While there has been a rigorous effort to disprove these findings, new evidence is continually emerging, especially throughout North America. One such find is a fossilized human finger found in a quarry of a layer formation deemed to be Cretaceous and 100 million years old.[39] Barring the obvious controversy of verifying such an old age, this still puts this relic of a human being (obviously buried quickly in some catastrophic event) well within the past existence of dinosaurs. Other interesting sites are well-known by the indigenous Indians, such as the Navajo near Tuba City, Arizona, where people can go on a guided tour to see dinosaur prints, human footprints, and amazingly, giant human footprints within the same vicinity.[40] These provocative findings demonstrate the validity of the Book of Job within God's Word.

While God's Word describes such a creature as a sauropod-type dinosaur, certain versions of the Bible actually set out to dismiss this entirely. In the New International Version, a footnote to Job 40:15 states:

> The Behemoth was a large animal, possibly an elephant or hippopotamus.[41]

While it is a fact that the elephant or hippo did frequent ponds and other waterways, both did not have tails like cedars; both certainly do eat vegetation (however, hippos eat meat as well), and both of these animals can be subdued by humans (humans can ride elephants). Based on this, one is led to conclude that the sole reason for the publishers of the NIV to present this ambiguous, somewhat preposterous, footnote was to align with the secular educational system's teaching on the Theory of Evolution. This position perpetuates the foundational tenet that the existence of man and dinosaur is separated by some sixty-five million years (a period of time that simply cannot be officially verified).

This ambiguity will extend to our next example. In the Book of Job we come across a description of yet another perplexing creature, the Leviathan. Only, this description goes into far more detail than what we saw pertaining to the Behemoth.

Job 41:1–34
Canst thou draw out leviathan with an hook? or his tongue with a cord *which* thou lettest down? Canst thou put an hook into his nose? or bore his jaw through with a thorn? Will he make many supplications unto thee? will he speak soft *words* unto thee? Will he make a covenant with thee? wilt thou take him for a servant for ever? Wilt thou play with him as thou *with* a bird? Or wilt thou bind him for thy maidens? Shall the companions make a banquet of him? shall they part him among the merchants? Canst thou fill his skin with barbed irons? or his head with fish spears? Lay thine hand upon him, remember the battle, do no more. Behold, the hope of him is in vain: shall not *one* be cast down even at the sight of him? None *is so* fierce that dare stir him up: who then is able to stand before me? Who hath prevented me, that I should repay him? *whatsoever* is under the whole is heaven is mine.

I will not conceal his parts, nor his power, nor his comely proportion. Who can discover the face of his garment? *or* who can come *to him* with his double bridle? Who can open the doors of his face? his teeth *are* terrible round about. *His* scales *are his* pride, shut up together *as with* a close seal. One is so near to another, that no air can come between them. They are joined one to another, they stick together, that they cannot be sundered. By his neesings a light doth shine, and his eyes *are* like the eyelids of the morning. Out of his mouth go burning lamps, *and* sparks of fire leap out. Out of his nostrils goeth smoke, as *out* of a seething pot or caldron. His breath kindleth coals, and a flame goeth out of his mouth. In his neck remaineth strength, and sorrow is turned into joy before him. The flakes of his flesh are joined together: they are firm in themselves; they cannot be moved. His heart is as firm as a stone; yea, as hard as a piece of the nether *millstone.* When he raiseth up himself, the mighty are afraid: by reason of breakings they purify themselves. The sword of him that layeth at him cannot hold: the spear, the dart, nor the habergeon. He esteemeth iron as straw, *and* brass as rotten wood. The arrow cannot make him flee: slingstones are turned with him into stubble. Darts are counted as stubble: he laugheth at the shaking of a spear. Sharp stones *are* under him: he spreadeth sharp pointed things upon the mire. He maketh the deep to boil like a pot: he maketh the sea like a pot of ointment. He maketh a path to shine after him; *one* would think the deep *to be* hoary. Upon earth there is not his like, who is made without fear. He beholdeth all high *things:* he *is* a king over all the children of pride.

There are two main aspects to this chapter in Job. One is based on an actual, physical overview. The other aspect is based on a metaphorical, spiritual overview. We will consider the physical aspect first.

Carefully considering all thirty-four verses, overall we learn that the Leviathan cannot be subdued by any human intervention. It cannot be tamed. It cannot be leashed. It is extremely fierce and evokes fear in the mighty. Its strength can overcome both iron and brass. When it moves through the sea it makes the surrounding water boil from the strong agitation of its movement. Arrows, spears, swords, and protective coats of mail (habergeon) are useless against it. It has very large, thick, and sealed scales. It is large and has very sharp claws. It has enormous jaws with an array of large, sharp teeth. It has a thick and strong neck. Its eyes have a menacing glow about them.

This is a significant, ominous, and frightening creature. Yet, the next part of the description puts the Leviathan in a whole new category. It is described as having "burning lamps," "sparks" and "flames" proceeding from its mouth. Smoke exits its nostrils as from a cauldron (a large fire pit). This is none other than a fire-breathing dragon. A fire-breathing dragon? "Preposterous nonsense!" one might say, and yet this is *exactly* what God's Word is stating. May I also point out, once again, that this creature co-existed with humans? A dragon, much more a fire-breathing dragon, would conceivably be a specific species of dinosaur.

Let us take a look at another footnote reference to Job 41:1 found in the New International Version of the Bible:

> While Leviathan usually refers to a seven-headed sea monster in old Canaanite myths, it probably means crocodile here.[42]

Really? While the crocodile is certainly a formidable creature, and had attained a larger size in ancient times, the last time I checked crocodiles can be subdued by humans through various means—often through the use of poles, ropes, and lassoes. And crocodiles do not exhale sparks and flames of fire through their jaws, nor plumes of smoke through their nostrils. This seems to be another concerted effort to relegate this detailed description of a fire-breathing dragon to the realm of myth and pure fantasy.

Speaking of myths, this NIV footnote assumes that the Leviathan is an old Canaanite myth. As we covered in Section One, the Canaanite giants (including Goliath and King Og), the mighty men of renown, and other genetically altered hybrids may have their basis in actual fact rather than simply as myth. Also previously stated, the evidence of their destruction and annihilation is found all over world, buried deep within both the earth and various oceans. I encourage you to search the internet, as there are hundreds of newly discovered sites of ancient cities and megalithic structures previously unknown to modern researchers.

What we just covered was a consideration of the physical aspect of Job 41. Now let us consider the spiritual aspect.

The dragon is a creature of great significance within Scripture. Throughout the description of the Leviathan in this chapter, not only do we see physical attributes of this dragon, but we also see attributes of characterization. We are asked, will this dragon "make any supplications unto thee" (will this persona receive any prayer requests from man)? Will "*he* speak soft words unto thee" (emphasis added: suggesting a male persona that can speak)? Will "*he* make a covenant unto thee" (emphasis added: suggesting this persona will make a binding agreement with man)? More implorable, or perhaps deplorable, "wilt thou take *him* for a servant for ever" (emphasis added: suggesting a possible binding allegiance to this persona, by man, for eternity)? The question is also asked, "shall they part *him* among the merchants" (emphasis added: will man separate this persona from the merchants of the world's system of commerce)?

God Himself answers these questions: "Behold, the hope of him is in vain: shall not *one* be cast down even at the sight of him?" God is warning us about this dragon, about this persona. He goes on to say, "Upon earth there is not his like, who is made without fear. He beholdeth all high *things:* he *is* a king over all the children of pride." Here, the mounting clues finally reveal who this dragon, this persona really is. It is none other than the god of this world. Satan.

On one level, we are presented an actual fire-breathing dragon, a physical creature that existed alongside human beings, stated in God's Word in a matter of fact way. On another level, we are presented a metaphoric image that symbolically represents Satan as the dragon. We are reminded:

Revelation 12:9
And the *great dragon* was cast out, that old serpent, called the Devil, and Satan, which deceiveth the whole world: he was cast out into the earth, and his angels were cast out with him. (Emphasis added)

We are also told in this same chapter of Revelation:

Revelation 12:3–4
And there appeared another wonder in heaven; and behold a *great red dragon*, having seven heads and ten horns, and seven crowns upon his heads. And his tail drew the third part of the stars of heaven, and did cast them to the earth: and the dragon stood before the woman which was ready to be delivered, for to devour her child as soon as it was born. (Emphasis added)

This describes the initial fall of the angel Lucifer, who transformed into a dragon with seven heads, ten horns, and ten crowns. This dragon drew one third of the "stars of heaven" (the one-third group of all other fallen angels). Lastly, this dragon waited (over millennia) before the woman (a metaphor for Israel), conniving for the time where she would bring forth her child (Jesus Christ, the Son of God, King of the Jews) and then attempted to eradicate Him (King Herod ordered the death of all first-born males in the ancient land of Israel in an attempt to prevent the prophesied coming of the Messiah). This, of course, is one example of the influence of Satan over man. It is by God's grace, planned through Mary and Joseph, that this attempt failed.

As we covered, prior to the First Coming of our Lord, Jesus Christ, ancient Israel was indeed the Land of Canaan—the land of false worship of false gods, and the land of genetically altered lifeforms. So, it is no wonder the dragon, the seven-headed sea monster (the Leviathan) has its roots in ancient Canaanite folklore (described as myth in the previous NIV footnote). It was certainly Satan (the dragon) at the centre of this manipulation and genetic contamination in this ancient fallen land.

Where this juncture of myth and reality of the dragon intersect is described in *Dragons or Dinosaurs?: Creation or Evolution?* by Darek Isaacs. Darek writes:

We can continue to explore the evidence by considering the significance of February 5, 2000. To most of us, it was just a winter day like no other. On the Chinese calendar, however, that date was the beginning of the year 4698, named the Year of the Dragon.

A series of twelve animal names are used to denote a sequence in the Chinese calendar. In order, these names are rat, ox, tiger, hare, dragon, snake, horse, sheep, monkey, fowl, dog, and pig.[43]

Notice that amongst animals that are familiar to people around the world lies the dragon—a creature that has been thought to be only a myth. Yet, one of the *oldest* societies in the world has used the dragon as a cultural icon and for centuries the Chinese have included the dragon in a list of common animals like the sheep, rabbit and dog.

…The dragon is the only so-called mythical creature. By making no distinction between the reality of a dragon and any of the other animals, they give a powerful testimony to the reality, at least from their perspective, of the dragon.[44]

11.
ANCIENT TEMPLES, MEGALITHS AND OTHER CULTURES

As we covered in Section One, after the time of Noah's Flood, humanity began rebuilding a society. This particular society grew and flourished in the same general region as the initial Garden of Eden. The ancient Sumerians are officially recognized by historians as the first culture on Earth to develop in the Fertile Crescent, Mesopotamia—known as the Cradle of Civilization. This is the beginning of post-flood, modern society. We covered that these people began to build a great city called Babylon. They built a great tower, called the Tower of Babel. God saw what they were doing and knew their intentions to "reach unto heaven" would begin a repeated progression of heavenly contact (Second Heaven) of the fallen angels (Genesis 11:4). God destroyed this tower, confounded (confused) their language, and then dispersed the people throughout the earth to prevent any further contact. We learned this is where one common language became multiple languages and when one culture (ethnic race) became multiple cultures throughout the world.

However, the people remained defiant. Wherever the people migrated, megalithic temples and altars were constructed. The evidence of this is seen throughout the world. We are going to continue to take a closer look at some examples and we discover how all this ties in to the bigger picture.

12.

PUMA PUNKU

PUMA PUNKU IS A LARGE COMPLEX OF TEMPLE STRUCTURES LOCATED NEAR Tiwanaku, Bolivia. It was subsequently discovered by early Spanish explorers. It had great reverence to the Inca culture, as they believed it to be the location where the world was created.[45]

This site comprises large mounds of earth and an impressive array of interlocking stone blocks and large stone slabs. Many of these blocks weigh up to eighty-five metric tons, and the largest weighs up to one hundred thirty-one metric tons. It is believed the blocks of red sandstone were quarried about six miles away, near Lake Titicaca.

Perplexingly, the site is thirteen thousand feet above sea level, where the air is thin and above the existing tree line. This brings into question the use of timber rollers, or the lack thereof, to move such blocks over long distances and steep inclines. This becomes especially problematic when considering that the other andesite blocks came from a quarry nearly sixty miles away.

While it is estimated that the site is less than two thousand years old, with the culture peaking between 500 and 1000 A.D. and some stonework being indicative of Bronze Age technology, there are remnants of stonework suggesting a much older origin and a superior level of technology. The red sandstone blocks at this site are of a material that is relatively easy to carve and shape, whereas the andesite blocks are much harder to shape, carve, and polish. In fact, some of the smooth faces and precise cut inserts suggest the use of power tools, such as drills. While this cannot be verified, what is verifiable is the fact that this workmanship is next to impossible to duplicate without the use of power tools. This is especially true of some of the large stone blocks that have been fashioned from hard granite and basalt discovered throughout both Bolivia and Peru. Some speculate that laser-cutting devices may have been used in the formation and cutting. The workmanship of these particular blocks is far beyond the scope of primitive hand tools and chisels. The following illustration demonstrates two key aspects of this profound workmanship.

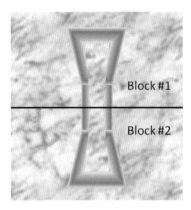

Block #1

Block #2

Carved Insert   Keystone Cut

The image on the left shows an example of a carved insert in the shape of a Swiss cross. This symbol is carved twice within itself, revealing precise skill. These carved inserts are found throughout the site.

The image on the right shows an example of a keystone cut used to join two separate blocks. The resulting trough was then filled with a molten bronze alloy to hold the blocks together. This technique has been discovered at other ancient sites throughout the world, such as in Egypt and South Asia. Amazingly, the space between the two surfaces where the blocks meet together is so precisely flat that it would be difficult to slip a thin razor blade between the two.

Other blocks found at this site, known as H blocks, were cut at specific angles to allow for a precise interlocking method of construction. These H blocks are somehow magnetized and adversely affect the readings of a compass.[46] This phenomenon has also been documented at the ancient site of Easter Island off the western coast of Chile. This is basically a fragmented circular temple site with massive stone heads, weighing up to thirteen tons, with the majority of them having their backs turned to the ocean. A compass does not function properly on this island, especially within close proximity to the head stones.[47]

It has been documented that this electromagnetic interference is also experienced within real crop circles, as opposed to hoax circles. This was observed by researchers Colin Andrews and Pat Delgado while investigating successive crop circle formations concentrated around the site of the circular temple of Stonehenge located on England's Salisbury Plain.[48] We will take a closer look at Stonehenge later on.

Another amazing aspect suggests that this site is much older than two thousand years—namely the discovery of an ancient artefact that has been determined to be of ancient Sumerian origin. This is known as the Fuente Magna Bowl, discovered near Lake Titicaca. This artefact displays forms of ancient hieroglyph and cuneiform engraved writing.[49] As covered previously, the Sumerian culture represents the very first form of human society (post-flood) and began in the fertile crescent of Mesopotamia—the original location of the Garden of Eden (pre-flood), now in southern Iraq near the Persian Gulf. The ancient site of the Garden of Eden has been declared a World Heritage Site by UNESCO (July 2016).[50] Again, coming full circle, the discovery of the Fuente Magna Bowl is clear evidence of the dispersion of the people of ancient Babylon, cited in Genesis 11, to the far side of the world.

This historical connection extends to the foundation of the ancient tribes of Bolivia and Peru, such as the Incas. As a reminder, the Incas believed that their god Virococha was the creator of all things, especially the sun, rain, and storms.[51] He was called a "watcher," one of the terms used to refer to an angel found in both the Book of Daniel (4:13, 17, 23) and various passages in the Book of Enoch. He could shapeshift between serpent and human form. It was believed that Virococha created a race of giants who were eventually destroyed by way of a great flood. This flood would have had to have been "great" since as mentioned the site of Puma Punku is thirteen thousand feet above sea level, and yet there is evidence that some sort of cataclysmic event took place here, since many of the heavy blocks are toppled and strewn about as though a massive tsunami swept through. The evidence is clear that Puma Punku has been subsequently rebuilt a few times since its original days.

The ancient flood scenario seems to be a point of agreement between various researchers such as Eric Von Daniken, David Childress, Casey Hematyaar, and Giorgio Tsoukalos. Researcher John Tylor Hepner writes:

An Aymare elder, Rene Quispe, explains the legends, beliefs and traditions of his Bolivian descendants regarding Puma Punku. Quispe explains that Viracocha, their invisible sun god, is depicted on the Gateway to the Sun. He sat by the water, as a "Watcher," the term ascribed to the Fallen Angels in the apocryphal book of Enoch. Quispe further explains how Viracocha created a race of giants, and the Bolivians believe that there were once giants there (Tsoukalos). Quispe maintains that the giants carried, cut, and polished the stones that are at Puma Punku. In Genesis, giants or the Nephilim, are the product of the fallen angels coming to Earth to seduce women in the time of Noah, "There were giants in the earth in those days; and also after that, when the sons of God came in unto the daughters of men, and they bare children to them, the same became mighty men which were of old, men of renown" (King James Version, Gen. 6:4). Most important is the fact that they agree with Posnansky; that Puma Punku was built before the Great Flood.

A flood explains why the structure is scattered and spread out in its ruinous state as well as its age. Casey Hematyaar, a forensic structural engineer, studied the ruins and when asked if the destruction was caused by an explosion of some sort, "The size of these stones, the weight of them, the mass and the way I look at the pictures of the remains of these, it's my opinion that it would be very remote that that would've been the cause. The concept of flood would make more sense to me" (Hematyaar). He explains further, "The soil becomes almost liquid. Getting saturated by water, it loses its stability, and therefore it's not capable of providing support to the structure above anymore. And with the movement of water itself, that can cause movement of these objects" (Hematyaar, Tsoukalos). In addition, evidence of seashells and fossils of fish have been found in this area even though the nearest body of water is more than ten miles away (Tsoukalos). This evidence suggests that Puma Punku was destroyed by a flood, which supports the theories that it was built before the Great Flood, thousands of years ago.

Those who favor the idea of extraterrestrial visitations to Earth have also hinted the Fuente Magna Bowl, a vessel bearing Sumerian hieroglyphs and cuneiform that was found in Lake Titicaca near the site of Puma Punku (Childress). This bowl suggests to some that the

Sumerian Annunaki came to South America. So it only offers, however, further evidence of the validity of the Fallen Angels from the Bible.[52]

The point needs to be stressed here, as it has been throughout this book, that many researchers and academics are looking at the overall evidence through the lens of the presumption of past extraterrestrial interaction with ancient man. This is simply a matter of intellectual, secular reasoning dismissing any link of the factual evidence to the reality of advanced beings, with superior knowledge of the creation, originating from a Spiritual dimension. Not only do some refuse to acknowledge where the facts actually lead, others simply cannot see what is staring them right in the face.

13.

THE DOGON TRIBE

COMPARED TO MODERN SOCIETY, THE DOGON TRIBE IS CONSIDERED TO BE A very primitive culture and, for the most part, one of the last remaining cultures that has been able to cling to their ancient traditions.

The Dogon have settled in the districts of Bandiagra and Doventia in the West African country of Mali. This is a region made up of plains, a plateau, and an array of cliffs. Some of these cliffs rise up to two thousand feet high. Many of the villages are found close to the Niger River. Villages found on the plains comprise mud huts for dwellings. Other villages are literally carved out of the sandstone cliffs. The original construction of these is of a previous, unknown ancient culture. The previous known inhabitants in this region were the Toloy culture (3rd to 2nd century B.C) and the Tellum culture (11th to 15th century A.D.). It is postulated that the Dogon culture migrated from Egypt, making their way to Libya, then on to Mauritania and Guinea.[53] In 1490, they fled to the Bandiagra region, escaping the Islamic expansion at that time. Current estimates of the Dogon population are between four and five hundred thousand, dispersed throughout more than seven hundred villages.

The Dogon culture comprises three main religious sects: the Awa, the Labe, and the Binu.

The **Awa** are known as the cult of the dead. They participate in lavish ceremonies using various masks and dress. These ceremonies are done for the general purpose of leading the *spirits of the dead* to their final resting place. The Awa believe it is their purpose to reorder spiritual forces from a state of disorder. They believe the spiritual realm was disrupted and altered by the death of the Nommo/Nummo, who are considered to be their ancient ancestors of *extra-terrestrial* origin.

The name **Lebe** means earth god and god of land fertility, also chief priest. The high priest is known as a Hogon. It is believed that the god Lebe visits the Hogons nightly in the form of a *serpent* and licks their skin to purify them and to infuse the "life force" into them, as well as passing on *wisdom* and *knowledge* to them.

The **Binu** are a sect based on a totemic system of worship similar to the North American First Nations tribes who display totem poles on the west coast. The Dogon totem emblems are displayed in sacred areas of worship, places of communication with *spirits* and sacrificial offerings of crops. These sacred sites are considered to be related to the creation of the world involving the Nommo/Nummo. The shrines are said to hold the *spirits* of these ancient, *extraterrestrial* ancestors who arrived before the appearance of *death* amongst mankind. It is said the Binu *spirits* appear in the form of various animals, hence the totem emblems.

Considering all aspects of these three sects of the Dogon in relation to what we've covered in Section One, the following points should be considered:

- ► The Awa are known as *the cult of the dead*. Satan is referred to as the Lord of the Dead and this title crosses over to other ancient gods that can be traced back to Satan himself, such as Osiris and Horus in pagan Egyptian worship.

- ► The Awa are involved in leading the *spirits of the dead* to their final resting place. The wandering and familiar spirits are in fact the released spirits of the deceased Nephilim and Rephaim giants.

- ► The titles of the god Lebe, "earth god," "god of land fertility" and "chief priest" parallel the titles of the god Baal, which also can be traced back to Satan.

- ► Lebe takes on the form of a serpent. Satan also appears in the form of a serpent.

- ► Lebe, as the serpent, imparts knowledge and wisdom to the Hogon priests. Satan, as the serpent, tempted Adam and Eve with the fruit of the Tree of Knowledge of Good and Evil.

▸ The Nommo/Nummo are said to be beings of *extraterrestrial* origin, interacting with ancient humans. The fallen angels presented themselves to ancient humans as gods originating from Second Heaven, the Cosmos, or the Universe.

▸ The Nommo/Nummo arrived before the appearance of death within mankind. Upon the arrival of Satan on earth, it was the fall of Adam and Eve, at the Garden of Eden, where sin, and subsequently death, entered into the world.

▸ The Binu spirits appear in the form of animals. Both fallen angels and terrestrial spirits can shapeshift, transforming into various forms, including animal form.

Beginning in the 1930s two French anthropologists, Marcel Griaule and Germaine Dieterlen, embedded themselves for fifteen years amongst the Dogon people. Amazing stories of their ancient past were shared, much of which had passed down through oral tradition for thousands of years. Further information on this can be explored through two books: *The Pale Fox* (Griaule and Dieterlen) and *Conversations with Ogotemmeli: An Introduction to Dogon Religious Ideas* (Griaule).

It was discovered, apparently for the first time for these modern researchers, that the Dogon tribe was well aware of the Sirius star system near the Orion Belt star system. This in itself is not significant, as Sirius is easily seen as the brightest star in the sky, which they called Sigi Tolo (*tolo* meaning star). However, what is groundbreaking is that the Dogon also knew about a second star, which they called Po Tolo (*Po* meaning smallest seed, alluding to a smaller star). This star cannot be seen with the naked eye, as it is a White Dwarf star in its final stage of existence—having the same mass as our sun, but condensed to the size of Earth. Our sun has the equivalent mass of 1.3 million Earths.[54] This White Dwarf star is extremely dense and emits very low luminosity, its internal fusion all but done.

The existence of this second star was not verified until the nineteenth and twentieth centuries through astronomy research using telescopes. It was initially suspected in 1844 that Sirius had a companion star due to a detected gravitational wobble. This was confirmed in 1862 by Alvan Clark of Massachusetts, and later confirmed as a White Dwarf in the 1920s. The star is now known as Sirius B, which rotates around Sirius A every fifty years. This verifiable information would be divulged to Griaule and Dieterlen within a decade of time in 1931 by the Dogon who stated that Po Tolo was very small and very heavy, rotating on its axis and orbiting Sigi Tolo every fifty years!

However, the Dogon divulged details even further, stating that there is a third star in the system called Emme Ya Tolo, which has a planet that orbits around it called Nyan Tolo. Emme Ya Tolo was described as being larger than Po Tolo, yet lighter. In 1995, gravitational studies conducted by French researchers Daniel Benest and J.L Duvent indicated the possible presence of a Red Dwarf star. This would indeed be lighter in mass than a White Dwarf and reddish in colour, and therefore somewhat harder to detect.

Loy Lawhon, a researcher for *UFO Evidence,* writes:

The Dogon have a special reverence for Sirius. The elders told Griaule that Sirius is not just one star, but three. The one we see, Sigi Tolo (Sirius A) is just the largest and brightest. It is orbited by a smaller star, Po Tolo (Sirius B) which is named after a tiny grain that is also called Digitaria. They believe that this tiny star is the heaviest thing in the universe and that it is made of a metal called sagala. This tiny star orbits Sigi Tolo every fifty years, in an elliptical orbit. The third star in the system is called Emme Ya, the sun of women. It is four times lighter in weight than Po Tolo, and it travels in the same direction around Sigi Tolo, but in a larger orbit. It moves much more quickly through space, so that it takes the same amount of time to complete an orbit around Sigi Tolo. Emme Ya has a satellite or planet of its own, called the Goatherd or the star of women. There are drawings on the four-hundred-year-old sigui mask that represent this cosmology.[55]

Sirius Triple Star System

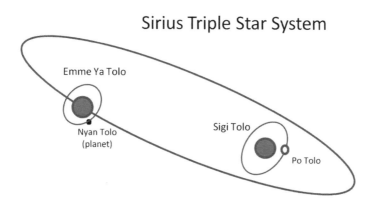

According to the Dogon, the Nommo/Nummo were humanoid/fish-like hybrid creatures believed to be *extraterrestrials* who originated on a planet that orbited Sirius A (Nyan Tolo). The Nommo were called "Masters of the water," "The Monitors" and "The Teachers."[56] It was believed they were created by the "sky god" called Amma.[57] Due to their unusual hybrid appearance, they were also referred to as serpents and lizards. The Nommo also appear in ancient folklore within the ancient Babylonian, Acadian, and Sumerian cultures.[58] It is interesting that there is a close resemblance of the name Amma compared to the pinnacle god of the Sumerians, An or Annu, which we covered previously:

An (Anu—Annu): father and king of the gods; god of heaven; god of the sky; ruler of the Annunaki; creator of demons and lord of the spirits

Despite these interesting correlations, there has been some controversy surrounding these stories and claims. The famous cosmologist Carl Sagan asserted that the Dogon must have been coached or somehow socially contaminated by western culture, since the French anthropologists had made long-term contact only after scientists had documented the presence of Sirius B.[59] However, the fact remains that the extreme density of Sirius B was officially determined only a few years before the recorded Dogon story accounts. In addition, amongst Dogon ceremony (called a sigui) a particular dance, known as the Sigi dance, is performed every sixty years, passed down from generation to generation since the thirteenth century A.D.[60] This involves a headdress that has a long wicker stem of some fifteen feet with an attached ball at the end. The high priest whips this extended ball, representing the orbit of Po Tolo, in a circular pattern around his own head, representing Sigi Tolo. It is estimated that many of the current masks used in these ceremonies are as much as four hundred years old, as stated in the previous quote by Loy Lawhon. This certainly trumps Carl Sagan's assertion that the Dogon culture was influenced by western knowledge of the Sirius star system.

Besides the detailed knowledge of the Sirius system, the Dogon also had celestial knowledge of the rings of Saturn and of some of the major moons of Jupiter.

As mentioned, it is believed the Dogon tribe had originally migrated from ancient Egypt. The goddess Isis is sometimes associated with the star Sirius in ancient pagan Egyptian worship. In fact, there are mural paintings depicting Isis traveling in a boat along with two other companions. Some postulate this is a symbolic reference to the two other companion stars to Sirius, Sirius B and Sirius C.

14.

THE PYRAMID OF KING KHUFU

THIS LEADS US TO A CLOSER LOOK AT ONE OF THE LARGEST PYRAMIDS IN THE world, the Great Pyramid at Giza, Egypt. This is the pyramid of King Khufu, also known as the Pyramid of Cheops in Greek. Khufu was the second Pharaoh of the fourth dynasty of ancient Egypt. The pyramid is considered one of the Seven Wonders of the World, built between 2584–2561 B.C. This pyramid is the oldest and largest of the three pyramids that form a mirror image of the three-star Orion's Belt constellation. The third star offset of 19.5º is duplicated exactly by the deliberate site placement of the third pyramid at Giza. This purposeful alignment was the foundation for the blockbuster film *Stargate* (1994), which brought forth the conceptual relationship between pyramids and star travel to the general population. There is a saying amongst occultists and New Age philosophers: "As above, so below." In other words, what is displayed in heaven is also displayed or mirrored here on Earth.

The word *pyramid* is actually comprised of two root words in the Greek language, *pyra* (meaning fire) and *mid* (meaning in the middle). It literally means "fire in the middle." Now, for the most part this meaning has either gone unnoticed, or it has not been completely understood. This is primarily because, while the general population is aware of the external grand presence of the Great Pyramid itself, most are oblivious to the elaborate and significant *internal* construction. While some people understand that the structure itself serves as an immense burial tomb, housing the king's chamber within the centre, many do not realize that there are functional aspects about the deliberate construction, which may be of profound significance.

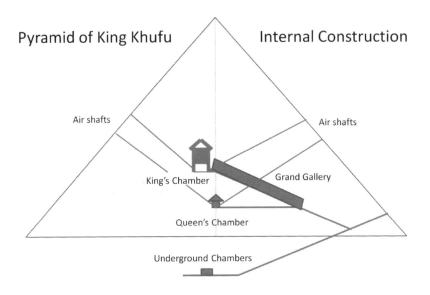

Pyramid of King Khufu   Internal Construction

Air shafts   Air shafts

King's Chamber   Grand Gallery

Queen's Chamber

Underground Chambers

Looking at the diagram of the internal construction of the Great Pyramid, we see the Grand Gallery leading up to the King's Chamber where the sarcophagus (tomb) of Khufu was located. When an individual enters the King's Chamber, they are entering a room roughly 5.25 (17 ft.) by 10.5 metres (34 ft.). One only notices that they are standing within a rectangular walled room with a 6-metre (19.5 ft.) tall flat ceiling composed of nine granite beams, some weighing up to 80 tons for a total ceiling weight of 650 tons.[61] However, what is not readily noticed is the elaborate structure that starts at the ceiling level and continues for another 17.25 metres (56 ft.).

The following diagram reveals a very deliberate and perhaps purposeful structure above the King's Chamber. For some reason the ancient Egyptians went to great lengths to install 50-ton granite slabs, separated and supported by limestone spacer blocks. Finally, two 70-ton granite slabs were installed as angled roofing trusses. This seems like an exercise of extreme overkill, especially since modern tower cranes can only lift 20 tons (40,000 lbs.).[62]

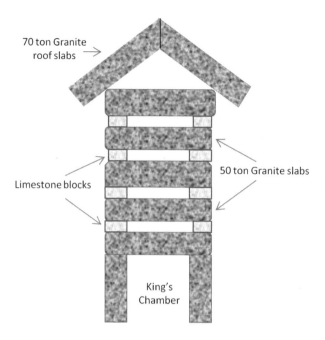

70 ton Granite
roof slabs →

50 ton Granite slabs

Limestone blocks

King's
Chamber

Some researchers speculate that this elaborate structure was meant to stabilize the overall pyramid. However, most people with knowledge of construction would have to conclude that, despite the immense size of this particular internal structure, it is still dwarfed by the overall size of the pyramid itself. The Great Pyramid is built out of 2.3 million blocks, reaching a height of 147 metres (476 ft.) and covers an area of 13.3 acres. So the idea that this relatively tiny internal structure provides any structural reinforcement is a grand assumption not based on observable evidence.

However, it's very interesting that the large 50- and 70-ton slabs are made out of granite. Granite falls under the category of a holocrystalline rock, a material composed of crystalline substances, in this case mainly feldspar, quartz, and mica. These *crystalline* slabs are then separated by blocks of limestone, a sedimentary rock. In fact, the 2.3 million blocks that comprise the pyramid structure are also made of limestone, each weighing 2–3 metric tons. The ancients' deliberate use of these granite slabs for the King's Chamber is unique and very particular, apart from the majority of the construction, which makes this even more intriguing. Especially since the granite was transported 900 km by boat from a quarry south in Aswan.[63]

Crystalline substances can be affected by heat, vibration, pressure, or light. In fact, it is through the use of crystals that many of our modern electronics function. Quartz crystals are often used in watches and clocks to keep accurate time. Quartz is also used in oscillators and various digital circuitries. Quartz crystals can produce electricity when pressure is applied to them.[64] Limestone, on the other hand, is relatively inert and has the property of an insulator.[65] Essentially, you have crystalline, conductive material stacked and separated by inert, non-conductive material acting as insulators. It seems this structure is partially conductive and partially non-conductive. This is exactly the configuration of an electronic component known as a semi-conductor.

> Although an electrical insulator is ordinary thought of as a non-conducting material, it is better described as a poor conductor or a substance of high resistance to the flow of electrical current. Different insulating and conductive materials are compared with each other in this regard by means of a material constant known as resistivity. *See also* semiconductor.[66]

Both of these materials, used together, in this deliberate structural configuration, require serious contemplation of the following points:

(1) As illustrated in the following diagram, there are four airshafts that converge in two pairs of north and south alignments to both the King's Chamber and the Queen's Chamber.

Pyramid of Khufu /Cheops

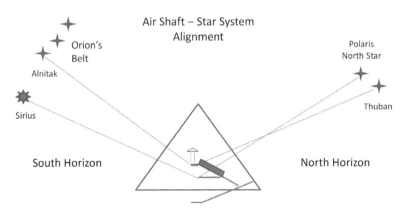

Air Shaft – Star System Alignment

Orion's Belt

Alnitak

Sirius

Polaris North Star

Thuban

South Horizon

North Horizon

(2) These airshafts were originally aligned with specific stars in the night skyline. This alignment has shifted from the original alignment over millennia.

(3) It is one thing to have airshafts for workers to breath fresh air within a deep, remote chamber; it is another to have these "airshafts" purposely aligned with the stars in the southern skyline Sirius and Alnitak (Orion's Belt), and the stars in the northern skyline Thuban and Polaris (the North Star).

(4) The north-south centre line crosses the King's Chamber.[67]

(5) Through all the looting and vandalization of the King's Chamber over the years, the mummified body has never been found. The lid to the granite burial tomb is also missing. However, it is known that the ancient Egyptian kings were buried in sarcophagi plated in gold, such as King Tutankhamen. Many of these gold sarcophagi were moved and reburied in the Valley of the Kings due to the ongoing looting. Gold is highly conductive of electrical current.

(6) Is it possible some form of light or electrical current was received from the cosmos (Second heaven) to activate the 24-metre-tall semi-conductor?

(7) Again, as we have covered, the very word *pyramid* itself brings an enhanced level of understanding as the defined meaning is the clear description: fire in the middle.

(8) As covered in Section One, the name Lucifer means light bringer, as he is known as the angel of light.

(9) The star Polaris, also known as the North Star and the brightest star in Ursa Minor, happens to be the same Greek word Polaris, which also translates to Satan.[68]

(10) The star Thuban, the brightest in Ursa Major, is known as the dragon in Greek and the serpent in Arabic (*Al Thuban*).[69]

(11) As covered in Section One, the ancient Egyptians worshiped Osiris, who they believed originated from the star system of Orion's Belt. Osiris was known as the lord of the dead—the same title Satan is well-known for, through many synonyms throughout history. The Egyptians were preoccupied with death and the *afterlife*.

(12) As covered in Section One, the ancient Egyptians believed the Nephilim were the offspring of Osiris.

Much like their predecessors of ancient history, the Egyptians initially engaged in human sacrifice. This was a common practice with all the pharaohs during the first dynasty. One such example is the tomb of Djer, known to have 338 humans buried with him. Animals were also sacrificed, such as donkeys, thought to be used for transporting goods in the afterlife. The practice of human sacrifice ended with the first dynasty.[70] Despite this latter absence of human sacrifice, the pharaohs continued to be entombed with many of their riches and earthly possessions to assist them in the afterlife. Of course, as mentioned, most of these items were subsequently pillaged during ongoing looting and, obviously, these items did not transcend into the afterlife as they were physically left behind. To emphasize this false doctrine of belief, Satan is also known as the "father of lies" (John 8:44).

As a final note, the following describes an amazing phenomenon that positively links these ancient, megalithic structures throughout the world, intrinsically, by the direct influence of satanically inspired knowledge. The researcher mentioned is Hugh Harleston Jr., an American civil engineer who did extensive research of the pyramid complex at Teotihuacan, Mexico. The following quote is from the exhaustive text *Mysteries of the Mexican Pyramids* (1976) by Peter Tompkins:

> Harleston was able to witness a unique event. As the sun crossed the zenith at 12:35'30" (local noon at the longitude of Teotihuacan), the lower west part of the fourth face of the pyramid, which is in shadow during the morning, became illuminated as the sun's rays moved from south to north. The whole effect occurred in 66.6 seconds, a phenomenon which makes the Sun Pyramid a perennial clock, still transmitting its silent message, exactly as does the Great pyramid of Cheops, or as does the south corner of the Castillo at Chichen Itza, each equinoctial day of the year. All these structures would have had to be designed by architects aware of the considerable astronomical and geodetic data required to achieve such effects—*before* the buildings were begun.[71]

15.

STONEHENGE

PERHAPS ONE OF THE MOST RECOGNIZABLE ANCIENT STRUCTURES, OTHER THAN the Great Pyramid, is the ancient site of Stonehenge. This ancient temple is located in the region of Wiltshire, England, in the area of Salisbury Plain. It was proclaimed a World Heritage Site by UNESCO in 1986.

It's been determined Stonehenge was built over three main, separate phases. The first phase, estimated between 2950 and 2900 B.C., consisted of a large circular ring of wooden post holes and/or bluestones that measured 360 feet in diameter. The second phase, around 2600 B.C., consisted of bluestones forming a double circle configuration. The third, around 2400 B.C., consisted of large sarsen stones erected in pairs with stone lintels spanning their tops. These formed a horseshoe configuration within the centre of the complex. Another circle, comprising large sarsen stones, surrounded this inner horseshoe complex and was connected at the top with more stone lintels. It is estimated that by 2300 B.C. additional bluestones were added to form a smaller horseshoe configuration inside the main sarsen horseshoe and another circle erected between the main sarsen horseshoe and the main sarsen outer ring. It is believed the bluestones, weighing up to four tons, were quarried from different sites in western Wales and transported as far as 225 kilometres (140 miles). The sarsen stones, nine metres high (30 ft.) and weighing an average twenty-five tons each, are believed to have been quarried in the area of Marlborough Downs some 32 kilometres (20 miles) away.[72]

There has been much speculation regarding the purpose of this elaborate structure. The majority consensus, stemming from both scientific circles and

New Age philosophies, is that Stonehenge is simply an astrological structure, as it is purposefully aligned with the rising sun, especially marking the celestial events of the winter and summer solstices. Some researchers have noted more complex celestial relationships within the alignments. This has fueled a lighter side of understanding, to the general populace, based on the surface-level recognition of nature or cosmic worship (albeit paganistic). However, there is definitely a darker side to this temple known as Stonehenge.

> Recently researchers have also discovered a massive wooden building which may have been used for burial rituals. Also, dozens of burial mounds have been discovered near Stonehenge indicating that hundreds, if not thousands, of people were buried there in ancient times. At least 17 shrines, some in the shape of a circle, have also been discovered near Stonehenge.[73]

Mike Parker Pearson, a former professor of archeology at the University of Sheffield, and head of the Stonehenge Riverside Archeology Project, has this to say:

> It is now clear that burials were a major component of Stonehenge in all its main stages…Stonehenge was a place of burial from its beginning to its zenith in the mid third millennium B.C. The cremation burial dating to Stonehenge's sarsen stones phase is likely just one of many from this later period of the monument's use and demonstrates that it was still very much a domain of the dead.[74]

Stonehenge Salisbury Plain, England

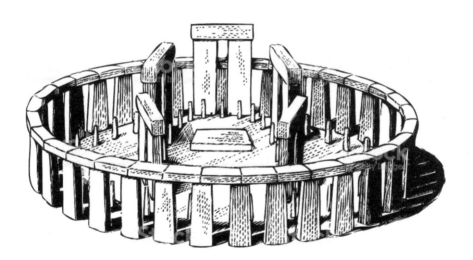

Illustration of the original stone alignment

Viewing the images of Stonehenge on the next page, we see both a photo of the original site and an illustration of the original configuration. Taking this into consideration, there is one aspect of this ancient temple not commonly mentioned—the existence of an altar near the centre, within the horseshoe sarsen stones. The Altar Stone, known as stone 80, was excavated in the 1950s and has been identified as part of the phase three modification.[75]

While it is obvious Stonehenge is directly associated with death and burial, it is not widely understood that this ancient megalith was actually a temple altar of human sacrifice. While it is not clearly understood who actually built Stonehenge, we do know that an ancient priesthood, the Druids, were the subsequent occupiers of this temple of the dead. In modern times, the druidic belief system is regarded as a paganistic organization of nature worship. This is simply a gross oversight of the actual historical and foundational roots of this ancient priesthood.

Druids are commonly recognized as having a heritage stemming from the Celts, which are commonly recognized as having settled in Ireland and throughout the British Isles. However, they were also known to have settled in Brittany, a region in northwestern France. Megalithic temples are also found in this region. Going further back in history, one learns that the Celts had occupied Gaul, which was the major central region of France, both east and west. Going back even further, we discover that the Celts had settled many other regions of central Europe, including parts of Germany west of the Rhine River and the southern regions, parts of Switzerland, and parts of Italy, Belgium, and Denmark. Based on this, the Celts were historically rooted in central Europe, primarily Gaul and Bavaria. We will revisit this last point later.

The Celts were known to have been a formidable adversary in battle. The Romans fought the Celts on several occasions, recorded in the writings of Julius Caesar when he invaded Gaul in 56 B.C. As we will discover, the Druids, as the priesthood of these ancient Celts, were also considered to a formidable group, but not necessarily in the normal sense of confrontation.

The word *Druid* defined means a priest, a magician, and a soothsayer as described by the online Oxford Dictionary. The old Irish word *drui* means druid or sorcerer. An ancient Celtic word *druwids* means "they who know the oak" or "oak knower."[76] This last defined term is very significant as stated by researcher and occult expert Gene Aven, who, when interviewed on *100 Huntley Street* in the mid-1990s said,

The name 'druid' actually means 'men of the oak trees' in reference to their ancient Bavarian roots. The Druids would cut down a large oak tree, deep in the forest, and would use this large stump round, some being six feet across, as an altar for human sacrifice.

Gene went on to show actual photographs of himself standing near some of these sacrificial oak tree stumps.

Through his studies of comparative religions in relation to Christianity, Gene Aven became a consultant to law enforcement agencies throughout North America regarding criminal cult activities. In his book, *Oranges and Onions: Volume 1*, Gene goes on to describe this ancient priesthood:

The celebration of Halloween predates the Christian church by several centuries, an ancient Druid rite dating back into antiquity. It was the high holy day of the year for Druids honoring Samhain, the lord of the dead, their name for Satan.

Druids are mentioned by name in some thirty references by Greek and Roman writers between the 2nd century B.C. and the 4th century A.D. Druids are a member of the Celtic religious order of mystic priests who originated in ancient Britain, Ireland, and France. The word Druid means "the men of the oak trees" and rituals were frequently performed out of doors in forests or caves.

Druids have a mixture of mystical-occult theological beliefs. They worshipped the sun, moon and stars. And the famous Stonehenge in Southwestern England is a Druid altar.

The Druids themselves came out of the Celtic culture, which practiced human sacrifice. They sacrificed adults as well as infants, and had ritual drowning. Such mysticism and occultism became a part of the Druid tradition.

Today, Druids have given us our modern form of witchcraft, and Druid priests still practice animal and human sacrifice.[77]

It is believed and taught by the Druids that on October 31st Samhain called together all the wicked souls who had died within the past twelve months and had been condemned to inhabit the bodies of animals (hence the origin of animal sacrifice). These souls demanded to be placated by the living through provisions of acceptable food, shelter and sacrifice. If acceptable food, shelter and sacrifice were not provided these evil spirits would cast spells, cause havoc and terror, and haunt and torment the living.

Druids believed that human sacrifice offered the ultimate appeasement of Samhain. After this sacrifice was given, a large pumpkin was hollowed out and the smiling face of Samhain was carved out and a candle of human tallow placed inside. The lit finished product was a sign that Samhain had been appeased.

If the victim to be sacrificed was not willingly provided, the home was cursed by the Druids by placing the sign of the six pointed star enclosed by a circle upon the door and through the same evil power that takes a life in voodoo rituals, a life would be involuntarily taken. This drawing of the hexagram is where we derive the term "putting a hex on someone.

These activities on the 31st of October led to the practice amongst ordinary folks of placing food offerings outside their door to attempt to appease Samhain, the demons and Druids. It did not take long for the poor to discover that dressing like the devil or a demon or a Druid and going door to door pretending to be these personages was a pretty good way, in just one evening, to fill the larder for the winter.

Even though most people have forgotten the origins of this occult holiday, these practices are what evolved to our celebration of Halloween: a cartooned reenactment of ancient Druid witchcraft rites. We dress the children in costumes and send them out door to door to collect their food offerings. Even the phrase we teach them, "trick or treat," simply means: "if you don't want the trick, you had better appease us with the treat, the food offerings due the demons." The trick today means that at the very best you will get your windows soaped and your garbage cans turned over. Originally they played a little rougher.

The date of this celebration was the last day of October, the end of the Celtic new year. It was a time of falling leaves and general seasonal decay and it seemed appropriate to celebrate death. And that is just what Halloween is all about: a celebration of death. It honored the god of the dead and the wicked spirits of the dead.[78]

It is clear Stonehenge was a significant sacrificial altar used by the Druids, substantiated by the presence of hundreds, if not thousands, of buried sacrificed humans all around this site. This is a direct, unbroken link to the satanic influence of other ancient cultures we have covered, such as the sacrificial blood pyramid of the Mayans.

While Stonehenge is commonly recognized as an astrological calendar and marker of the cosmos, it is more accurately designated as a temple of worship to Satan, the lord of the dead, and to the other fallen angels who were the former stewards, under God, of the aspects of Second Heaven—the sun, the moon, and the stars. This is simply a continuation of Satan's arrogance and insistence that he is proclaimed and exalted on a higher seat than God Himself (Isaiah 14:13–14).

Finally, it is through the pervasive influence of the ancient Druid priesthood throughout regions of ancient Europe where the roots of modern-day witchcraft and occult ceremonies began. Regarding key symbolism of Satanism and the Occult, Gene also states:

> The word pentagram comes from the Greek "pente," meaning "five," and "gamma" meaning "letter." In the science of magic the pentalpha is called the holy and mysterious pentagram. The triple triangle is called "Pentalpha" because in its configuration it represents the form of the Greek letter alpha, or 'A', in five different positions. Cornelius Agrippa (philosophy, occult) says of this figure, that, "by virtue of the number five, it has great command over evil spirits because of its five double triangles and its five acute angles within and its five obtuse angles without, so that this interior pentangle contains in it many mysteries." The Druids wore it on their sandals as a symbol of their deity, and hence the Germans called the figure "Druttenfuss," a word that originally meant "Druid's foot," but which now has come to mean "Witch's foot." As an ancient druidic symbol, it was used to represent a goat's head in worship of the goat god. When the symbol is shown with two points up, it depicts the goat and is considered a representation of black witchcraft, or conscious Satan worship. When shown with one point up it is considered to be a symbol of white witchcraft, or neutral magic.[79]

Diagrams of Pentagrams and Satan's Goat Head

Satan and the fallen angels were known as morning stars prior to their initial fall, when they were cast out of Third Heaven into Second Heaven and subsequently down to First Heaven. It should not be construed as a mere coincidence that the pentagrams depicted above are also basic illustrations of heavenly stars. In addition, as we covered in Foundational Point Four of Section One, the very first Scripture where the word "devils" appears is in Leviticus 17:7, which is derived from the Hebrew word *saiyr*, meaning "a devil, *a goat*, hairy."

It is also interesting to consider the word *Druttenfuss* as an ancient German word for both Druid's foot and Witch's foot as cited by Gene Aven. We covered previously that the ancient Celts can be traced back to ancient Bavaria. When this point is taken into consideration with the Druids as the architects of witchcraft, it should not come as a surprise that the modern-day secret society, the Illuminati, was founded in Bavaria (Ingolstadt, Germany) by Adam Weishaupt in 1776. This just happens to be the same year many members of the Masonic Lodge in America (another secret society), such as George Washington, John Adams, Thomas Jefferson, Benjamin Franklin, and John Hancock, signed the Declaration of Independence and/or the Constitution of the United States of America. We will continue to explore this historical connection in an upcoming chapter, Secret Societies and the Coming Antichrist, in Section Three.

This ancient influence of Druid occultism was deeply rooted in both Germany and Austria. Gene Aven noted that modern-day Germany has one of the highest participation numbers of its population involved within Occult and New Age belief systems. This unbroken thread has been noted and documented by many researchers and authors pointing out the glaring occult overtones and symbolic relics of Hitler's Nazism and proposed Third Reich. Some of these deep, dark undertones sprang from inner circle involvement within secret societies such as the Thule Society founded in 1918 by Rudolf Von Sebottendorf, head-quartered in Berlin. Not surprisingly, the foundation of Aryan race supremacy in Germany has been traced back to this particular secret society. Also not surprising, this foundational ideology fostered an unrelenting contempt and hatred towards the Jewish people. This can be traced to Satan's influence and manipulation throughout human history. After all, Satan attempted to prevent the birth of Jesus Christ, King of the Jews, by working through King Herod to murder all the first-born babies in the land. The attempted genocide and scattering of the Jewish people through the Nazi regime was simply another step in Satan's plan to prevent the prophecy of Israel becoming an official nation. Despite this, God's will and purpose for the Jewish people, and for the nation of Israel, remains in play to this very day.

As an interesting note, director Steven Spielberg incorporated many aspects of Nazi occultism and spiritism in his famous Indiana Jones film series, starting with *Raiders of the Lost Ark* (1981), even incorporating the extraterrestrial facet in *Indiana Jones and the Kingdom of the Crystal Skull* (2002).

As a final note to the satanically inspired, pervasive influence of the Druids, stemming from Bavaria, and subsequently well established at Stonehenge, England, there is an old tradition in the Germanic cultures of Europe that remains today. This is the folklore of Krampus.

Krampus is known as an *anthropomorphic* creature defined as "having the attributes of human traits, emotions and intentions bestowed to a non-human entity." Krampus is described as a half-demon/half-goat who walks upright like a human being. According to folklore, Krampus is a partner to Saint Nicholas just before the Christmas season (December 6) to bring punishment to the children who have misbehaved throughout the previous year.[80] Of course Saint Nicholas is thought to be, by many, the origin of the personification of Santa Claus. We will closely examine the true origin of Santa later in Section Three.

Again, much of this folklore, occultism, and spiritism can be traced to the heritage of the Celtic Druids. However, they were not the only group that had a high sacred investment in a megalithic, circular temple. Megalithic, circular temples such as Stonehenge are found throughout the world. We will now cover another, lesser-known example.

16.

GILGAL REPHAIM

The Gilgal Rephaim is a monolithic circular temple found in the Israeli area of the Golan Heights, sixteen miles east of the Sea of Galilee. It is centered on a large plateau and comprises concentric circles formed from piles of volcanic, basalt stone. The outermost circle wall is 160 metres (520 ft.) in diameter and 2.4 metres (8 ft.) high. This makes this temple much larger than a modern football field at 173 yards in overall length. At its centre is found a *tumulus*, a mound of earth and stone piled over one or multiple graves. The site itself is surrounded by hundreds of *dolmens*, megalithic stone burial tombs dating back between 3000 and 4000 B.C. This should not come as a surprise, since it matches Stonehenge's direct connection to human sacrifice and death. The Gilgal Rephaim may in fact be the ancestral precursor to Stonehenge.

This megalithic temple is known as Rujm el-Hiri in Arabic. The word *rujum* in Hebrew refers to a tumulus, a tomb. The Hebrew word *Refa'im* means ghosts or spirits. *Gilgal Rephaim* in the Hebrew means ghost circles, wheel of ghosts, or wheel of spirits.[81] The name is also translated to "wheel of the giants" and is often referred to as the "temple of the giants" based on the Hebrew word *Rephaim* (Rephaites), which refers to a race of giants that inhabited the region of Bashan (Land of Canaan) that extended from Gilead in the south to Mount Hermon in the north (in fact, due north). As we covered in Section One, Mount Hermon was the exact location where the fallen angels began their campaign of genetic manipulation of humankind, and that King Og of Bashan is stated to have "remained of the remnant of giants," one of the last of the giants (Deuteronomy 3:11). It is at this juncture of Gilgal Rephaim that there is a direct correlation between ghosts/spirits and the released spirits of the deceased giants indicated by both the Hebrew words *Refa'im* and *Rephaim*.

It is interesting to note that this temple was also built on a relatively high place in relation to the immediate region. Also, due to its enormous size, spanning a large area, the full view of this structure can only be fully appreciated from an aerial vantage point. Once again, this temple has been deliberately situated to coincide with the movements of the sun, marking both the solstice and equinox throughout the year.[82] These two points bring into the focus the relationship of First and Second Heavens pertaining to the subsequent realm of the fallen angels. The following photo is another example of a circular megalithic temple at Mount Gilboa ninety miles south of Mount Hermon. Note the striking similarity to Stonehenge.

Mount Gilboa Megalith, Northern Israel

17.

MEDICINE WHEELS

WE HAVE COVERED THE HISTORICAL MIGRATION OF ANCIENT PEOPLE AND THE progression of ancient megalithic structures, such as pyramids and circular temples, throughout the world as a result of the initial dispersion at the Tower of Babel, the first post-flood organized society and the first post-flood mega structure ever built. We are going to have a brief look at yet another example of the progression of the utilization of circular type temples, this one known as the medicine wheel.

Similar to Gilgal Rephaim, medicine wheels are commonly constructed with piled stones, consisting of all, or a combination, of the following traits: (1) a central stone *cairn* (pile of stones) which is associated with either a marker, astronomy, or burial of some kind (a landmark or of memorial significance); (2) one or more concentric stone circles; and (3) two or more lines of stones that radiate outward from the centre of the wheel.[83] Often, four radiating lines of stone are formed that denote the four directions of East, West, North, and South. Medicine wheels were not built on the same scale as Gilgal Rephaim, but can be as large as seventy-five feet in diameter.

One of the most famous examples is the Medicine Wheel in Big Horn County in Wyoming. However, these structures are found in large numbers throughout the central-northern U.S.A. and throughout central-southern Canada, mostly in Alberta and Saskatchewan. It comes as no surprise that medicine wheels were constructed by the indigenous, First Nations tribes of these regions. Again, this is a direct result of the dispersion of the tribes of ancient people, bringing with them ancient knowledge, from the Tower of Babel. Medicine wheels have been dated as far back as 2500 B.C.[84]

Medicine Wheel, Wyoming (Insert depicting typical configuration scaled down)

I personally have settled in a region rich with the history of the First Nations in Canada. When I became a dedicated Christian believer, declaring and receiving Jesus Christ as my Lord and Saviour, I was baptized by full water submersion by Pastor Elwood McLean (now deceased). Elwood's brother, Dr. Glen McLean (also deceased), was a recognized paleontologist and pioneer of Creation Science research during the 1950s. Elwood was prominently known in the local area and spent much of his life as the last Circuit Rider Pastor amongst the Cree First Nation people of central Alberta and Saskatchewan.

Elwood told me stories of his experiences on various First Nations reserves. It was through Elwood that I first learned about medicine wheels. He explained that medicine wheels in the area were usually made of medium-sized stones, and that the circles were not overly large as the tribes were often nomadic, wandering the land based on weather and hunting cycles. This made the medicine wheel portable in some cases. He also told me the medicine wheel was a type of altar, where the medicine man (chief tribal priest) would enter, sit at the centre, and *fast* (not eat) for a long period of time to receive a spiritual vision. According to tribal doctrine, the medicine man could not leave the circle before receiving the vision. Should the tribal priest leave prematurely, a curse or even death could result. Elwood further explained that the centre of the wheel was a place of safety from evil spirits.

I found this information very enlightening. It also directly correlates with my past research of the Occult when I learned that, within the encircled pentagram as previously described by Gene Aven, the individual would be in a position of safety at the centre. This central part forms the shape of a pentagon.

The centre of safety and security of the United States happens to be the pentagon-shaped military headquarters known as the Pentagon. It is also interesting to note that the ranking system of the highest military officials is based on an insignia of *stars*, denoted from a one-star general to the highest position of a five-star general. In fact, it seems that the *star* is the insignia of choice of most military organizations of the world, including Russia and China. This bit of correlating information brings into focus that Satan (the fallen morning star) is truly the god of this world, both directly and indirectly, influencing and manipulating the nations of the world, where the military complexes in the world are the protectors of these nations. More specifically, a nation can be ultimately defined by its military, the ability to protect itself and destroy its enemies. This is further amplified in the latter days, converging towards the arrival of the coming Antichrist (Satan's son and global leader) and the compounded progression towards Armageddon (the location of the ultimate final battle of the world's military forces of our current modern age). This end result is alluded to in the Book of Daniel, as the Antichrist does not worship the almighty God, yet he pays homage to the military forces of the nations, some of which are under God (capital G). Throughout history, God has drawn and led various leaders and nations into battle.

Daniel 11:37–38
Neither shall he regard the God of his fathers, nor the desire of women, nor regard any god: for he shall magnify himself above all. But in his estate shall he honour the God of forces: and a god whom his fathers knew not shall he honour with gold, and silver, and with precious stones, and pleasant things.

In Section Three, we will explore in more depth the implications of all that we have covered thus far as it relates to the current and ongoing development of a technologically advanced and knowledge-driven modern society.

SECTION II ENDNOTES

21 Article, *Archeological Proof of David VS. Goliath Battle on Display in Jerusalem,* Anna Rudnitsky, Tazpit Press Service, August 31, 2016, Breaking Israel News, Latest News biblical Perspective, website: https://www.breakingisraelnews.com

22 Reference, *Mysteries of the Mexican Pyramids*, page 11 (side note), Peter Tompkins, Harper and Row, 1976

23 The "Cradle of Civilization," referring to ancient Sumeria, isn't exactly the very 'beginning of structured humanity' as according to secular historians through recorded history. What secular historians don't recognize is that there was another world dominating kingdom, a world kingdom, without an official name, that lasted exactly 1656 years—and a world kingdom that didn't remain intact, yet to the surprise of many, has also left obvious artifacts to be found as recorded history by modern day historians. In fact, it was an ancient civilization that was completely destroyed by a major cataclysm so extensive that it affected the entire planet—the Great Flood. Sometime later, after civilization had rebuilt itself, a written record of this prior ancient civilization was given to a man called Moses, who was summoned to a mountain through spiritual means where he met God, the creator of all things. The account of this lost civilization became the Book of Genesis. The interesting thing is that this lost ancient civilization also had its beginnings at this exact same location—known as the 'Cradle of Civilization.' How do we know this? Well, we read in Genesis:

Genesis 2:10–14

And a river went out of Eden to water the garden; and from thence it was parted, and became into four heads. The name of the first *is* Pison; that *is* it which compasseth the whole land of Havilah, where *there is* gold; And the gold of that land *is* good: there *is* bdellium and onyx stone. And the name of the second river *is* Gihon: the same *is* it that compasseth the whole land of Ethiopia. And the name of the third river *is* Hiddekel: that *is* it which goeth toward the east of Assyria. And the fourth river *is* Euphrates.

So, as God's Word states, those four rivers flowed into one river at the location of the Garden of Eden. We are told that the fourth river was the Euphrates River, which still remains to this day. The third river was called the Hiddekel River. This happens to be the ancient Hebrew name for the Tigris River, which we also know remains today. The second river was called the Gihon River. Which is the ancient Hebrew name for the Karun River and that river is also still present in modern times. And lastly, the first river mentioned, the Pison River, which flowed through the entire ancient land of Havilah has been recently discovered through satellite imagery as an ancient dried river bed. The other interesting aspect about this region is the fact that it is currently mostly desert with marshy swamp areas, which makes up much of the landscape of the modern country of Iraq. However, ironically, secular researchers do recognize that this region, during ancient times, was once a thriving, rich area for agriculture. Obviously, the landscape has changed drastically. It is also a known fact that the ancient Sumerians, and various other ancient civilizations, clearly recount and describe the event of the Great Flood.

24 The observable evidence clearly demonstrates that, in the process of pro-creation, each specific species remains completely intact. No *transitional* lifeforms have ever been observed within nature, or documented within the observable fossil record. Any purported *transitional* lifeforms, either proclaimed in the recent past or currently proclaimed in the present, have all been categorically discounted under rigorous scrutiny (i.e. misleading facts, absence of facts and, in some cases, complete falsification of facts). All species, either adapt to the natural environment, or they perish due to the natural environment. At the DNA level, adaptations are allowable changes (built in) that help the species to adapt to environmental change. Adaptations due not cause or promote *transitional* change. Mutations, on the other hand, are changes to the DNA that are either 75% harmful or 25% neutral to the sustaining of any particular species. Natural selection preserves the strongest of the species. It *preserves* the species. Natural selection does not allow, or promote, the *transitional* change of any species into some 'other' species that it simply is not.

25 Daniel Chapter 7 describes four World Dominating Kingdoms, which are portrayed in the metaphoric sense as distinct 'beasts.' The first three beasts are described as a 'lion,' a 'bear,' and a 'leopard' (Daniel 7:1-6). These beasts are described as being distinct and diverse from each other. They each

represent a clearly distinct ethnic culture of people. The fourth metaphoric beast that appears is a composite of the first three beasts before it (confirmed in Revelation 13:1-2). The first three beasts eventually lose their dominion, power and status in the world, but their ethnic heritage continues to be represented within the Fourth World Kingdom (Daniel 7:12; 7:23). Overall, Daniel Chapter 7 is describing a historical progression towards the advent of a fourth and final World Dominating Kingdom, occurring in the last days, as being racially and ethnically mixed—which, in the end, will be judged and subdued by the authority of Christ's Second Coming (Daniel 7:14; 7:26-27). This is exactly what we are witnessing today—a world that has transformed into a truly multi-cultural global kingdom as migration and immigration throughout has progressed over centuries of time.

26　Reference Video, *The Bible: The Key to Understanding*, segment: Pyramids, Dr. Glen McLean, Roger Oakland, Larry McLean, 1988

27　Article, *Ancient Man and His First Civilizations: The Olmec and the Americas—The Olmec*, website: http://realhistoryww.com/world_history/ancient/Olmec_the_Americas.htm

28　Article, *Part 1. Chinese Pyramids: facts and evidences*, World Pyramids, Maxim Yakovenko, 2008, website: http://world-pyramids.com/china/facts_pyramids.html

29　Quote Pages 14–15, *The Nature of Our Enemy*, 2000, Jon Hamilton, Published by Central Educational Broadcasting, Inc., Vero Beach, Florida

30　Quote, *An Autobiography of Buffalo Bill (Colonel W. F. Cody)*, Chapter Six, 1920, Cosmopolitan Book Corporation Book Corporation, Farrar & Rinehart Incorporated, On Murray Hill, New York. Printed in the U.S.A. by Quinn & Boden Company, Inc. Rahway, N.J. Ebook Release Date: June 25, 2004 [EBook #12740]

31　Article, *Thunderbird Meaning as a Native American Symbol*, What's Your Sign? Website: http://www.whats-your-sign.com/thunderbird-native-american-symbol.html

32　Article, *Why Don't We Find Human and Dinosaur Fossils Together?* Bodie Hodge, Answers in Genesis, November 1st, 2007, website: https://answersingenesis.org/dinosaurs/humans/why-dont-we-find-human-dinosaur-fossils-together/

33　Article, *The Destruction of Pompeii—God's Revenge?* Herschel Shanks, February 20th, 2014, Bible History Daily, website: *www.biblicalarchaeology.org*

34 Derived from the writings of 19th Century Greek Historian, Diodorus Siculus, Heracles in Latium [4-21-5] and Heracles and the Giants of Phlegra [4-21-6], website: http://www.theoi.com/Text/DiodorusSiculus4B.html

35 Quote: *Why Does the Bible Mention the Mythical Unicorn?* By Matt Slick (not dated); Section: Questions About the Bible; website: *www.CARM.org*

36 Article, Alvis Delk Cretaceous Footprint, Creation Evidence Museum of Texas, 2000, website: http://www.creationevidence.org/displays/alvis_delk_cretaceous_footprint.php

37 Article, *Evidence that Dinosaurs and Humans Co-existed*, website: http://www.bible.ca/tracks/tracks.htm

38 Article, *Human and Dinosaur Footprints in Turkmenistan?*, Answers in Genesis, Sergei Golovan, September 1, 1996, website: https://answersingenesis.org/dinosaurs/footprints/human-and-dinosaur-footprints-in-turkmenistan/

39 Article, *Fossilized Human Finger*, The Creation Evidence Museum of Texas, 2013, website: http://creationevidence.org/displays/fossilized_finger.php

40 Article, *The Tuba City Dinosaur and Human Tracks*, Revolution Against Evolution, Doug Sharp, July 7th, 1999, website: http://rae.org/pdf/tuba.pdf

41 Footnote to Job 40:15, *Life Application Study Bible*, New International Version, 1997, Tyndale House Publishers, Inc., Carol Stream, Illinois and Zondervan, Grand Rapids, Michigan

42 Footnote to Job 41:1, *Life Application Study Bible*, New International Version, 1997, Tyndale House Publishers, Inc., Carol Stream, Illinois and Zondervan, Grand Rapids, Michigan

43 Quote: *Dragons or Dinosaurs? Creation or Evolution?* Pages 29-30, Darek Isaacs, 2010, Bridge Logos, Alachua, Florida

44 Tiwanaku, *Encyclopedia of Anthropology*, Jo Ellen Burkholder, Editor James H Birx 2006. Thousand Oaks, CA: SAGE Publications, Inc.

45 *Art and Design: The Mystery of Puma Punku and the Fallen Angels*, Citations 2016, Journal of Undergraduate Research, LaGrange College, Sponsoring Faculty Member Dr. Dorothy Joiner, John Tyler Hepner, Page 22, website: http://www.lagrange.edu/academics/citations/2016/index.html

46 *Easter Island—Rapa Nui Explorer, Brief Itinerary, Day 2*, published by Cascada Expediciones, website: www.cascadatravel.com

47 *Circular Evidence, Mysterious Events*, page 172, Colin Andrews and Pat Delgado, 1989 Phanes Press, Grand Rapids, Michigan

48 *The Decipherment of the Fuente Magna Bowl,* Archeology index, University of California Riverside, website: www.faculty.ucr.edu/~legneref/archeol/fuentema.htm

49 *Iraq: Garden of Eden Named World Heritage Site,* Carey Lodge, Christian Today Journalist, July 21, 2016, website: http://www.christiantoday.com/article/iraq.garden.of.eden.named.world.heritage.site/91124.htm

50 *Narrative of the Incas,* Juan de Betanzos, ed. Dana Buchanan, tr. Roland Hamilton, University of Texas Press, 1996

51 Quote: *Art and Design: The Mystery of Puma Punku and the Fallen Angels,* Citations 2016, Journal of Undergraduate Research, LaGrange College, Sponsoring Faculty Member Dr. Dorothy Joiner, John Tyler Hepner, Pages 24-25, website: http://www.lagrange.edu/academics/citations/2016/index.html

52 Article, *Dogon Cosmology and Egyptian Hieroglyphics Writing,* New Dawn, David Jones, August 11th, 2013, website: http://www.newdawnmagazine.com/articles/dogon-cosmology-egyptian-hieroglyphic-writing

53 Cool Cosmos, website: http://coolcosmos.ipac.caltech.edu/ask/5-How-large-is-the-Sun-compared-to-Earth-

54 Quote: *Dogon:* Article/Document, Loy Lawhon, from UFO Evidence website, www.ufoevidence.org, 2011

55 Article, *The Dogon Tribe,* Library of Halexandria, website: http://www.halexandria.org/dward109.htm

56 Article, *Dogon,* Crystalinks, website: http://www.crystalinks.com/dogon.html

57 Article, *Dogon Legend of the Nommos Fish People,* Galactic Connection, Oct 8th 2014, website: http://galacticconnection.com/dogon-legend-of-the-nommos-fish-people-video/

58 Article: *Did Ancient Aliens Impart Advanced Astrological Knowledge to the Dogon Tribe?* Tara MacIssac, Epoch Times, January 2nd, 2015, website: http://www.theepochtimes.com/n3/1174627-did-ancient-aliens-impart-advanced-astronomical-knowledge-to-the-dogon-tribe/

59 Article, *Sigi Festival,* Dogon Country, website: http://www.dogoncountry.com/about-pays-dogon/festivals/

60 Article, *King's Chamber in Pyramid of Khufu (Cheops),* June 2008, website: http://www.khufu.dk/article/kings-chamber.htm

61 Article, *How Tower Cranes Work,* How Stuff Works, Science, Marshall Brain, website: http://science.howstuffworks.com/transport/engines-equipment/tower-crane2.htm

62 Article, *Sarcophagus in Pyramid of Khufu (Cheops)*, July 2008, website: http://www.khufu.dk/article/sarcophagus.htm

63 Article, *How is a Quartz Crystal Used in Electronics?* Subramani Vinay, April 26th, 2015, Quora, website: https://www.quora.com/How-is-a-quartz-crystal-used-in-electronics

64 Insulator, Physics, Encyclopedia Britannica, Editors, website: https://www.britannica.com/science/insulator

65 Quote, Insulator, Physics, Encyclopedia Britannica, Editors, website: https://www.britannica.com/science/insulator

66 Article, *Sarcophagus in Pyramid of Khufu (Cheops)*, July 2008, website: http://www.khufu.dk/article/sarcophagus.htm

67 Article, *The Great Pyramid*, Section 9, *The Pit and the End of the World*, General Notes by Phil Scovell; website: http://www.redwhiteandblue.org/christian/plstexts/PYRAMID.HTM

68 Reference, Biblical Astronomer, number 100, *Witness of the Stars*, pages 53-56, Gerardus D. Bouw, Ph.D.; website: http://www.geocentricity.com/constellations/draco.pdf

69 *The Oxford History of Ancient Egypt*, page 68, Ian Shaw, Oxford: Oxford University Press, 2000

70 Quote, *Mysteries of the Mexican Pyramids*, page 252, Peter Tompkins, Harper and Row, Publishing Inc., 1976

71 Article, *Stonehenge: Facts and Theories About Mysterious Monument*: Live Science, Owen Janus, Live Science contributor, Oct 3, 2014, website: http://www.livescience.com/22427-stonehenge-facts.html

72 Quote, *Stonehenge: Facts and Theories About Mysterious Monument*: Live Science, Owen Janus, Live Science contributor, Oct 3rd, 2014, website: http://www.livescience.com/22427-stonehenge-facts.html

73 Quote, *Scientists: Stonehenge Was Ancient Burial Ground*, Fox News, Associated Press, May 29th, 2008, website: http://www.foxnews.com/story/2008/05/29/scientists-stonehenge-was-ancient-burial-ground.html

74 Article, *Altar Stone (Stonehenge)*, Wikipedia, website: https://en.wikipedia.org/wiki/Altar_Stone_(Stonehenge)

75 Word definition, *Druid*, Online Etymology Dictionary, Douglas Harper, 2001-2016, website: http://www.etymonline.com/index.php?term=druid

76 Quote, *Oranges and Onions Volume 1*, pages 57-59, Gene Aven, self-published Gene Aven Ministries, Bow, Washington, 1977

77 Quote, Ibid.

78 Quote, *Oranges and Onions Volume 1*, page 36, Gene Aven, self-published Gene Aven Ministries, Bow, Washington, 1977

79 Article, *Who is Krampus? Explaining the Horrific Christmas Devil*, Tanya Basu, National Geographic, December 19th, 2013, website: http://news. nationalgeographic.com/news/2013/12/131217-krampus-christmas-santa-devil/

80 Article, *Rujum el-Hiri; Stonehenge of the Golan*, Bill Slott, The Times of Israel, July 26th, 2016, website: http://blogs.timesofisrael.com/rujum-el-hiri-stonehenge-of-the-golan/

81 Article, *Rujm el-Hiri (Golan Heights)—Ancient Observatory*, Kris Hirst, archeologist, April 8th, 2016, website: http://archaeology.about.com/od/archaeoastronomy/a/rujmelhiri.htm

82 Article, *Medicine Wheel*, Wikipedia, website, https://en.wikipedia.org/wiki/Medicine_wheel

83 Article, *Alberta Aboriginal History Timeline*, Royal Alberta Museum, website, http://www.royalalbertamuseum.ca/research/culturalStudies/archaeology/timeline.cfm

84 Article, *Alberta Aboriginal History Timeline*, Royal Alberta Museum, website, http://www.royalalbertamuseum.ca/research/culturalStudies/archaeology/timeline.cfm

RELEVANCE IN A MODERN SOCIETY

2 Thessalonians 2:8–10

And then shall that Wicked be revealed, whom the Lord shall
consume with the spirit of his mouth, and shall destroy with
the brightness of his coming: Even him, whose coming is after
the working of Satan with all power and signs and lying wonders,
And with all deceivableness of unrighteousness in them that
perish; because they received not the love of the truth,
that they might be saved.

18.

LUCIFER'S ANCIENT THRONE

As mentioned at the beginning of this book, in Foundational Point One, Jesus made this very profound statement:

Matthew 24:37
But as the days of Noah were, so shall also the coming of the Son of man be.

In a plain and simple sense, Jesus is stating what happened in Noah's time will repeat itself prior to His Second Coming. This has extreme and profound implications for us in a modern society. Before we explore these implications, we are going to return once again to the very beginning, to an ancient time—a time that seems so far removed from the thoughts of everyday people, and yet, the result of which is actually staring us right in the face, today. It is unfathomable to know that most individuals, even highly intellectual individuals who are well schooled, can't seem to see what is either clearly visible, or which is occurring, right before us in plain sight. This brings into focus the biblical term of being spiritually blind.

First, we are going to have a close look at a few areas of Scripture, some of which have not been investigated deeply enough and some that have simply been misrepresented. We will follow this process again in other subsequent chapters, but for now we will start with Ezekiel 28, which has garnered much speculation and debate amongst Bible scholars and researchers.

In the beginning of Ezekiel 28, God's Word draws attention to a figure referred to as the "prince of Tyrus" (v. 2) and also referred to as the "king of Tyrus"

(v. 12). Tyrus, also known as Tyre in modern times, was an ancient Phoenician city on the Mediterranean coast of southern Lebanon. It was heavily fortified, having two harbours.

At first glance, pertaining to the prince or king, one would assume God is talking about a mere mortal man, since He refers to this figure in the context of a man (v. 2 and v. 9). This is also amplified as one reads the previous chapters and can see the clear descriptions of a leader, a wealthy city, and its pervasive influence. However, as one contemplates the first twelve verses of Ezekiel 28 more intently and continues to read the remainder of the chapter, it becomes clear that God is not just talking about a mortal man. This "man" displays attributes beyond the scope of a normal, mortal man. In fact, God draws the attention of this figure to the "Son of man," a term usually reserved for the Son of God, Jesus Christ, but used here in reference to God's prophet, Ezekiel. This is very interesting, because Ezekiel is an Old Testament book, written prior to the First Advent of Jesus Christ to our world. Overall, it becomes clear that God is talking about something in the context of two different, yet related, levels of understanding.

This brings into focus one of the five distinct ways God presents His Word to the reader, which I call *multi-level interpretation*. This method is perhaps one of the least understood by studiers of the Word. The other four methods of conveyance being (1) the direct, *literal sense*, which is the most common; (2) the *parable sense*, simply telling a story to illustrate one or more lessons of truth and principle, a method Jesus used often; (3) the *metaphoric sense*, which is presenting something, usually a singular object or action, that is symbolically representing something else. This extends to the *allegoric sense* which presents multiple facets that symbolically represent a more complex theme based on moral or political issues and, (4) something which I call *encoded revelation*, which is Spiritual knowledge God has encoded within His Word (both ancient and modern languages) that have remained hidden and are locked until they are meant to be unlocked and understood at God's prescribed time and by God's anointed person(s).

Encoded revelation has been a topic of contention and controversy between various researchers and church denominations, yet it has been documented within God's Word. An example is found at the back of this book, entitled Hidden Encoded Scripture in Genesis.

Based on the method of multi-level interpretation, Ezekiel 28 presents two possibilities of verifiable understanding. These two levels of understanding are based on the same parameters of a king, a kingdom and the pervasive influence of both.

As we continue, another important point is the fact that this prince or king has proclaimed to exalt himself to the same level as the almighty God.

Ezekiel 28:1–2
The word of the LORD came again unto me, saying, Son of man, say unto the prince of Tyrus, Thus saith the LORD God; Because thine heart is lifted up, and thou hast said, I am a God, I sit in the seat of God, in the midst of the seas; yet thou art a man, and not God, though thou set thine heart as the heart of God...

This is reinforced in verse six:

Ezekiel 28:6
Therefore thus saith the Lord GOD; Because thou hast set thine heart as the heart of God;

God goes on to state:

Ezekiel 28:11–12
Moreover the word of the LORD came unto me, saying, Son of man, take up a lamentation upon the king of Tyrus, and say unto him, Thus saith the Lord GOD; Thou sealest up the sum, full of wisdom, and perfect in beauty.

Notice that the two titles, prince and king are presented in lowercase. This is subtle evidence that God has demoted the legitimacy of this figure, especially after declaring himself on the same level as God.

Ezekiel 28:13
Thou hast been in Eden the garden of God; every precious stone was thy covering, the sardius, topaz, and the diamond, the beryl, the onyx, and the jasper, the sapphire, the emerald, and the carbuncle, and gold: the workmanship of thy tabrets and of thy pipes was prepared in thee in the day that thou wast created.

Here, it is now absolutely clear God is not just talking about a mortal man. Apparently this figure was present in the Garden of Eden. At the time of Ezekiel (post-flood), the Garden of Eden was long gone. Of course, Adam was certainly a man (the only man) who once resided in the Garden of Eden, but as we continue it is also clear that God is not talking about Adam.

Ezekiel 28:14
Thou art the anointed cherub that covereth; and I have set thee so: thou wast upon the holy mountain of God; thou hast walked up and down in the midst of the stones of fire.

This Scripture makes a statement that is direct and unambiguous: this figure, this man, is none other than Satan. More specifically, God is talking about Satan as the "cherub that covereth," the angel Lucifer prior to the fall. Cherubim are a specific order (or race) of angels that have two sets of wings, large enough to cover an area when spread out (Ezekiel 1:4–6, 10:5).

We are told in this passage that Lucifer was an "anointed cherub"—a special angel that was set, meaning placed in a specified place or position, which is described as "the holy mountain of God." Based on this, it is no coincidence that Satan and the select group of two hundred fallen angels had descended at a significant place on Earth: a high place—Mount Hermon. In his quest to be like God, Satan often replicates or mirrors the things of God.

We are also told Lucifer "walked up and down in the midst of the stones of fire." We will address this statement momentarily.

Ezekiel 28:15
Thou wast perfect in thy ways from the day that thou wast created, till iniquity was found in thee.

Initially, Lucifer was an adorned and brilliant angel. We see in verse 12 that he was beautiful to look at and was full of wisdom. We see in verse 13 that he was adorned with many precious jewels. He was also bestowed with much talent as alluded to with the tabrets and pipes (percussion drums and horns) he had fashioned (fabricated and built) on the very day he was created by God.

It is further still no coincidence Satan is referred to as the *prince and power of the air* (Ephesians 2:2). The modern term airways is used to describe the broadcasting of radio and television signals, which transmit music to households, vehicles, and now smartphones all over the world. It is also not a coincidence to contemplate that those who excel to a highly revered position in the music industry are exalted to *stardom*—commonly cited as country *star*, pop *star*, and rock *star*. Again, this is reminiscent of the pervasive influence of the chief morning star.

Despite Lucifer's God-given greatness, "*iniquity* was found in him" which is the presence of wickedness, impropriety, and evil—simply sin.

Ezekiel 28:16
By the multitude of thy merchandise they have filled the midst of thee with violence, and thou hast sinned: therefore I will cast thee as pro-fane out of the mountain of God: and I will destroy thee, O covering cherub, from the midst of the stones of fire.

Lucifer defied God's will, opening the door for sin to enter in, something that cannot remain in God's holy kingdom. This first act of rebellion saw the emergence of the first sin. Lucifer was cast out of the mountain of God, and cast out of the holy Kingdom of Heaven (Third Heaven). In addition, by using the connecting word "and," God states that he "will destroy thee, O covering cherub, from the midst of the stones of fire."

This is now the second time God has used the phrase "the midst of the stones of fire" within Ezekiel 28. What does this statement actually mean?

Regarding the interpretation of this phrase, there are varying trains of thought. One explanation is that the stones of fire represent the stone tablets of the Ten Commandments that were written by fire, the signature of God (Deuteronomy 5:22, 9:10). As such, it is reasoned that Lucifer once abided by the law, "*walked up and down in the midst of the stones of fire*" (v. 14), but then rebelled and transgressed the law, at which point God states, "*I will destroy thee, O covering cherub, from the midst of the stones of fire*" (v. 16). However, bear in mind that the Ten Commandments, in the form of stone tablets, were given to Moses on Mount Sinai a time much later in history after Lucifer's rebellion in the Kingdom of Heaven. Despite this glaring fact, it is also reasoned that Mount Sinai can be attributed as the "mountain of God." Yet again, in the context of Ezekiel 28:16, the fact remains that Lucifer was cast out of the Kingdom of Heaven, not Mount Sinai.

In another related train of thought, the stones of fire are explained as literal sparkling jewels or precious stones. Pertaining to the Ark of the Covenant, which was constructed as a communication device (an oracle) between man and God, two carved images of Cherubim were attached to the top. The Ark was carried by pole handles and held the stone tablets of the Ten Commandments, along with other holy artifacts, within. The high priest would wear a breastplate adorned with twelve precious stones, each representing the original twelve tribes. Upon establishing communication with God, the precious stones would flash in a fiery light in various sequences according to the inquiries and answers between the priest and God. This is described by a commentary written by Jonathan Bayley in 1867:

> But we must not forget that the Breastplate was not a thing of beauty only: it was a Breastplate of judgment, by its means the Divine Will was made known, in all times of difficulty and perplexity. The High Priest, with this Breastplate on, laid his own inquiries, and his own sorrows, or those of the people, before the Lord, in the Holy of holies; and received from Him infallible direction. The Divine Light shone upon the precious jewels, and conveyed the instruction of heaven and its sanction as the case might be. "And thou shalt put in the breastplate of judgment the Urim and Thummim; and they shall be upon Aaron's heart when he goeth in before the Lord: and Aaron shall bear the judgment of the children of Israel upon his heart, before the Lord continually."[85]

This was done in the near presence of the Ark of the Covenant itself. However, again we must recognize this was at a time much later than the actual rebellion of Lucifer.

Another train of thought is that the stones of fire are precious stones laid before the throne of God in Third Heaven. Dr. Daniel K. Olukoya, a Nigerian evangelist, writes:

> This is the emergence of Lucifer as the first sinner and his sin was rebellion. The above verses established the fact that he had many privileges. For example, the last sentence in verse 16 says: "O covering cherub, from the midst of the stones of fire." The last sentence in verse 14 says, "Thou hast walked up and down in the midst of the stones of fire." Not all angels could do that. The stones of fire refer to the Holy ground upon which the throne of God was placed. Not all angels could walk upon these stones. This is the history of the first sinner and unfortunately, all his children are still like him up till today.[86]

There is also an interesting correlation between the twelve precious stones on the breastplate of the high priest before the Ark of the Covenant and the twelve gates, three per side, of Third Heaven—both representing the twelve original tribes before the dispersion at Babylon (Revelation 21:12–13). This information brings the researcher somewhat closer to both the actual location and the ancient timeline of Lucifer's initial rebellion.

It should be noted that a description of twelve precious stones are attributed to the *walls* of the new heaven, post Thousand-Year Reign, and not specifically attributed to any *laid* stones before the throne room of God (Revelation 21:17–20).

This particular point is an important one that I believe has been widely misunderstood. This brings into focus the term "mountain of God" in Ezekiel 28:14 and 28:16. As mentioned, there is a particular set of methods God uses to convey various meanings of His Word to the reader, one of which I refer to as multi-level interpretation.

We recognize that Moses was called to a high mountain, Mount Sinai (also known as Mount Horeb and Mount Paran), to meet with God to receive the Ten Commandments. The term "mountain of God" has also been used to describe the mountain adjacent to Jerusalem (Mount Zion) also referred to as the city of David, the old city, where God's Temple (Solomon's Temple) is located. This also correlates with the new heaven, the new earth and the New Jerusalem where Christ will reign over the nations of the earth for eternity. This is also presented as the mountain of the Lord:

Isaiah 2:1–4
The word that Isaiah the son of Amoz saw concerning Judah and Jerusalem. And it shall come to pass in the last days, that the mountain of the LORD's house shall be established in the top of the mountains, and shall be exalted above the hills; and all nations shall flow unto it. And many people shall go and say, Come ye, and let us go up to the mountain of the LORD, to the house of the God of Jacob; and he will teach us of his ways, and we will walk in his paths: for out of Zion shall go forth the law, and the word of the LORD from Jerusalem. And he shall judge among the nations, and shall rebuke many people: and they shall beat their swords into plowshares, and their spears into pruninghooks: nation shall not lift up sword against nation, neither shall they learn war any more.

This is echoed by the prophet Micah (Micah 4:1–3). So far, we see that there are physical examples of the mountain of God *on earth* in ancient times, of which some still remain today, as well as a physical example *on earth* prophesied for our destined future. However, pertaining to the rebellion and fall of Lucifer, in conjunction with the stones of fire, there is another understanding of the mountain of God on a heavenly level. This is important to understand before we can clearly define the meaning behind the stones of fire.

When Jesus was brought before Pontius Pilate and confronted before being sentenced to His crucifixion, He said:

John 18:36
...My kingdom is not of this world: if my kingdom were of this world, then would my servants fight, that I should not be delivered to the Jews: but now is my kingdom not from hence.

Jesus' kingdom is not of this world. This is simply because His Second Coming to usher in the Millennial Kingdom and subsequent Eternal Kingdom between the Kingdom of Heaven and Earth has not happened yet, although it is coming. This is reinforced within the Lord's Prayer, a prayer that many have heard yet, perhaps, have not fully realized its prophetic implication: "...Thy kingdom come. Thy will be done in earth, as it is in heaven..."

Jesus also spoke of the temple of God. There is the temple of God, in the physical sense, on earth (Matthew 21:121); there is the temple of God, in the Spiritual sense, within the born-again believers on Earth (in the body of Christ, 1 Corinthians 3:16–17); and there is the temple of God, in the heavenly sense, in the Kingdom of Heaven (Revelation 11:19).

Based on this, the mountain of God can refer to a meeting place, of various locations, between man and God on Earth; it can refer to the stationary place of God's temple in the city of Jerusalem; and it can also refer to the actual Throne Room of God within the Kingdom of Heaven.

Considering Ezekiel 28:13, we are told the angel Lucifer was at one point in the Garden of Eden, on Earth. The same verse goes on to describe how Lucifer was adorned with many precious stones and bestowed with great talent, such as music.

Ezekiel 28:14 calls the angel Lucifer a "Cherub that covereth," set or installed by God Himself; and states that he was also, at some point, upon the "mountain of God," referring to the Throne Room of God in the Kingdom of Heaven (not referring to earth in this context); and that he has "walked up and down in the midst of the stones of fire." It is here the confusion begins. This statement is not talking about Earth; neither is it talking about the Throne Room in the Kingdom of Heaven. This is now referring to what lies between the two. This is referring to Second Heaven, as previously mentioned throughout this book, also known as the cosmos, the realm of all the heavenly bodies (planets and stars) within God's created universe. Ezekiel 28:14 is simply describing Lucifer's ability and experience to have travelled and visited Eden (under First Heaven on Earth), the "stones of fire" (Second Heaven of the Universe), and the Throne Room of God (the central part of Third Heaven, the Kingdom of Heaven).

This is reinforced as God's Word clearly states in Ezekiel 28:16, "I will cast thee as profane out of the mountain of God" (now with the all-important connecting 'and') "*and* I will destroy thee, O covering cherub, from the midst of the stones of fire." Two separate, yet connecting, events are occurring here: (1) Lucifer is cast out of the Kingdom of Heaven, and (2) God will destroy him from within Second Heaven.

Regarding the statement "...walked up and down in the midst of the stones of fire," the term "walked up and down" is also found within both Job 1:7 and 2:2 pertaining to Satan's visitations to Earth:

Job 1:7
And the LORD said unto Satan, Whence comest thou? Then Satan answered the LORD, and said, From going to and fro in the earth, and from walking up and down in it.

Here, the term "walking up and down in it" is referring specifically to the Earth itself. Bear in mind this is a reference in the singular sense, as the Earth is one planet, of a system of planets within our solar system. Also, bear in mind that the Earth and the rest of this solar system lay within the realm of Second Heaven, the universe.

We have established in Section One that Satan lost his permanent residence in the Kingdom of Heaven, yet retains the ability to present himself before the Throne Room of God (Job 1:6, 2:1) to accuse the believers on earth, day and night (Revelation 12:10). Generally overlooked is that between Satan's visits before God and his visitations on Earth he has the ability to traverse the entire solar system, and even beyond this—to travel to all the heavenly bodies of the universe. This ability will change and be restricted in the future. This will be covered in more detail in upcoming points.

Based on what we have covered thus far, there is still another train of thought, one that has recently been brought to light. It is an explanation that considers multiple, yet seemingly diverse, Scriptures, and ties all this together with actual physical evidence—the recently discovered reality of which has eluded any serious plausible explanation by many intelligent scientists, researchers, and serious studiers of the Word.

I believe this is an alternate explanation that brings focused clarity to our ancient history, our origin, and to our future. I believe this glaring, physical evidence is staring us all, all humanity, right in face. Despite this, it needs to be stated that this proposed explanation has garnered some sharp criticism by some, in the circles of theology, and has simply been dismissed and ridiculed by others, in the circles of scientific and historical research. I will simply say, I feel strongly that they are wrong. Therefore, as we continue, we are going to explore this explanation in more detail.

First of all, we have just determined that the Earth itself is a singular planet amongst other planets in our solar system. We have also established that the phrase "walking up and down" directly refers to the planet Earth in Job 1:7 and 2:2 and the phrase "walked up and down" refers to the term stones of fire in Ezekiel 28:14. So the obvious question is, is there a relationship between the stones of fire and the planet Earth?

When considering the term stones of fire, we find that the word stone is derived from the Hebrew word *eben*, which means built stones. This word is also related to the Hebrew *banah*, which also means to build or to set up. This implies *created* stones by the hand of God. Certainly, this understanding can be related to God's creation of precious stones, such as diamonds, rubies, sapphires, etc. However, this understanding can also be related to the planet Earth and other heavenly bodies. Consider that the Earth itself is composed of stone, which gives it its form. Even gaseous planetary giants, such as Jupiter and Saturn, have solid cores. Considering further, the word fire is derived from the Hebrew word *esh*, which means burning, fiery, fire, flaming, hot. It is known that Earth has a burning, fiery, and flaming hot central core that escapes to the surface of our planet in the form of lava flow and volcanic eruptions. This has been discovered as ancient activity on other planets, such as on Mars, and witnessed as current activity on other heavenly bodies, such as the moon Io that orbits Jupiter.[87] Our Sun is a massive heavenly body constantly radiating burning fire and heat in the form of plasma in a process of nuclear fusion. Our Sun is just one of billions of other stars that display a fiery glint in the night sky of our own atmosphere (First Heaven). Certainly, we need to also recognize that precious stones themselves can give off a fiery glint, as we saw concerning the high priest's breastplate worn in the presence of the Ark of the Covenant. Therefore, the term stones of fire can be used to describe either precious stones or heavenly bodies, such as planets. Both are built stones in the sense of God's creation. This is further demonstrated by many astrologists and New Age spiritualists who relate certain precious stones as representing the planets themselves, which can vary substantially between different belief systems.[88] Nonetheless, in the context of Ezekiel 28, we are going to explore the connotation of planetary bodies more closely.

We have established that the phrase "walking up and down" directly refers to the planet Earth in Job 1:7 and 2:2 and the phrase "walked up and down" refers to the stones of fire in Ezekiel 28:14, and therefore, there is a direct relationship between the *planet* Earth and the stones of fire. However, Earth is one planet of many in our solar system, a stone of fire (singular), and the phrase stones of fire is plural. Moreover, God's statement in Ezekiel 28:16, *"...and I will destroy thee, O covering cherub, from the midst of the stones of fire,"* suggests He is going to destroy Lucifer in the *midst* of the *planets*. This specific action is stated immediately following God's previous action of casting Lucifer from out of the Kingdom of Heaven: *"I will cast thee as profane out of the mountain of God..."* As mentioned, the two separate actions are connected in succession by the word "and." The first action occurred in Third Heaven and the second action occurred in Second Heaven. The word midst is defined in most common dictionaries as a noun as "middle, center, midpoint" and as a preposition it is defined "in the middle of." What does this mean? Well, quite simply, God's second action is that He destroyed Lucifer from the *midpoint*, or from the *middle of the planets*. Lucifer was destroyed from the middle of our solar system. However, this must be taken into context, as Lucifer himself was not destroyed. Albeit, at this stage of his banishment, Lucifer, the chief angel became Satan, the chief fallen angel. He was not destroyed in the sense of having been annihilated—in the context of the finality of death. No, Satan is still quite alive—*"...roaring lion, walketh about, seeking whom he may devour"* (1 Peter 5:8). Considering this, we need to understand that Lucifer lost his pinnacle position in the Kingdom of Heaven, but he also lost something else—he lost his *throne* amongst the stones of fire, amongst the planets of our solar system. More specifically, he lost his *throne* from *in the middle* of the planets of our solar system. In this context, God's second action was to destroy both Satan's physical throne within our solar system of Second Heaven and to cast out (dethrone) his pinnacle position within Third Heaven as a first action. To summarize, God did not destroy Lucifer in the sense of death, He destroyed Lucifer's reigning position. Regarding the existence of Satan's ancient throne—is this possible? Perhaps, more importantly, is this verifiable?

The first aspect we are going to examine is the premise that Lucifer once had a throne. Recognizing that God and the Kingdom of Heaven existed prior to the creation of Second Heaven (the universe), and that Second Heaven existed prior to the creation of First Heaven (the firmament, atmosphere of Earth), we must also recognize that God created the angels prior to the creation of both Second and First Heavens. The angelic hosts were given specific duties as stewards (overseers) of God's creation. Initially, this was the stewardship of Second Heaven, and subsequently became the stewardship of First Heaven, with the subsequent advent of mankind itself. An example of this is found in Revelation:

Revelation 7:1
And after these things I saw four angels standing on the four corners of the earth, holding the four winds of the earth, that the wind should not blow on the earth, nor on the sea, nor on any tree.

Obviously, as stated, four angels had the specific task of either holding back or unleashing the four winds on Earth stemming from the four directions of north, south, east, and west. However, despite this realization, many people don't know that there are actually nine orders of angels having specific duties.[89] The list and overview as follows:

THE FIRST SPHERE (THIRD HEAVEN):
Angels who serve God and the Son of God in the Kingdom of Heaven:

Seraphim: Six-winged angels who are servants of God's throne and sing continual praises to the almighty God (Isaiah 6:1–8).

Cherubim: Four-winged angels having four faces of a man, cherub, lion, and eagle (Ezekiel 10:12–15). Their wings are lined with eyes. Their body is of a lion with the feet of oxen. Cherubim are guardians of the throne room of God (Revelation 4:6–8) and were placed as guardians of the entrance of the Garden of Eden in preventing Adam and Eve from returning to the Tree of Life after their removal from Eden (Genesis 3:24).

Thrones or Ophanim: Oddly shaped as wheels with eyes around the perimeters. They move only when other spiritual beings move (Ezekiel 1:18–21).

THE SECOND SPHERE (SECOND HEAVEN):

Angels who serve as both heavenly governors of the creation and guiding the spirits:

Dominions: An order of angels that rarely appear to humans, yet have the appearance of humans themselves with feathered wings. Dominions are described as carrying swords or scepters that radiate brilliant light from a source described as an orb. They relegate authority to other, lower orders of angels. Dominions are mentioned in Ephesians 1:21 and Colossians 1:16.

Virtues: An order of angels that bring signs and miracles to the world. Virtues are mentioned indirectly in Ephesians 1:21 derived from the Greek word *dynamis* in reference to the word *might*. This is also described as "virtuous powers" in relation to "powerful deeds" and "marvelous works." Virtues are also associated with the heavenly choirs.

Powers: Powers oversee the movements of the celestial bodies with the purpose of ensuring order within the cosmos. Powers are described as warrior angels wearing full armour and carrying weapons. Powers are mentioned in Ephesians 1:21 and 6:12.

THE THIRD SPHERE (FIRST HEAVEN):

Angels who provide protection and are heavenly guides and messengers to human beings:

Principalities: Also known as Rulers or Authorities (Ephesians 1:21, 3:10). An order of angels designated to protect and guide nations, peoples, specific institutions, and the foundational church (i.e. the church under the leading of the Holy Spirit). Principalities are the facilitators of various bands of angels (as described below). Not only are they guardians of humankind, they are also the educators of humans, said to inspire the areas of art and science.

Archangels: The order of Archangels is derived from the Greek word *archangelos* meaning "chief angel," which is also translated from the Hebrew word *ravmalakh*. Archangels are mentioned in 1 Thessalonians 4:16 and Jude 1:9 and one is named, Michael, in the Bible as cited in Revelation 12:9 leading the battle against Satan and his angels. Only seven archangels are collectively named when considering 1 Enoch as a source. These are Gabriel, Michael, Raphael, Uriel, Raguel, Phanuel (considered to have replaced the fallen Remiel), and Sariel.

Angels: These are known as the common angels derived from the Hebrew word *malakhim* (plural) and *malakh* (singular). They are the messengers and guardians of human beings. Therefore, based on this interaction, they are the most recognized class of angels, and as we have previously covered, often appear in human form on Earth. However, also previously covered, their human form is a transfigured form or shapeshifted form from their original, spiritual state of being.

Based on these nine orders of angels, and the hierarchy of service and duties assigned to each, the fallen realm of angels under Satan's control is essentially a mirror image of this heavenly hierarchy, representing one third of the former morning stars that fell.

It is at the point of the rebellion that we get an understanding that Lucifer once had an ancient throne, a pinnacle position, over the nine-order hierarchy of angels, which is clearly stated in the Book of Isaiah:

Isaiah 14:12–15
How art thou fallen from heaven, O Lucifer, son of the morning! how art thou cut down to the ground, which didst weaken the nations! For thou hast said in thine heart, I will ascend into heaven, I will exalt my throne above the stars of God: I will sit also upon the mount of the congregation, in the sides of the north: I will ascend above the heights of the clouds; I will be like the most High. Yet thou shalt be brought down to hell, to the sides of the pit.

Here we see the emergence of the famous five "I wills" defiantly spoken to God by the pinnacle angel, Lucifer, in rebellion.

His first "I will" states that he "will *ascend* into *heaven*" (emphasis added). Although, we understand Lucifer was once present in Eden, as cited in Ezekiel 28:13, this is clearly speaking about Lucifer ascending from Second Heaven in to Third Heaven. This point will be verified as we continue. It is important to understand this statement is made just prior to him being cast out of Third Heaven, since he is referred to here as the angel Lucifer—not as the *fallen* angel, Satan. Also interesting, the word ascend is derived from the Hebrew *alah*, which carries many connotations, some of which are "exalt, restore, set up, take away."

Lucifer's second "I will" states that he "will exalt my *throne* above the stars of God" (emphasis added). Lucifer is emphatically threatening God by stating he will exalt (raise) his *throne* from Second Heaven higher than the throne of God Himself, and more specifically, exalting his throne above the *stars* of God. We can take this understanding in the context of actual stars (heavenly bodies God has created), or we can take this understanding in the context of the loyal morning stars (angels God has created). The latter understanding suggests Lucifer had threatened to elevate his throne above all the other loyal angels of God as well. This latter connotation is reinforced by the following Scripture, which describes Lucifer becoming the great, red dragon that convinces (draws) one third of the morning stars to join him in the rebellion. The morning stars simply referred here as stars:

Revelation 12:4
And his tail drew the third part of the stars of heaven, and did cast them to the earth: and the dragon stood before the woman which was ready to be delivered, for to devour her child as soon as it was born.

We will examine the other three "I wills" in the upcoming chapter, Secret Societies and the Coming Antichrist. For now, let it be clearly recognized that Lucifer once had a throne, and that his throne was once located in the midst of the planetary bodies of our solar system, within Second Heaven.

The second aspect we're going to look at is based on the obvious question that arises from what we have just covered. If Satan had a throne in the midst of our planets, then which planet are we talking about? This becomes a very interesting question, one most people—and quite frankly, most Christian believers—have not asked or even *thought* to ask. Incredibly, the answer to this ultimate question is staring us all right in the face. Are you ready for the answer? Strap on your seatbelt—here we go!

Our solar system is made up of nine planets. Starting from the closest to our Sun outward they are Mercury, Venus, Earth, Mars, Jupiter, Saturn, Uranus, Neptune, and Pluto. In 2006, the outermost body, Pluto, was downgraded as a dwarf planet by the International Astronomical Union (IAU) since the discovery of similar (some larger) dwarf planets beyond Pluto that exist within the Kuiper Belt, a massive asteroid belt that encircles our outer solar system. While many asteroids are composed of rock and metals, the trillions of objects within the Kuiper Belt primarily comprise methane, ammonia, and water.[90]

In addition to the Kuiper Belt, another asteroid belt exists *within* our solar system, known as the Main Asteroid Belt. This system of asteroids lies between the orbits of Mars and Jupiter. The following full-page diagram is a basic illustration of our solar system that displays the position of the Main Asteroid Belt within it. Although this illustration is not exactly to scale, do notice the position of the Main Asteroid Belt in relation to the positional orbits of all the planets of our solar system; then draw your attention to the Main Asteroid Belt's position specifically in relation to the orbits of Mars and Jupiter.

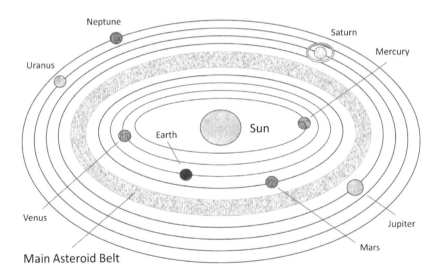

Our first observation is that the Main Asteroid Belt lies proportionally in the middle of our solar system in relation to all the planets. The second observation is that the Main Asteroid Belt lies proportionally between Mars and Jupiter, in the middle of these two planets. This brings into clear focus God's second action within Second Heaven, "…and I will destroy thee, O covering cherub, from the *midst* of the stones of fire" (emphasis added). The third observation is that the Main Asteroid Belt is primarily locked into an elliptical orbit that is similar to all the other planets of our system. Essentially, the Main asteroid Belt fills a 'gap' where a planet should be. Based on these three basic observations, what is the significance of this?

According to scientists, the Kuiper Belt (outside our solar system) represents leftover material in the early formation of our solar system. The theory of evolution (living matter) as an intrinsic extension of the Big Bang Theory (non-living matter) is an alignment of the proposed idea that dispersed material from an explosion somehow eventually formed (evolved) stars, planets, and subsequently, all life as we know it. It is thought that the early Universe was composed of basic materials and gases, such as methane, ammonia, and water along with other carbon-based molecules such as the materials that primarily make up the Kuiper Belt.

However, the Main Asteroid Belt is not like the Kuiper Belt. It is not primarily made up of *basic* materials, gases, and ice.

Most of the asteroids in the Main Belt are made of rock and stone, but a small portion of them contain iron and nickel metals. The remaining asteroids are made up of a mix of these, along with carbon-rich materials. Some of the more distant asteroids tend to contain more ices. Although they aren't large enough to maintain an atmosphere, but there is evidence that some asteroids contain water.[91]

This article also states:

Early in the life of the solar system, dust and rock circling the sun were pulled together by gravity into planets. But Jupiter, the largest planet, kept a number of the pieces from coalescing into another planet. Instead, its gravity disrupted the formation process, leaving an array of unattached asteroids.[92]

Based on the first quote, we discover that the Main Asteroid Belt is primarily composed of objects made of more complex stone substances, and complex metal substances, such as iron and nickel. Based on the second quote, it is hypothesized that these more complex substances, somehow remained as separate asteroid bodies and did not complete the continued formation of a planet such as the fully formed neighbours Mars or Jupiter. The reason stated is that Jupiter's gravitational influence prevented the continued formulation of a complete planet. But is this a reasonable assumption? Especially, if we were to accept and follow this cosmological premise of particle attraction, would not both Jupiter and Mars have been, at the same time, in their infancy of formulation as well? In addition, the previous illustration shows these billions of asteroids are in a similar orbit as the other planets around our Sun. In fact, the asteroids, albeit separated and somewhat scattered, are travelling in a consistent, concise, and deliberate orbit. The majority of these objects are so far away from the gravitational pull and influence of the planet Jupiter, in fact, many are orbiting on the complete opposite side of the solar system!

This becomes even more confusing by the following statement from the same article:

> The Main Belt once contained enough material to form a planet nearly four times as large as Earth. Jupiter's gravity not only stopped the creation of such a planet, it also swept most of the material clear, leaving far too little behind for a planet of any size to form. Indeed, if the entire mass of the Main Belt could somehow create a single body, it would weigh in at less than half of the mass of the moon.[93]

Somehow this material's formulation into a planet was interrupted. Yet, this same belt system somehow contains billions of objects formed of a variety of complex substances (i.e. fully formed metals). The next statement furthers the mystery:

> Some asteroids are large, solid bodies—there are more than 16 in the belt with a diameter greater than 150 miles (240 km). The largest asteroids, Vesta, Pallas and Hygiea, are 250 miles (400 km) long and bigger. The region also contains the dwarf planet Ceres. At 590 miles (950 km) in diameter, or about a quarter of the size of our moon, Ceres is round yet is considered too small to be a full-fledged planet. However, it makes up approximately a third of the mass of the asteroid belt. Other asteroids are pile of rubble held together by gravity. Most asteroids aren't quite massive enough to have achieved a spherical shape and instead are irregular, often resembling a lumpy potato.[94]

Out of billions of asteroid objects within the belt, only one, Ceres, has been identified as a *round* dwarf planet. The rest are irregular, some simply piles of rubble held together by their own degree of gravity.

What if the *entire* asteroid belt is a pile of rubble? What if Ceres, the lone spherical object, is actually a former moon of a planet? More specifically, of a *former* planet? What if the entire Main Asteroid Belt is in fact the remains of a former planet? Not a planet that was in the early stages of formation, but a planet that was fully formed, just as the rest of the planets of our system are fully formed; a former planet that was reduced to "rubble" by some *unknown* destructive force.

As an interesting personal testimony here, I was just finishing this segment of writing after learning about this unique and peculiar spherical body called Ceres. I had not heard of Ceres, nor was I aware of its existence within the Main Asteroid Belt. I decided to take a break and flipped on the TV to watch a bit of news, when, within not more than ten minutes, the newscaster spoke of a major announcement by NASA, regarding the dwarf planet Ceres to be made the following day. Needless to say, I just about fell off the couch in amazement! Well, sure enough, the very next day, the announcement described a NASA probe mission named Dawn had discovered organic material on the surface of Ceres. Now this changes everything, especially challenging the cosmological notion that Ceres is part of this incomplete formulation of a full planet. The following quote is very revealing:

> The discovery adds to the growing list of bodies in the solar system where organics have been found. Organic compounds have been found in certain meteorites as well as inferred from telescopic observations of several asteroids. Ceres shares many commonalities with meteorites rich in water and organics—in particular, a meteorite group called carbonaceous chondrites. This discovery further strengthens the connection between Ceres, these meteorites and their parent bodies.
>
> "This is the first clear detection of organic molecules from orbit on a main belt body," said Maria Cristina De Sanctis, lead author of the study, based at the National Institute of Astrophysics, Rome. The discovery is reported in the journal Science.
>
> Data presented in the Science paper support the idea that the organic materials are native to Ceres. The carbonates and clays previously identified on Ceres provide evidence for chemical activity in the presence of water and heat. This raises the possibility that the organics were similarly processed in a warm water-rich environment.[95]

The statement, "This discovery further strengthens the connection between Ceres, these meteorites and their parent bodies" is strongly suggesting that these meteorites, asteroids, and possibly Ceres itself were once part of some larger parent body. The other possibility is that Ceres itself, as a former moon of a destroyed planet, received foreign organic debris deposited on its surface.

The statement, "This raises the possibility that the organics were similarly processed in a warm water-rich environment" is glaring evidence that this material came from the presence of a body of water. Perhaps, more specifically, this is evidence of organic material and clay originating from a sea or ocean at some point in the past. It should be noted that clay substances on Earth are considered to be formed through *weathering* processes.

> Weathering, disintegration or alteration of rock in its natural or original position at or near the Earth's surface through physical, chemical, and biological processes induced or modified by wind, water and climate.[96]

Therefore, this leads to the conclusion that this destroyed planet not only contained water, in the form of seas or oceans, it may have had atmosphere and subsequent weather patterns in the past.

We all have seen various illustrations of our solar system depicting the orbits of the planets around our Sun. As mentioned, these illustrations are not drawn to actual scale. In fact, the *actual* distances between planets would reduce the planets too small to see on a scaled diagram, and the *actual* size of the planets would not accurately display the true distances between them on a scaled diagram. What this means, in terms of the Main Asteroid Belt, is that if this is truly the remains of a former planet, then this particular planet was the victim of a *direct* strike, either by some abnormal, natural catastrophe, a direct strike on a grand scale by another planetary body, or destroyed by some other *unknown* destructive force. The first scenario, the occurrence of a *random* natural catastrophe, is truly in the realm of astronomical odds, since the immense distances between planetary bodies is not conducive to regular planetary collisions. This makes the lone presence of Ceres as a possible moon even more intriguing, as a direct strike on its former planetoid partner may not have directly, albeit did somewhat indirectly, adversely affect its own ongoing existence.

Overall, we are left with three options as to the origin of the Main Asteroid Belt: (1) it was formed by the interrupted and partial formation of a tenth planet in our system, (2) it was formed by the catastrophic destructive force of an *unknown* source upon a once existent planet, or (3) billions and billions of irregular objects came from outside of our solar system and somehow 'parked' themselves, one by one, in a concise orbit around our Sun that just happens to be an elliptical orbit in the middle of our solar system, and exactly in the middle orbital position between Mars and Jupiter. I would stress that this involves billions of fragmented objects in an orbital position between Mars and Jupiter where the presence of another planetary body would likely have been. This third scenario, when seriously considered, is simply not a reasonable possibility. However, these are the three, the only three, possibilities that explain the existence of the Main Asteroid Belt.

It is interesting that the educational system and scientific institutions of our society only recognize and support one or two of these scenarios (not surprisingly, ignoring option #2). How many of you remember learning about the asteroid belt in science class, yet never fully understood, or were even taught, the reason for its existence? Perhaps, even more interestingly, how many of you, as Bible-believing Christians, have attended a Bible study that explained the existence of the asteroid belt using the Creation Model as stated in God's Word? We are told God's initial creation was perfect. If the truth is that the existence of this asteroid belt is the remains of a past destroyed planet, then how does this anomaly fit within God's perfect creation? Does the Bible, God's Word, support this scenario that a former planet was destroyed? Is there other physical evidence that this scenario actually occurred sometime in our ancient past?

There are two forces at work here. First of all, the scientific community and educational system does not want to recognize a scenario other than natural forces causing the formation of the asteroid belt. To say otherwise is a serious proposition—one that would challenge, threaten, and subsequently turn these ingrained institutions completely upside down. All the "factual" text books would have to be rewritten. Secondly, on the other hand, the religious community would have to recognize that science itself is not the enemy. God gave us a mind and intellect to figure things out. Science itself is not the enemy; it is the foundational principles of secular science that may be in question. This is something that also challenges, threatens, and subsequently forces one to re-evaluate their *personal* positions of certain areas of doctrinal belief, leading those who are Spirit-filled, to go even deeper in their understanding of their faith—going beyond the common, surface-level type of biblical understanding and teaching.

We are going to explore this profound possibility from scientific, geological, and historical perspectives and explore what God's Word has to say about this ancient catastrophic event.

19.

AN ANCIENT PLANET DESTROYED

UP TO THIS POINT, WE'VE EXPLORED THE FACTUAL EVIDENCE THAT LUCIFER HAD a throne, as stated in God's Word. We have determined that this throne was located within Second Heaven. We also explored the distinct possibility that Lucifer's throne was located on an ancient planet somehow destroyed in our ancient past, leaving behind billions of fragments adrift in its former orbit.

When one does serious research into our ancient past, and more specifically, serious research into ancient cultures, surprising revelations begin to surface. Many ancient cultures had prior knowledge, and in some cases, detailed information regarding various planets, moons, and other star systems. They knew about these things despite having, in some cases, a level of technological knowhow that may seem quite primitive by today's standards. This was a major aspect of the Dogon civilization we covered previously. However, some civilizations displayed areas of amazing advancement that actually supersede our own modern abilities today. We touched on a few areas of this regarding many of the megalithic structures of ancient times found all over the world.

Since the scientific and information revolution of the 20th Century, various researchers have been searching the historical archives discovering important pieces of the puzzle that seriously challenge the official narrative of our past. While some alternate hypotheses may be in error and don't fit or line up completely with all the facts, some info brought to the table, pieces of the preverbal puzzle, do bring clarity to the overall picture. I will briefly mention some of these notable researchers.

Immanuel Velikovsky: a Russian-Jewish scholar born in 1895 and died in 1979. Through much time studying the historical archives of ancient cultures,

Velikovsky concluded that Earth had been drastically affected by multiple cat-astrophic events caused by direct impacts of foreign objects from space and by indirect near-impact events of other planets, namely Mars and Venus that he asserts now rest in their current stationary orbits. Velikovsky wrote *Worlds in Col-lision* in 1950, presenting the historical evidence of ancient cultures, and *Earth in Upheaval* in 1955 that presented the archeological evidence for these catastrophic events. Additionally, strong in his Jewish faith, he tied his research to the histor-ical events described in the Old Testament of the Bible, such as Noah's flood.

On a personal note, I attended a lecture seminar by Velikovsky in 1975 when I was sixteen. I was fascinated by his proposed explanations of our his-torical past, much of which were contrary to and far beyond the mainstream educational system. This attracted much defiance and ridicule from his peers in the scientific community. His Russion-Jewish heritage may have further pro-voked his discrimination, especially during the 1950s–60s era of the Cold War. However, the bottom line is that his proposals have provoked serious thought and consideration. This was summed up by Professor Harry Hess of Princeton University in a letter to Velikovsky on March 15, 1963:

We are philosophically miles apart because basically we do not accept each other's form of reasoning—logic. I am of course quite convinced of your sincerity and I also admire the vast fund of information which you have painstakingly acquired over the years.

I am not about to be converted to your form of reasoning though it certainly has had successes. You have after all predicted that Jupiter would be a source of radio noise, that Venus would have a high surface temperature, that the sun and bodies of the solar system would have large electrical charges and several other such predictions. Some of these predictions were said to be impossible when you made them. All of them were predicted long before proof that they were correct came to hand. Conversely I do not know of any specific prediction you made that has since been proven to be false. I suspect the merit lies in that you have a good basic background in the natural sciences and you are quite uninhibited by the prejudices and probability taboos which confine the thinking of most of us.

Whether you are right or wrong I believe you deserve a fair hearing.[97]

Eric Von Daniken: a Swiss author of many books who is perhaps best known for *Chariots of the Gods?* published in 1968, in which he claimed many ancient cultures were directly affected by *extraterrestrial* visits. Von Daniken also related historical and archeological evidence with his interpretations of the Old Testament to support these claims. Although Von Daniken's research overwhelmingly demonstrates *physical* aspects, he does not necessarily present comprehensive information regarding *spiritual* aspects. Generally, his hypothesis contends that religions are a result of historical *alien* influence on mankind. This premise extends to modern TV programs such as *Ancient Aliens* where Von Daniken has often appeared as a guest commentator. However, despite various challenges by critics on specific claims, his hypothesis overall has provoked serious thought and discussion by many fascinated with the prospects and possibilities of what lies beyond Earth and human understanding.

Zecharia Sitchin: a Russian-American author, born in 1920 and died in 2010. Sitchin explored ancient Sumerian cuneiform (earliest form of writing) and developed the hypothesis of *alien* influence on ancient man presented in his famous book *The 12th Planet* published in 1976. Sitchin asserts that an *alien* race, which the Sumerians called the *Anunnaki*, originated on an undiscovered planet called *Nibiru*, which is said to follow an extensive orbit from beyond Neptune to passing close to Earth every 3600 years. Sitchin also maintains that catastrophic events involving the celestial bodies of various planets and moons have occurred in our ancient past. Some of his strongest critics have pointed out that life, as we know it, is unlikely to survive the barren reaches of outer space far from the warmth of our Sun.

Sitchin's research also brings attention to the possibility of another planetary body that once existed between Mars and Jupiter as described by the Sumerians.

Sitchin also explores various passages of the Bible as support for his claims. It is interesting to note that the name *Anunnaki* refers to "those who from heaven came down to earth." However again, the point of contention here is the important understanding that *aliens* are in fact fallen angels and as such, contrary to physical life, are indeed able to exist beyond the warmth of our Sun.

As we previously covered, the Sumerians' principal god was An or Anu, known as the sky god and the Anunnaki are described as, "…the Sumerian deities of the old primordial line; they are chthonic deities of fertility, associated eventually with the underworld, where they became judges…"[98] Of course the glaring correlation of all of this—it is Satan, as the sky god, as the "prince and power of the air" (Ephesians 2:2) and both Satan and the fallen angels are from the ancient of days, "the old primordial line," as well as *eventually* associated with the underworld" (emphasis added), the kingdom of darkness, from where they currently reign, after (eventually) their first banishment from Third Heaven. Not to mention, Baal, one of a lineage of Satan's alternate names, was in fact known as the principal "deity of fertility."

Other notable contemporary researchers in this area of study are Steve Quayle, L.A Marzulli, David Flynn, David Childress, Tom Horn, and Dr. Chuck Missler who has an extensive biblical research background.

As the revolutionary Information Age continues, more and more vital pieces of the puzzle begin to emerge. Despite various errors in fact and some misleading trains of thought, one thing keeps confirming itself, over and over again—a planet once existed between Mars and Jupiter and the ancient Sumerians knew about it.

We can consider the ancients' understanding of this knowledge, as held by the Sumerians, as a simple result of being the first society to spring up, post-flood, in the exact same region of the former location of the Garden of Eden, the initial, pre-flood introduction of mankind to Earth. Naturally, being the direct descendants of Noah, the Sumerian culture held and retained this profound knowledge. It is reasonable to understand that Noah, including seven other people, would have brought and preserved certain first-hand knowledge from a former, destroyed world via the Ark. Mount Ararat, where Noah's Ark rested after the waters receded from the Great Flood (Genesis 8:4), is pretty much straight north of the former region of Babylon-Eden. Based on this, the Sumerians readily recognized the event of the Great Flood, as do many other ancient cultures of the world, even retained by the Pawnee Indians of North America as we covered regarding the famous William Cody (Buffalo Bill) journal entries.

The Sumerians placed great emphasis on the mythological, primordial goddess Tiamat, who they believed was the mother of all creation out of Chaos (a formless cosmos), which in turn brought about the appearance of all subsequent gods in antiquity. Tiamat is described as the goddess of the ocean (salt water) who married the god Abzu (fresh water), and through this union the younger gods came into being.[99]

As the ancient folklore describes, Tiamat was involved in a cosmic battle against a god named Marduk that vowed to assume the pinnacle position in the cosmos.[100] Marduk is also associated with the planet Jupiter.[101] Tiamat lost this battle and was slain and severed into two halves, one becoming the Earth and the other becoming the sky (heaven) of Earth.[102] Based on this, Tiamat became an ancient name to describe the planet Earth.[103]

Zechariah Sitchin asserts that Earth was the planet once located between Jupiter and Mars. According to Sitchen, Earth was struck by a moon of the twelfth planet Nibiru and broke in half, where one half reformed in its current state and orbit, as the third planet from the Sun, and the other half, remaining in rubble, formed the current Main Asteroid Belt.[104] However, a glaring problem that arises in research of the Sumerian/Babylonian culture is that the name *Nibiru* is also associated with the planet Jupiter.[105]

As one researches this area of study, it becomes clear that certain aspects are consistent, while others seem confusing, convoluted, and simply misleading. There is a good reason for this. While the ancient Sumerians knew much of their history that stemmed prior to the event of the Great Flood (knowing the truth), they eventually succumbed under Satan's second wave of influence and his continued attempt to gain control and manipulate God's creation, once again, post-flood. As we covered, this came to a head at the Tower of Babel, causing God to confound and disperse the people throughout the world. Pockets of strongholds remained in isolated regions in the Land of Canaan and notably on the other side of the world pertaining to the Aztecs, Mayans, Incas, and First Nations indigenous peoples. Based on this influence and manipulation, the narrative of the truth of their origins, through folklore, religious belief systems, and traditions, Satan has effectively altered and twisted some of these facts over time. This is why we see consistent aspects that do cross over from culture to culture, globally, yet conflicting, confusing, and misleading aspects which are sometimes mixed into the overall narrative as well.

An interesting note, which will come into focus as we continue, is that the goddess Tiamat was also described as a multi-headed *dragon* or sea *serpent*, having the attributes of arrogance, greed, hate, spite, and vanity.[106] Bear in mind that God's Word tells us a seven-headed beast will rise out of the *sea* in the last days before the Tribulation Period (Revelation 13:1). This is actually a metaphor for the coming conglomerate of nations (Revelation 13:2–3), whose historical lineage is linked to the previous world kingdoms (Daniel 7), under the control of the coming Antichrist (Revelation 13:11–12), who all receive their respective power directly from Satan (Revelation 13:4–5). It should be noted that Tiamat is female, while Satan is male. This may seem confusing to some. However, when one considers the entity known as *Baphomet* (another representation of Satan), this creature is a composite of male (body), female (breasts), goat (head), and angel (wings). As mentioned, Satan is able to shapeshift into various forms and, according to some witnesses, this includes the female form.

Keeping this narrative of the planet that was Tiamat in mind, there is another name for this destroyed planet in our system. Only, in this narrative, this particular planet was completely destroyed. It did not move out of orbit to form planet Earth as the third planet from the Sun. In this narrative, false gods and goddesses were not involved in its destruction. In this narrative, it is the almighty God, the true Creator of the Universe, who reduced this planet to rubble. This planet's name, in the Hebrew language, is known as *Rahab*.

For many theologians, church leaders, and researchers of God's Word, the name Rahab is readily recognized. However, it is readily recognized as a *person*, not as a *planet*. We are told of a story in the Book of Joshua where a prostitute, named Rahab, assisted the spies of Joshua's forces in the campaign to bring down the fortress of Jericho.

Joshua 2:1
And Joshua the son of Nun sent out of Shittim two men to spy secretly, saying, Go view the land, even Jericho. And they went, and came into an harlot's house, named Rahab, and lodged there.

There are some notable points worth mentioning here: (1) this is at a time in history when Joshua was commanded by God to forth into the Land of Canaan and systematically eradicate the cities, fortresses, and valleys of the Promised Land of the Nephilim giants, any other genetic abominations, and all humans participating and perpetuating in the false worship, rituals, and interaction of the fallen angels; (2) the Land of Canaan was a region where sexual immorality was rampant, and the presence of prostitutes was very common, especially within certain temples of worship; and (3) prostitutes were, and are, often named after both precious stones and heavenly bodies (stones of fire), such as Ruby, Sapphire, Pearl, Venus, Neptune, Jupiter, etc., so it shouldn't come as a surprise to learn that the prostitute Rahab, especially living in a satanically controlled region, was most likely named after the former planet called Rahab.

How do I know this for certain? There is actually another, distinctly different, Rahab in the Scriptures. In the Book of Psalms, King David speaks with reverence regarding the strength of the almighty God.

Psalm 89:8–11
O LORD God of hosts, who is a strong LORD like unto thee? or to thy faithfulness round about thee? Thou rulest the raging of the sea: when

the waves thereof arise, thou stillest them. Thou hast broken Rahab in pieces, as one that is slain; thou hast scattered thine enemies with thy strong arm. The heavens are thine, the earth also is thine: as for the world and the fulness thereof, thou hast founded them.

God has the power and ability to calm a raging sea. Continuing in verse 10, David acknowledges that God's power and strength has the ability to break "Rahab in pieces." This is simply not speaking about breaking a prostitute into pieces. David goes on to state how this action relates with the rest of Second Heaven: "The heavens are thine, the earth also is thine: as for the world and the fulness thereof, thou hast founded them." In other words, God is righteous and just to destroy the planet Rahab, since it is He who created the heavens and the Earth in the first place.

This next Scripture found in the Book of Isaiah is even more revealing:

Isaiah 51:9
Awake, awake, put on strength, O arm of the LORD; awake, as in the ancient days, in the generations of old. Art thou not it that hath cut Rahab, and wounded the dragon?

Here, the strength of the almighty God is once again confirmed. The Scripture goes on to mention the "ancient of days" in the "generations of old," referring to ancient times, even at the time of the prophet Isaiah, who lived in the eighth century B.C. In comparison, the prostitute Rahab lived sometime between mid-1300 B.C and mid-1200 B.C.;[107] a difference of some four centuries would hardly qualify as a reference to the "ancient of days." That would be like us calling the 1600s ancient times. Olden days yes, but not exactly ancient.

Again, we have another reference to God harshly dealing with the planet Rahab. Likewise, this is simply not speaking about the prostitute Rahab. If it were, is it reasonable to think God would turn against the prostitute Rahab who clearly had a change of heart to do His will? This is reinforced in Hebrews 11:31. Why would God decide to cut the very person who assisted His chosen men of God in a victory over the enemy? Investigating more deeply, one discovers that the prostitute Rahab is also synonymous with the Hebrew word *Rachab*, which as an adjective [7342] means "roomy, broad, large, breadth—also, proud" and as a proper name [7343] means "proud, a Canaanitess" referring to a woman of Canaan.

In Isaiah 51:9 the word cut also comes into focus. About six months before writing this portion of the book, I was led to do a Bible study on Ezekiel 28 which included the two Scriptures mentioned previously. I was closely considering Isaiah 51:9 when the Holy Spirit prompted me to look up "cut" in the *Strong's Exhaustive Concordance.* What I discovered truly amazed me! Out of the forty-one references where the word cut is derived from various Hebrew words, and where certain references are repeated throughout Scripture (some over a hundred times), the Hebrew word *chatsab* also *chetseb* [2672] is only found exclusively pertaining to Isaiah 51:9. It is not found anywhere else in the Old Testament. This Hebrew word *chatseb* means to "cut or divide stone or other material." This is exactly what God did to the planet Rahab; He cut and divided the various materials of Rahab, namely stone, into billions of fragmented pieces, leaving them adrift to become the Main Asteroid Belt we know today. To the best of my knowledge, this piece of information has not been brought to light or formally published until now. The reason for this is simply that "cut" is a common word without any perceived profound connotation—until one realizes the profound implications of this specific usage in Isaiah 51:9. This point of understanding has lain dormant, completely unnoticed, until now—and whether other individuals have also discovered this still has no bearing that this piece of information was, for me personally, unlocked by the leading of the Holy Spirit!

Many theologians have equated Psalm 89:10 and Psalm 51:9 as a reference to Egypt, with the interpretation that it is Egypt who is "broken into pieces." This is often equated with other Scriptures such as Job 9:13 and 26:12, Psalm 87:4, and Isaiah 30:7.[108] However, as one reads the adjacent Scriptures, these passages also describe great cosmic upheavals within Second Heaven, including Earth, and other grand actions by the hand of God, such as the parting of the Red Sea (which is associated with Egypt). Overall, these Scriptures are referring to events on a grander scale than just pertaining to one mere nation here on earth. On this basis, I believe the interpretation of Rahab as a destroyed ancient planet is seriously overlooked and misunderstood. Again, cut is referring to literal *stone* pieces or fragments, not a metaphor in relation to Egypt. In addition, Psalm 89:10 describes the scattering of "thine enemies" (plural) in relation to the destruction of Rahab. This is not speaking of a singular nation or entity. I submit that this is a reference to the other fallen angels (former stewards) caught up in this cataclysmic event and scattered throughout Second Heaven.

Not only is this action clearly defined in Isaiah 51:9, it is also clearly linked with the wounding of the dragon. Lucifer, as Satan (the dragon), was wounded in the exchange of his banishment from the Kingdom of Heaven and the destruction of his throne on the ancient planet Rahab. The wounding of the dragon did not occur at the time of the Exodus from Egypt. As a note to this, various Hollywood movies, such as *Angel Heart* (1987), often depict Satan, in the form of a man, as a cripple, requiring either a wheelchair or a cane to walk, as a result of an injury to his left leg. This will come up again in a later chapter, The Man from the North Pole.

Bearing in mind Lucifer's previous throne and banishment as the serpent, God's almighty power, a former destroyed planet once having seas or oceans, and a cosmic cataclysm on a level that would shake the very foundation of Second Heaven, consider yet another passage of Scripture:

Jeremiah 26:9–14
He holdeth back the face of his throne, *and* spreadeth his cloud upon it. He hath compassed the waters with bounds, until the day and night come to an end. The pillars of heaven tremble and are astonished at his reproof. He divideth the sea with his power, and by his understanding he smiteth through the proud. By his spirit he hath garnished the heavens; his hand hath formed the crooked serpent. Lo, these *are* parts of his ways: but how little a portion is heard of him? but the thunder of his power who can understand?

Rahab, other than the named prostitute, is defined in the Hebrew language as "proud, boastful, insolent, embolden," which is an accurate description of Lucifer's fall into prideful iniquity as he challenged God, his own maker, with the five "I wills" in Isaiah 14. This also intertwines with the attributes of Tiamat, as we covered. Yet, the name Rahab is still also considered as an epithet for Egypt. This peripheral connection to Egypt will come up in other points as we continue. Rahab is also associated with a mythical sea monster, especially with cultures in the ancient Land of Canaan.[109] So, it is very interesting that Rahab, Tiamat, and Satan are all intertwined and linked as a *dragon, serpent,* or *sea monster*.

Following this distinct possibility of an ancient planet destroyed, we will explore other physical evidence to substantiate this cosmic cataclysm.

20.

MARS: THE ANGRY RED PLANET

THE TWO CLOSET PLANETS TO THE EARTH ARE VENUS AND MARS. WHILE VENUS is similar in size to Earth, its close proximity to the Sun makes it a poor candidate for life (as we know it) and would be a very inhospitable planet for manned spacecraft missions. Mars, on the other hand, while much smaller than the earth, is somewhat conducive to planned, manned missions in the future. This second smallest planet (as compared to Mercury) has impact craters, similar to our moon. It has high mountain peaks, open desert plains, deep canyons, polar ice caps, and an atmosphere, although much thinner than Earth's. Due to its smaller size, the gravitational strength is one third of Earth's. The climate can range from a chilling low of -143° C (-225° F) at the polar ice caps to an occasional high of 27° C (81° F) during the summertime season at the equatorial regions.[110]

After collecting much data from orbiting mapping satellites and various surface rovers, scientists have increasingly speculated that Mars once had large oceans on its surface. In addition, it is becoming clear that Mars once had an atmosphere similar to Earth's. Based on these two foundational conditions, anticipation is high that Mars once supported some form of life.

With respect to the many long and deep canyons common to this planet, some ranging 4000 km (2500 miles) long, 200 km (125 miles) wide, and 10 km (6 miles) deep,[111] there are two interesting aspects: (1) the deepest regions of our oceans on Earth have substantial canyons, known as ocean trenches, which are common to the Pacific Ring of Fire, but are found in all the oceans of the Earth.[112] Similarly, the long and deep canyons of Mars may have been the deepest recesses of former ancient oceans on the planet and, (2) it has been reasoned that the Grand Canyon in Arizona was formed (carved out) by a massive deluge of water in our past. This explanation is based on the research of many scholars who point to the rapid formation of sedimentary layers and a similar, yet smaller, formation of a new canyon after the major eruption at Mount St. Helens.[113] With these two points in mind, there is also growing and strong evidence that the Martian surface was inundated with a major, planetary flood at some point.[114]

A flood on Mars? The next obvious questions: what happened to the oceans on Mars? And what happened to the original atmosphere? The answer to these questions is, again, staring us all right in the face. Consider this following quote posted on *Hidden Mysteries: The Magazine*:

Satellites sent to Mars in 1976 collected information concerning the geologic nature of Mars, and its atmosphere. The images from the orbiters mapping sequence made it clear that Mars had experienced nearly unimaginable catastrophic episodes.

With the evidence of oceans of water having once flowed on Mars' surface in huge quantities, it was apparent that the Martian atmosphere was once more dense, the climate much more hospitable. Sometime in the remote past, for reasons still being debated by astrophysicists, there was a cataclysm on Mars. The Martian oceans washed over the surface of the planet, inundating continents. The vast atmosphere was ripped away, and the once Earth-like environment was laid waste.

In the 1987 October edition of Science magazine, D.P. Cruikshank and R.H. Brown reported a startling piece of news. They had discovered organic compounds on three asteroids: Murray, 103 Electra and Orguiel. Utilizing the process of spectral analyses of reflected light from these three asteroids, Cruikshank and Brown detected amino acids. More startlingly, "aqueous alteration products" such as clay were found, suggesting that the parent body had been affected by water. If these asteroids did in fact contain sediment, it could not have been deposited without large quantities of liquid water laid down over a length of time. This would have also required an environment of gravitation strong enough to hold the dense Martian atmosphere and these vast quantities of water. But these were asteroids—relatively minute chunks of rock hurtling around the sun from a common area between the orbit of Mars and Jupiter. The evidence found on these asteroids could only mean that they were from a parent body possessing an atmosphere and oceans. This parent planetary body was broken up in a cataclysm that shouldn't be a mystery if one is familiar with the Bible.

The accepted theory for the creation of the asteroid belt is usually the failed planet accretion theory. This theory states that during the primordial beginning of the solar system a planet which astronomers call Astera was forming in the place now occupied by the asteroid belt. Jupiter's gravitational influence on the incipient planet was too strong for it to fully solidify. Because of Astera's insufficient mass early in its development, it fragmented. This theory cannot be correct. The facts are becoming more obvious…both the planet Mars and this mysterious parent body of asteroids once sustained oceans and atmospheres.[115]

It is interesting that modern astronomers call this former planet *Astera,* side-stepping the Hebrew name Rahab. Even more intriguing is the name *Astera,* which means "star-like," often associated with the word star.[116] Once again, an intrinsic connection to the fallen morning star.

The clear answer before us is the scenario that Mars suffered an epic cataclysm so intense it literally moved the oceans from one side of the planet to the other. The force of this cataclysm stripped the Martian atmosphere right off the planet, leaving but a trace of its former presence behind—a very thin atmosphere. Without the protective layer of the original atmosphere to hold in natural humidity and dense moisture, such as clouds and rain, the oceans of Mars simply evaporated into space, leaving frozen traces of its past existence in the North and South poles and frozen within underground pockets discovered recently.

Looking at Mars, we see evidence of multiple extreme impacts of meteors and small asteroids. But the interesting thing about these impacts is that most of them appear primarily on one side of Mars, as illustrated on the right side of the topographic map. One of the impact zones in the southern hemisphere is extremely large, situated dead centre of the overall impact regions. This central region is known as the Hellas Impact Basin, an impact zone 2300 km (1429 miles) in diameter and 7 km (4.35 miles) deep.[117]

On the exact opposite side of the Hellas Impact Basin is the Tharsis Montes Region. This region measures 4000 km (2485 miles) across and rises 10 km (6.2 miles) high from the original Martian sea level.[118] In fact, the highest mountain peak in this region, Olympus Mons, is 30 km (15.5 miles) high, dwarfing our own Mount Everest at 4.7 km (2.9 miles) high.[119]

Now the interesting thing is that the Tharsis region, which looks *pushed out*, is exactly 180 degrees from the opposite side of Mars, where we see the Hellas region, a major impact zone, that is *pushed in*. Looking at the topographic map, if you can imagine inserting a straight rod in the middle of the Hellas Basin (slightly south), and pushing it straight through Mars (slightly north), it would come out exactly where the highest points of Mars are located, at the Tharsis Montes Region.

It also appears the Hellas Impact Basin was the scene of multiple impacts— appearing very similar to a shotgun blast with a central, concentrated impact zone and having a surrounding sprayed area of smaller impacts. This obvious comparison is derived from the fact that planets are spinning in rotation on their axis. So, as Mars was spinning in rotation—this had to have been, overall, a single combined impact event. We see clearly that there are no signs of multiple impacts on the other side of Mars. Had there been multiple *delayed* events we would see impacts on *both sides* of the planet as the planet was rotating. It should be stated that the odds of random impacts of meteors and small asteroids of concentrating zones in the upper and lower central regions, most occurring in the southern hemisphere (on one side only) over long periods of time is extremely unlikely. Actually, it is not a plausible explanation. Not to mention the odds of a single massive impact area, occurring dead centre of the other surrounding impact regions, is also far off the scale of random possibilities. So, quite simply, the Hellas Impact Basin and the surrounding regions in the central and lower southern hemisphere of Mars are due to an overall combined, single event.

The next question becomes, what caused this massive, singular event of multiple foreign impacts on Mars? Well, I think we have already answered this question. When God destroyed Lucifer's seat and throne on the planet Rahab, fragments of this catastrophic event struck the nearby planet Mars with immense intensity. Mars was first in line to take a direct hit. As for Jupiter, it is quite possible that its thick, gaseous atmosphere is effectively hiding any evidence of catastrophic impacts.

When considering Mars as a planet, many overlook that Mars has two moons. But these are not moons in the traditional sense. Phobos is only 22.2 km in diameter and Deimos is even smaller at 12.6 km in diameter.[120] Both of these objects are the typical Idaho potato shape, demonstrating irregular formulation. These are hardly moons. However, they are consistent in the overall bombardment of large fragments from the exploding planet Rahab. These are no more than two large asteroids that parked themselves in orbit around Mars.

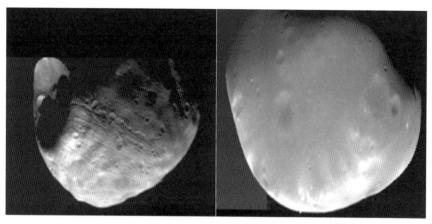

Phobos   NASA/JPL credited images   Deimos

Also interesting is that Phobos and Deimos were both names of Greek gods representing "fear, panic, terror and dread."[121]

As a note here, it has been declared that a meteorite that fell in Egypt in 1911 is an ancient fragment of Mars. Scientists say this specimen is suspected of being a fragment of Martian rock that ended up flying out into space after Mars was hit by meteor or asteroid—and landed here on Earth. This is also the famous Martian rock suspected of containing evidence of fossilized bacterial life.[122] This is provocative evidence of the aftermath of the catastrophic event of the destruction of Rahab.

We have just covered the real and distinct possibility of a physical connection between Rahab, the former *planet*, defined as boastful, insolent and proud…

and the planet Mars. As we continue, we're going to explore some other amazing information about Mars that will shed some light on the intrinsic connection of this planet with ancient Egypt, where some theologians equate the name Rahab (the proud) as a code word for this nation, usually citing Psalm 87:4.

21.

THE EGYPTIAN CONNECTION

On July 20, 1976, NASA successfully landed Viking 1 on the surface of Mars and beamed back the very first sequence of panoramic photographs of the Martian landscape and skyline. At the same time, the Viking Orbiter began detailed mapping and photographs of the Martian surface. Starting on July 25, 1976, a series of photographs would eventually be leaked to the general public in the early 1990s. These photo images, frame 035A72 and frame 070A13, taken in the region known as Cydonia, were originally considered misfiled until they were uncovered by NASA computer engineers Vincent DiPietro and Gregory Molenaar:

> In one of the images taken by Viking 1 on July 25, 1976, a 2 km (1.2 miles) long Cydonian mesa, situated at 40.75° north latitude and 9.46° west longitude had the appearance of a humanoid face. When the image was originally acquired, Viking chief scientist Gerry Soffen dismissed the "Face on Mars" in image 035A72 as a "trick of light and shadow". However, a second image, 070A13, also shows the "face", and was acquired 35 Viking orbits later at a different sun-angle from the 035A72 image. This latter discovery was made independently by Vincent DiPietro and Gregory Molenaar, two computer engineers at NASA's Goddard Space Flight Center. DiPietro and Molenaar discovered the two misfiled images, Viking frames 035A72 and 070A13, while searching through NASA archives.[123]

Twenty years later, subsequent NASA missions, such as the Mars Global Surveyor and the Mars Reconnaissance Orbiter sent back images using higher resolution cameras. These images seem to suggest that the former images of the Face on Mars were simply a result of a trick of light and shadow on the Mars surface. The following two photographs show the difference in the overall resolution and seem to reveal differences in features:

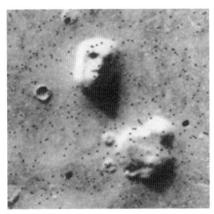 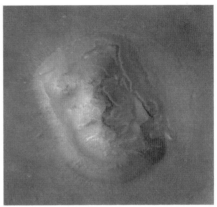

Viking Mission Frame 035A72   Mars Global Surveyor Mission

NASA/JPL credited images

However, despite this discrepancy between these two images, other researchers, such as Richard C. Hoagland (winner of the Nobel Prize for Astronomy 1997), who dispute and challenge this discrepancy and even suggest that the subsequent, high-resolution images have been purposely photo-shopped and brushed out to eliminate various strong features. Carefully consider this image with the next full-page photo of the entire Cydonia site, comparing the features of the face, and decide for yourself if the first image has been purposefully altered. Hoagland goes into lengthy detail regarding the Face on Mars and other Martian anomalies in his books *The Monuments of Mars: A City on the Edge of Forever* (1987) and *Dark Mission: The Secret History of NASA* (2007).

The next frame image of the overall landscape of the region of Cydonia not only seems to verify and support the presence of a face anomaly on the surface of Mars, it reveals striking images of possible unnatural, pyramid structures in the same vicinity.

Five Pyramids in Pentagon Formation

The 'Fortress'

Face on Mars

D & M Pyramid

Cydonia Region, Mars

NASA/JPL credited Image

Considering the real possibility that Mars suffered a catastrophic event in its ancient past, the structures revealed in the photo above may also reveal unnatural structures that are sand-swept from ongoing massive dust storms. The anomaly referred to as the fortress displays angular corners and straight wall faces that are simply beyond natural rock formations. This is very apparent upon viewing close-ups of this particular anomaly.

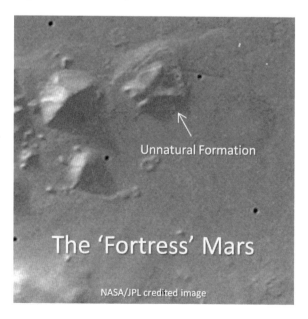

Unnatural Formation

The 'Fortress' Mars

NASA/JPL credited image

As an interesting note, the Hollywood film *Total Recall* (1990), starring Arnold Schwarzenegger, is a futuristic sci-fi movie principally set on Mars with one of the central locations referred as the Pyramid Mine. Coincidentally, this movie was released just prior to the time the actual images of the Cydonia pyramids were leaked to general public.

Another researcher, from a Christian perspective, is Stewart Best who released a documentary video production called *Project Red Star: Martian Genesis* (2002) that documents other revealing anomalies on Mars, such as roadways, walls, buildings, stepped ziggurat pyramids, and, amazingly, statues strikingly similar to Egyptian statues. All of these structures are located in a region on Mars called Tithonia, originally discovered on photo frame MO204505 from NASA's Mars Global Surveyor after 1997.

We have looked at the pyramids at Giza and how they are aligned/mirrored with the Constellation of Orion's Belt. These pyramids are just outside Cairo, the capital of Egypt. The name *Cairo* is derived from the Arabic word *al-Qahira* which translates to "the victorious." However, what is most intriguing, when further investigation is done, is the fact that one finds that the name *Cairo* is also derived from the Arabic *al-Qahir*, which translates to "city of Mars"!

Taking all this into perspective, various researchers, such as the late Zecharia Sitchin, tend to believe in the possibility of a pre-Adamic race (before the creation of Adam and Eve). I personally don't subscribe to this point of view, even with many of the unexplainable anomalies being discovered on Earth and beyond. However, I do firmly believe that God's Word does speak of an era before the advent of humankind on Earth, which I refer to as the pre-Adamic era of the angels. As we covered in Section One, God created the angels before He created mankind. Now, whether that former era involves conclusive evidence of *extraterrestrial* (beyond Earth) structures on other planetary bodies is yet to be fully determined.

What we have determined, thus far, is that Lucifer had an ancient throne—and that throne was once located on the planet Rahab, other than the planet Earth. It is also clear from the description of both the New Jerusalem and Kingdom of Heaven in Revelation 21 and 22 that structural aspects of a *city* are being described. There are walls and twelve gates mentioned (Revelation 21:10–12); it is measured in area dimensions (v. 15–17); the substance materials of its composition are listed (v.18–21). A *street* is described alongside a "pure river of water" extending from the throne of God (Revelation 22:1–2). It is Jesus, Himself, who clearly states that many *mansions* (dwellings) are being *prepared* (constructed) in

Third Heaven for a future time when all the saved, born-again Christians will be gathered together for eternity, starting at the events of the Rapture and the Second Coming:

John 14:2–3
In my Father's house are many mansions: if it were not so, I would have told you. I go to prepare a place for you. And if I go and prepare a place for you, I will come again, and receive you unto myself; that where I am, there ye may be also.

Keeping all this in mind, let's read this next intriguing passage from Jeremiah:

Jeremiah 4:23–26
I beheld the earth, and, lo, it was without form, and void; and the heavens, and they had no light. I beheld the mountains, and, lo, they trembled, and all the hills moved lightly. I beheld, and, lo, there was no man, and all the birds of the heavens were fled. I beheld, and, lo, the fruitful place was a wilderness, and all the cities thereof were broken down at the presence of the Lord, and by his fierce anger.

Various researchers point to this passage as evidence of a pre-Adamic era and race of beings, especially based on the reference to the Earth (v. 23) as "without form, and void, and they had no light" which is equated to Genesis 1:2, "And the earth *was* without form, and void; and darkness was upon the face of the deep…" This is known as the Gap Theory (a gap of time and history between the first two verses of Genesis), which postulates that there was prior civilization(s) created and destroyed before Adam. However, I would stress that God's Word clearly states that *death* itself was introduced into the world at the fall at the Garden of Eden, and not before then (Romans 5:12). I would also stress that, in this area of study, one should be careful not to confuse the pre-Adamic era of the angels with the idea of a pre-Adamic race of physical human beings.

Having said that, the possibility of ancient pyramid structures, and other Egyptian-type artifacts, existing on Mars brings into focus the pervasive influence of the fallen angels over an ancient culture, devoid of God, and the Egyptians' reciprocal devoted and tenacious worship of these false gods.

This provocative information also raises the distinct possibility that the level of interaction between fallen angels and humans may not be exclusively limited to the confines of Earth itself. This area of study is much too expansive to fully cover in this book, but as we continue, we will look at some key points.

22.
UFOS AND ALIEN ABDUCTIONS

THE IDEA OF LIFE BEYOND EARTH HAS BEEN PONDERED THROUGHOUT HUMAN history but, perhaps, has never been as prevalent as over the last century. This possibility has fostered many books, magazines, TV shows, and Hollywood movies. In fact, while the all-time top grossing Hollywood film has been *Gone With the Wind* (1939), the top grossing all-time *theme* of Hollywood films has been the UFO/Alien/Space genre.[124] This includes films such as *Star Wars* (1977), *Close Encounters of the Third Kind* (1977), *War of the Worlds* (1953, 2005), *Alien* (1979), *E. T. The Extraterrestrial* (1982), *Independence Day* (1996), *Avatar* (2009), and pseudo documentaries such as *The Fourth Kind* (2009) and *Area 51* (2015).

Serious research and study has been conducted over the last several decades by both scientific and military organizations and departments. This includes scientific programs such as SETI (The Search for Extraterrestrial Intelligence) and military research programs such as Project Sign, Project Grudge, and Project Blue Book (U.S.); Setko MO and Setko AS (Soviet Union); and Project Magnet and Project Second Storey (Canada).[125] Of course, there is the infamous Operation Majestic (MJ-12), describing U.S. government/military direct interaction with supposed *extraterrestrials*. I would highly recommend reading *Top Secret/Majic* by nuclear physicist Stanton Friedman on that subject.

The idea of interstellar travel and life on other planets has been the fodder for wondering, pondering, and wild speculation as to the profound possibilities. Before we consider life on other planets, let's take an honest look at the possibility of interstellar travel.

First, when considering interstellar travel, this is not talking about orbiting the planet Earth or a three-day journey to the moon. This is extensive travel in space, which is at minimum, a six-month journey (one way) to our nearest planet, Mars. Considering a six-month stay on the planet surface, the total journey would involve a minimum of eighteen months away from the familiarity of Earth. Consider the following points carefully:

- The distance between star systems and galaxies is immense. Some of these systems are millions, if not billions of light years away—this is also based on a one-way trip. So you would have to double each distance for a return trip. Physical life forms simply do not live long enough to travel these distances—even at the speed of light.

- The amount of energy required to generate the speed of light for a trip lasting, say, on a relatively short jaunt of 200,000 years is absolutely astronomical! It was Albert Einstein who said any form of mass approaching light speed would exponentially increase in weight the closer it gets to obtain this speed.

- Light travels in an arc, not a straight line. Therefore, great consideration of distance calibration would be required. This consideration would also extend to slowing down from light speed to a reached destination and the energy required in doing so.

- Solar radiation in space is extremely lethal. This is one of the reasons the shuttle craft was generally positioned to shield astronauts from the sun's radiation while on their space walks. Other suns (stars) in the universe can be much larger than our Sun. For instance, Quasar stars can be thousands of times larger than our own Sun, and therefore can emit massive amounts of solar radiation.

- If one is traveling at extreme speeds in space, any amount of meteorite or comet debris could slice through a spacecraft like a laser beam, instantly killing any occupants inside.

- It has been proven that prolonged exposure to weightlessness in space decreases bone density and muscle mass in humans.

- ▸ Massive amounts of food, water, and supplies would be needed to sustain generations of humans to reach a designated destination.

- ▸ Unknown variables in long-distance, deep space travel are not known, or understood to the fullest, to guarantee any successful voyage.

In a nutshell, interstellar travel, as far as physical humans are concerned, is an extremely dangerous proposition far more likely to be unattainable than attainable. In addition to the previous points, interstellar travel would require travelling at the speed of light to cover these immense distances between star and galaxy systems. The speed of light is 186,000 miles *per second*. To put that into perspective, this would be the equivalent of travelling around the world eight times per second! While *Star Trek* and *Star Wars* suggest light speed is somehow attainable, these depictions do not address the immense gravitational force stresses on both *physical* crafts and *physical* humans in order to achieve these velocities. For instance, fighter pilots, flying an F-16 jet, have a tough time coping with G-forces of mach-3 accelerations (three times the speed of sound, which is 760 miles per hour at mach-1). A sudden right-angle turn at mach-3 would be catastrophic to both the jet and the pilot, resulting in assured death.

Regarding the notion of life on other planets, this cannot be confirmed or denied at this point. We simply do not know. However, one thing is for certain: from a human perspective, everything we know of in the universe that God created, including life itself, exists on a *physical* level. This is important to understand, because if God has created *physical* life elsewhere (other than Earth), then those life forms are bound by the same *physical* laws of the universe as we are. These universal laws, such as gravity force, electromagnetic force, strong force, and weak force are known to be consistent and unchanging in how they affect and react throughout the creation. In addition, God created immense distances between star and galaxy systems. This may be for a profound reason. If the possibility of *physical* life exists elsewhere, then they cannot make the trip here, as we cannot make the trip there. Quite simply, interstellar travel is *physically* impossible.

However, considering this, all the while we have been earnestly searching for signs of life beyond Earth, *something* has been entering our airspace from beyond our Earth; *something* has displayed extraordinary accelerations, on occasion described as 14,000 Gs (somehow without breaking the sound barrier); *something* has been able to outmaneuver our scrambled fighter jets; *something* has displayed the ability to materialize from a ball of light into a craft the size of a football field and then dematerialize into a ball of light; *something* has been witnessed and reported by highly trained professionals, such as police officers, airline pilots, air traffic controllers, and specialized military personnel. Again, all the while we have been searching for signs of life beyond Earth, with our telescopes, listening devices, and satellites—these occurrences, in the millions, have happened right in our proverbial backyard. Perhaps, more amazingly, *something* has displayed *meta-physical* abilities beyond our universal physical laws.

What could it be? The answer to this question becomes clear and sobering when one views this phenomenon through the lens of the *spiritual*, rather than the *physical*. The secular world, especially secular scientists, are so wrapped up in empirical reasoning that they are completely closed off to any possibilities other than the five basic senses within a physical world. While the idea of other dimensions may be pondered, as with the study of quantum physics, somehow the idea or any acknowledgement of the *spiritual* dimension is completely discounted.

In the early 1990s I watched an episode of CBC's *Man Alive* that explored the possibility of *alien* sightings and abductions told by eye witness accounts. In one segment a group of researchers sat around a table in discussion. One of them said, "You know, there comes a time where technology and *magic* meet." That statement struck me to the core. I not only realized he had said something very significant and very profound, but the more I considered this statement, the more I realized that absolute truth had been spoken. Those words inspired me to eventually further define the following premise:

When considering the level of achievement and technological knowledge between a culture considered to be primitive, such as cave dwellers, and a culture considered to be ultra-advanced, such as the various cultures depicted in *Star Wars,* who are demonstrating interstellar travel, what is the defining factor between the two?

The answer is simply this: the ability to utilize electromagnetic energy forces and crystals. Further defined, electromagnetic energy sources include ultra-violet, infra-red, gamma ray, x-ray, microwave and radio wave frequencies which are all part of the Electromagnetic Spectrum of Light. Only 5 percent of this spectrum, such as incandescent light, is visible to the naked eye; the other 95 percent is invisible. As for crystals, this includes quartz, feldspar, and mica (as we saw concerning the Pyramid of Khufu). It also includes precious stones such as sapphires and rubies. Ruby crystals are the preferred crystal utilized in telecommunication devices such as radio telescopes and cell phones.[126] The ruby crystal was instrumental in the development of laser technology.[127] Obviously, the primitive culture, the cave dwellers, would be considered at a technological level of basic sticks and stones.

On the other hand, when considering the level of achievement and knowledge of *spiritism* between a simple person, such as a layman or peasant, and the advanced knowledgeable capabilities of a master sorcerer, what is the defining factor between these two?

The answer to this question is simply this: the ability to utilize electromagnetic energy forces and crystals. It is the exact same answer. A person involved in spiritism often utilizes crystal amulets and crystal balls, for instance. Sorcerers manipulate electromagnetic energy sources to accomplish such abilities as levitation, bringing the *unseen* into the realm of the seen, and altering molecular structure. It was the medieval alchemists who searched for the magic elixir to change base metal lead into precious gold.

Based on this revealing premise, when an eye witness describes an account of a large UFO craft materializing and dematerializing from and into a ball of light the size of a basketball, is this advanced technology they have witnessed, or is this advanced sorcery? When supposed *alien* beings, described by eye witness accounts, demonstrate the ability to walk through walls, appear out of mirrors, and shapeshift into human form, are they demonstrating advanced technology or are they demonstrating advanced sorcery? When *alien* abductees describe being levitated (telekinesis) from their beds in the middle of the night and describe an exchange of communication through their mind without speaking (telepathy), again, is this advanced technology, or is this sorcery? Truthfully, this is nothing less than a demonstration of witchcraft. The act of *alien* levitation and abduction in the still of the night, within one's private bedroom, is a clear violation of the privacy, sanctity, and safety of one's own home. This is also nothing short of a parallel scene right out of William P. Blatty's film, *The Exorcist* (1973).

When one researches this area of study, one discovers striking similarities between the stories of various eye witnesses (victims). I have personally heard, first hand, a few of the recounted stories of those who have experienced this evil infringement in their lives. Some witnesses have received strange marks and unusual burns on various places on their bodies. I have personally seen, first hand, the results of some of these marks. In addition, sudden nosebleeds and foreign object implants have been documented with abductees.[128]

Over the years, there have been various researchers concerned with this phenomenon, including Budd Hopkins, John Keel, Raymond Fowler, and John E. Mack, M.D., a Pulitzer Prize winner and a former professor at Harvard Medical

School. As a professional psychiatrist, he had counseled some sixty individuals regarding their personal experiences with *alien* abduction. He wrote the book, *Abduction: Human Encounters with Aliens* (1994), documenting these witness testimonies. I watched a video clip of an interview he did in the mid 1990s; referring to his many patients, he stated:

> If what they say is happening to them isn't really happening to them—then, tell me, what *is* happening to them?

Another researcher in the phenomenon of UFO sightings, considered by many of his peers as the top researcher of UFOs in the world, is French computer scientist and astronomer Dr. Jacques Vallée. In fact, Steven Spielberg modeled the lead UFO investigator Francois Truffaut after Dr. Vallée in *Close Encounters of the Third Kind* (1977).[129]

After years of extensive research and careful considerations, Dr. Vallée made the following statements based on his conclusions:

> Scientific opinion has generally followed public opinion in the belief that unidentified flying objects either do not exist (the "natural phenomena hypothesis") or, if they do, must represent evidence of a visitation by some advanced race of space travelers (the extraterrestrial hypothesis or "ETH"). It is the view of the author that research on UFOs need not be restricted to these two alternatives. On the contrary, the accumulated data base exhibits several patterns tending to indicate that UFOs are real, represent a previously unrecognized phenomenon, and that the facts do not support the common concept of "space visitors." Five specific arguments articulated here contradict the ETH:
>
> 1. unexplained close encounters are far more numerous than required for any physical survey of the earth
> 2. the humanoid body structure of the alleged "aliens" is not likely to have originated on another planet and is not biologically adapted to space travel;
> 3. the reported behavior in thousands of abduction reports contradicts the hypothesis of genetic or scientific experimentation on humans by an advanced race;

4. the extension of the phenomenon throughout recorded human history demonstrates that UFOs are not a contemporary phenomenon; and

5. the apparent ability of UFOs to manipulate space and time suggests radically different and richer alternatives.[130]

We are dealing with a yet unrecognized level of consciousness, independent of man but closely linked to the earth...I do not believe anymore that UFOs are simply the spacecraft of some race of extraterrestrial visitors. This notion is too simplistic to explain their appearance, the frequency of their manifestations through recorded history, and the structure of the information exchanged with them during contact.[131]

If they are not an advanced race from the future, are we dealing instead with a parallel universe, another dimension where there are other human races living, and where we may go at our expense, never to return to the present? From that mysterious universe, are higher beings projecting objects that can materialize and dematerialize at will? Are UFOS "windows" rather than "objects"?[132]

The 'medical examination' to which abductees are said to be subjected, often accompanied by sadistic sexual manipulation, is reminiscent of the medieval tales of encounters with demons. It makes no sense in a sophisticated or technical framework: any intelligent being equipped with the scientific marvels that UFOs possess would be in a position to achieve any of these alleged scientific objectives in a shorter time and with fewer risks.[133]

Dr. Jacques Vallée has written many thesis papers and books on this subject including, *Passport to Magonia: From Folklore to Flying Saucers* (1969), *Messengers of Deception: UFO Contacts and Cults* (1979), and *Revelations: Alien Contact and Human Deception* (1991). His latest book is *Wonders in the Sky: Unexplained Aerial Objects From Antiquity to Modern Times* (2010).

Quite interesting is Steven Spielberg's choice for the grand backdrop of the pre-arranged rendezvous with the *alien* mother ship and a U.N. special team in *Close Encounters of the Third Kind* (1977). The site chosen is a real U.S. national landmark, in the state of Wyoming, which is actually named Devils Tower! Once again, a high place, a high mountain!

Devils Tower, National Landmark, Wyoming

Another point worth noting is the apparent manipulation of space and time in the presence of both UFOs and *alien* beings. It is important to understand that within the *spiritual* realm, time itself is inconsequential. Time has no bearing on God's existence. A billion years to God is relative to a single second in time to human existence.

2 Peter 3:8
But, beloved, be not ignorant of this one thing, that one day is with the Lord as a thousand years, and a thousand years as one day.

While certain *physical* aspects are part of the spiritual realm, i.e. the Kingdom of Heaven is a *physical* place where *spiritual* beings reside (Revelation 21 and 22), time was given to mankind to gauge *physical*, finite life spans within a *physical* environment, under First Heaven. God created the sun and moon, within Second Heaven, to gauge time of human life spans through the account of morning, evening, days, weeks, months, and years.

Genesis 1:14–16
And God said, Let there be lights in the firmament of the heaven to divide the day from the night; and let them be for signs, and for seasons, and for days, and years: And let them be for lights in the firmament of the heaven to give light upon the earth: and it was so. And God made

two great lights; the greater light to rule the day, and the lesser light to rule the night: he made the stars also.

Based on this, it stands to reason that fallen angels are not only still functioning in First and Second Heavens in a *physical* environment, but are also functioning in and out of the *spiritual* realm, the unseen dimension (the 95 percent of the Electromagnetic Spectrum of Light that is invisible). It is a well known fact (in some cases documented) that houses haunted by *spirits* have seen effects on their electrical current, such as lights dimming and/or flickering and electronic devices and appliances suddenly turning on and off by themselves. Apparently, these same phenomena happen in the presence of *extraterrestrials*, described by many witnesses. This was highlighted by Spielberg within two scenes in *Close Encounters of the Third Kind* (1977): (1) the main character's (Richard Dreyfuss) work truck alternator, lights, and radio start to operate erratically in the presence of a UFO, and (2) the appliances, house lights, and child's toys begin to move and operate erratically in the presence of *alien* beings just prior to the abduction of the character of a young boy.

It needs to be noted that not all human experiences with *extraterrestrials* have been reported as being horrific or negative. However, it is important to fully understand that when one closely considers such "positive" events, they usually involve individuals who do not have a Christian background. Many of these individuals profess a belief in other world religions, or are involved in New Age philosophies or various cults. It seems, in many of these cases, the individual(s) have been purposely selected to propagate messages to the rest of humanity. These messages include: (1) all of humanity will soon enter into a new era of enlightenment, (2) global government and a world leader is coming, (3) all religions lead to the same place, (4) Jesus is just one teacher of many, (5) *we* are here to help you, and (6) there will be a removal of a large number of individuals from Earth. The latter point is perhaps the *alien's* involvement, falsely proclaimed, for the coming Rapture.

There are psychics who claim to have received telepathic messages from *extraterrestrials*. To be clear, the practice of psychic clairvoyance, "a consulter of familiar spirits," is occultic witchcraft and sternly forbidden in God's Word (Deuteronomy 18:10–13). One such example is the ongoing psychic contact of an *extraterrestrial* being named Ashtar. A comprehensive account of these deceptive communications and messages, covering the six messages previously mentioned, is found in the book *From Here to Armageddon: I Am Ashtar*.[134]

God's Word presents these warnings:

Colossians 2:18
Let no man beguile you of your reward in a voluntary humility and worshipping of angels, intruding into those things which he hath not seen, vainly puffed up by his fleshly mind...

Galatians 1:18
But through we, or an angel from heaven, preach any other gospel unto you than that which we have preached unto you, let him be accursed.

An example of this pervasive influence of UFOs/*extraterrestrials* on deceived individuals is the case of the Heaven's Gate cult in San Diego, California. This story made news headlines in 1997 when it was discovered that thirty-nine individuals were found dead in a housing complex due to an apparent suicide pact.

To many, this story seemed shocking and understandably foreign in terms of average, normal thinking. However, when one investigates the story on deeper level, it becomes abundantly clear what and where the centre of influence is derived.

The Heaven's Gate cult was founded in 1974 by Marshall Applewhite and Bonnie Nettles, who presented themselves as Do and Ti.[135] Their belief system was intertwined with prophetic passages from the Bible, New Age occultists such as Helen Blavatsky, and elements of reincarnation.[136] Central to this mixture of beliefs, Applewhite and Nettles proclaimed they were the two witnesses described in the Book of Revelation, and that the Earth was soon to be recycled and cleansed.[137] They taught various followers that the human body was merely a physical vessel, a temporary vehicle, to help them on their journey.[138] In order to escape from the purging of planet Earth, one would need to leave their body, spiritually, and board a UFO spacecraft they described as hidden in the tail of the comet, Hale-Bopp, as it was approaching close to Earth.[139] It was thought this would be a transition into the next higher level of existence, leaving all things of the old world behind, in exchange for a new body and a new utopia.[140] It was decided a suicide pact would be the only way to release the souls of the group to meet the UFO and transcend to the next level of existence, which was understood as "above human" existence.[141]

Between March 19 and 20, 1997, Marshall Applegate videotaped a farewell address. On March 26, thirty-nine bodies were found in partial decomposition.[142] All deceased followers were dressed in identical fashion: a purple shroud

UFOs and Alien Abductions

covering, brand new Nike runners, black sweat pants and shirts, and arm bands with Heaven's Gate and "away team" embossed within the form of a *pyramid* patch.[143] Each person had drunk a poisonous concoction and had secured plastic bags around their heads to ensure suffocation.[144]

An interesting aspect about this is all the followers were in a death formation (in bunk beds) in a similar, yet scaled down, fashion of the Valley of the Kings in Egypt (burial crypts). In fact, the Heaven's Gate logo, representing a keyhole in its design, is also very similar to the symbol of the Egyptian Ankh, which many researchers have associated as the symbol of life, but more specifically as the symbol of the afterlife.[145] You can search the Internet to find and compare the image of the Heaven's Gate logo with the image of the Egyptian Ankh below.

Egyptian Ankh

Ironically, the Ankh was always present during the Egyptian ceremonial funeral and upon death, without the provision of eternal salvation, a physical death, the first death, would assuredly lead to the second death, the spiritual death (Revelation 2:11, 20:6). In the final analysis, the *false* symbol of the Ankh was proclaimed by an ancient *false* religious deity, and in modern times incorporated by a *false* religious cult as the symbol of life. Essentially, both religious sects were influenced by the same false doctrine of the fallen angels of old. In the end, this deception results in an eternal death, not eternal life or heavenly afterlife at all—certainly not a recycled life commonly known as reincarnation.

We are reminded in God's Word:

Hebrews 9:27
And as it is appointed unto men once to die, but after this the judgment:

With the advent of personal video cameras and cell phone cameras and increased level of security camera surveillance systems over the past few decades, the level of eye witness accounts and captured video accounts of UFO encounters has increased dramatically. Obviously, some of these reports are hoaxes or can be attributed to natural phenomena. However, the internet is full of unexplained and provocative cases of UFO sightings on dedicated websites, YouTube videos, and official news organization sites.

What many have failed to recognize, and what puts this recent increase into perspective, is that Christianity is under attack. Some would argue Christianity has always been under attack, but there has been a marked increase in a concerted effort to overthrow foundational Christian values in recent decades. Even more specifically, many fail to recognize that there is a direct correlation with the amped up attack on Christianity and the increased UFO phenomenon. The more there is a falling away from the foundational tenets of Christianity, it seems, the more UFOs come out of the closet. It is the presence of the Holy Spirit, through believers (the body of Christ), that is holding back evil from completely taking over. As we covered with the *Progression of Sin* overview, when society fully rejects God, a spiritual vacuum results and the enemy rushes in to fill the void—unchallenged and able to inundate humanity. This brings into focus the Scripture of 1 Timothy 4:1, which we covered in Section One:

1 Timothy 4:1
Now the Spirit speaketh expressly, that in the latter times some shall depart from the faith, giving heed to seducing spirits, and doctrines of devils;

This is also highlighted in the following Scripture, where this falling away (departure from the faith) is a hallmark that precedes the coming Antichrist, the Devil's son, and the future one world leader:

2 Thessalonians 2:3
Let no man deceive you by any means: for *that day shall not come,* except there come a falling away first, and that man of sin be revealed, the son of perdition;

Again, as a reminder, Jesus warned:

Matthew 24:37–39

But as the days of Noah were, so shall also the coming of the Son of man be. For as in the days that were before the flood they were eating and drinking, marrying and giving in marriage, until the day that Noe entered into the ark, And knew not until the flood came, and took them all away; so shall also the coming of the Son of man be.

Also interesting is the Vatican's (Church of Rome) recent raised interest and focus on *extraterrestrial* life and UFOs. The Vatican has entered into a joint program with the University of Arizona, utilizing one of the largest telescopes in the world. The name of this joint project—are you ready for this? It is named Project *L.U.C.I.F.E.R.!*[146] Of course, L.U.C.I.F.E.R. is an acronym which stands for Large binocular telescope near-infrared Utility with Camera and Integral Field unit for Extragalactic Research.[147] Researcher Tom Horn documents this relationship between the Vatican and UFO research in his video presentation, *The Vatican, Pope and UFOs: How Are They Linked?*, available on Dr. Chuck Missler's *Koinonia House Resource Center*.[148] Many, off hand, would find this quite odd that a supposed Christian organization, thought to be based on the Creation Model, would be earnestly interested in pursuing *extraterrestrial* life, considered by many (of secular reasoning) to be at an advanced level on the evolutionary scale. Then again, this might not be so odd to accept when one understands that the official Vatican position is that God did not actually speak the universe into existence, but instead used the Big Bang and Evolution as His methods. This is completely contrary to God's Word, as the timeline of His creation spans seven literal days. As stated six times throughout Genesis 1, *"the evening and the morning were [each day]"* (Genesis 1:5, emphasis added) resting on the seventh day. It is perfectly clear that an evening and a morning comprise a literal day. When God repeats something twice, we should take notice. When He repeats something six times, we really need to pay attention to what He is stating.[149] This becomes even more alarming when one does further study into actual Vatican tenets. I highly recommend two books, *Preparing for Eternity* by Mike Gendron, and *The Vatican's Holocaust* by Avro Manhattan for further insight.

As a final note here, this is an interesting passage of Scripture:

Obadiah 1:3–4

The pride of thine heart hath deceived thee, thou that dwellest in the clefts of the rock, whose habitation is high; that saith in his heart, Who shall bring me down to the ground? Though thou exalt thyself as the eagle, and though thou set thy nest among the stars, thence will I bring thee down, saith the LORD.

What makes this passage relevant to our modern era, and to this topic of space travel, is this famous statement in human history: "The Eagle has landed." This was a triumphant declaration of the accomplishment of humankind when the Apollo 11 mission successfully landed on the moon. Coincidently, when considering (v.4), the Apollo Moon Lander was named the Eagle. It should be also noted that Apollo is one name in the hierarchy of false Greek gods. Despite humankind's accomplishment to "set thy nest amongst the stars" (v. 4), God is stating that nothing is greater or higher than He (v. 3). This has been an ongoing warning since the Garden of Eden, applicable to both humans and Satan.

23.

GENETIC MANIPULATON

We live in a modern era of increased knowledge, technological advancement, and increased rapid travel. Pertaining the latter days, this increase is alluded to in God's Word:

Daniel 12:4
But thou, O Daniel, shut up the words, and seal the book, *even* to the time of the end: many shall run to and fro, and knowledge shall be increased.

Nahum 2:4
The chariots shall rage in the streets, they shall justle one against another in the broad ways: they shall seem like torches, they shall run like the lightnings.

With all of these increases, advancements in genetic research have also continued. This includes stem cell research, disease detection, organ and tissue transplants, and genetic cloning.

While some of these advancements have been well received as positive, enhancing, and, at times, life-changing and life-saving, other advancements, heralded as major breakthroughs, may in fact be detrimental to human life. More notably, some of these advancements may be in violation of the Divine order of God's creation.

One such example is the experimental area of GMOs (Genetically Modified Organism). The result of this research has led to such breakthroughs as (1) sliced apples that don't spoil when left on the counter for an extended time, (2) farmed salmon that grow much faster and larger than wild, natural salmon in the ocean, (3) and corn, soybean, and canola crops that are resistant to herbicide spraying, and in some cases contain insecticide within the DNA of the seeds to prevent crop failure due to insect infestation.

The problem with all of this is no one knows for certain what the long-term effects on human health will be over ten, twenty or thirty years. Certainly, no studies have been conducted on the hereditary implications of such dietary changes either. One possible clue to this long-term effect may be revealing itself in a subtle, yet massive way. The farmed crops of corn genetically modified with insecticide kill the insect when it starts to feed on the crop, in turn reducing the need to spray insecticide over large areas.[150] Corn is a harvested crop that has many uses: (1) humans eat corn niblets and corn on the cob, (2) corn is used as cattle feed, which ends up in the food chain for humans in the way of beef, (3) corn is used to make corn syrup, which has all kinds of applications within processed foods, (4) and corn starch is often added to fructose to form High Fructose Corn Syrup (HFCS) as an additive to many soft drinks and added to canned and frozen fruits to preserve the flavor.[151] Bottom line, corn or traces of corn is throughout the human dietary food chain. This means people are continually ingesting a vegetable that contains traces of pesticide. While this may not kill a human as it kills an insect through its intestinal tract, it may certainly irritate the human intestinal tract, especially over prolonged exposure.

While the first genetically modified crop was in 1982, starting with tobacco, GMOs really started to take off in the early 1990s.[152] Coincidentally, ever since, the TV commercials for stomach acid and acid reflux relief products have also exponentially increased. Is there a connection? By the time we find out, it may be too late. This is just one aspect of many regarding the serious issues surrounding the implementation of GMO products. For more in-depth analysis on this topic, I highly recommend watching *Food Matters* (2008) and *Genetic Roulette* (2012).

Through many discussions on this topic with a good friend of mine, who is also a pastor, he pointed out something that was very subtle within the Scriptures, yet very profound.

Genesis 1:11–12
And God said, Let the earth bring forth grass, the herb yielding seed, and the fruit tree yielding fruit after his kind, whose seed is in itself, upon the earth: and it was so. And the earth brought forth grass, and

herb yielding seed after his kind, and the tree yielding fruit, whose seed was in itself, after his kind: and God saw that it was good.

Reading this passage, we see that God "said." As mentioned earlier in this book, God *spoke* everything into existence. Twice in this Scripture we discover it was God's intention that all vegetation would either yield the "seed after its kind" or the "seed was in itself." This is one tenet of God's overall creation—and it is an important one. For, without the seed bearing forth, ongoing propagation of any particular species of vegetation would not occur and would not continue the species. This vital part of the eco-system of God's creation would cease to exist. Lo and behold, along comes man and says, "I have a better idea! Let us make watermelons and oranges and such—without seeds!"

Now, this may seem trivial to many, especially to those who find eating a seedless watermelon more appealing, but there is a serious undertone here. Despite man's self-proclaimed ingenuity, seedless watermelons cannot reproduce themselves. This subtle change of genetics has led to further manipulation and alteration of God's intended creation. In fact, attempts to genetically clone various species of animals, has more often than not ended in absolute failure despite the heralded and famous "Dolly" the sheep successfully cloned in Scotland in 1996.[153] Secular scientists' push to elevate cloning to new heights, such as the cloning of humans, could produce results that may bring forth the unthinkable.[154] This was alluded to in Steven Spielberg's blockbuster film *Jurassic Park* (1993), in which DNA of extinct dinosaurs was found preserved in amber (fossilized tree resin) and revitalized and incubated within a surrogate ostrich egg. This may not be just the notion of science fiction anymore, as soft tissue and blood cells were recovered from the remains of an extinct Tyrannosaurus Rex, near Bozeman, Montana in 2005.[155] This announcement conjures up thoughts of wild possibilities, but at the same time brings a sobering realization that this creature may not be some seventy million years old. No, not at all. This discovery ultimately points to the real possibility that this creature was only thousands of years old, if not less. As we covered in Section Two, God's Word clearly describes humans and dinosaur-type creatures co-existing—not separated by sixty-five million years. The evidence continues to mount to support this.

When we consider the recent advancements of genetic research and pair these with the ancient knowledge brought to ancient humans—the genetic contamination through the direct interaction and manipulation of fallen angels, we begin to see and recognize what Jesus really meant when he said, "But as the days of Noah were…" (Matthew 24:37). God's word continues to describe this repetition of human experience over history:

Ecclesiastes 1:9–10
The thing that hath been, it is that which shall be; and that which is done is that which shall be done: and there is no new thing under the sun. Is there any thing whereof it may be said, See, this is new? it hath been already of old time, which was before us.

In Foundational Point Three we looked at the term "his way" (Genesis 6:12) as referring to Satan's way about the corruption of "all flesh" (genetic contamination). Obviously, this corruption was a result of the direct interaction and manipulation of ancient humans and God's creation. Again, as Jesus stated in Matthew 24:37, through scientists' recent exploration, manipulation, and alteration of genetics it seems this influence is repeating in modern times.

As we saw concerning the Tower of Babel, humanity is capable of amazing feats when people are unified of one accord. Unfortunately, in times of past and present, this includes being unified of one accord against the will of God:

Genesis 11:6
And the LORD said, Behold, the people is one, and they have all one language; and this they begin to do: and now nothing will be restrained from them, which they have imagined to do.

This defiance of the will of God stems from the original defiance of God by Satan. This has fostered an all-out defiance of what God has already created. On this basis, we are going to highlight a few Scriptures generally overlooked and/or misunderstood.

Genesis 3:13–15
And the LORD God said unto the woman, What is this that thou hast done? And the woman said, The serpent beguiled me, and I did eat. And the LORD God said unto the serpent, Because thou hast done this, thou art cursed above all cattle, and above every beast of the field; upon thy belly shalt thou go, and dust shalt thou eat all the days of thy life: And I will put enmity between thee and the woman, and between thy seed and her seed; it shall bruise thy head, and thou shalt bruise his heel.

This passage speaks about God discovering that Adam and Eve ate the fruit from the Tree of Knowledge of Good and Evil, a forbidden fruit (Genesis 2:16–17). God also discovers that this incident was manipulated and influenced by Satan (disguised as a serpent). However, focusing our attention on God's statement, "And I will put *enmity* between thee and the woman, and between *thy seed and her seed…*" (emphasis added), two points need to be highlighted: (1) enmity means hostility, animosity, resentment, and pertaining to ill feeling. It also refers to bad blood. This is between Satan and a human (the woman, Eve). (2) God clearly states that this enmity will also extend between "thy seed" (Satan's seed) and "her seed" (the human woman's seed). God is speaking about *two* different seeds here—the seed of fallen angels, specifically Satan, and the seed of humans. This is specifically referring to genetics and to genetic offspring. The word seed used here is derived from the Hebrew language as follows:

Seed—*Zera* (2233)—fruit, sowing time, carnally, child

However, this Hebrew word *Zera* is actually derived from the Hebrew word *Zara*:

Seed—*Zara* (2232)—to sow, bear, conceive

God's statement in this Scripture comes prior to the genetic lineage of Adam and Eve, the arrival of the fallen angels at Mount Hermon, and the advent of the Great Flood—the regrettable decision to destroy the majority of the genetically corrupted creation.

This is a definitely a foreshadow of things to come. While many mainstream churches preach and teach God's Word, the majority focus on certain Scriptures, from certain books of the Bible. For example, common teaching is usually derived from the book of Matthew, Mark, Luke, John, Acts, etc.; somewhat deeper teaching is usually derived from Romans, Corinthians, James, Timothy, etc.; but much of the Bible is left ignored. This is unfortunate and a real tragedy on many levels, since roughly thirty to forty percent of the Bible deals with prophecy—the things to come. The actual percentage of Prophetic Scriptures is an unknown variant dependent on the ongoing accumulation of biblical knowledge through research and Spiritual revelation. However, prophecy can be found from Genesis right through to Revelation. While many leaders and teachers in many churches either ignore prophecy or are simply afraid to teach about it, prophecy is not necessarily all about knowing the future. More specifically, it is a verification of who God is, and that He is who He says He is—with absolute, one hundred percent accuracy and certainty. The Apostle Paul alludes to the importance of prophecy:

1 Corinthians 14:4–6
He who speaks in a tongue edifies himself, but he who prophesies edifies the church. I wish you all spoke with tongues, but even more that you prophesied; for he who prophesies *is* greater than he who speaks with tongues, unless indeed he interprets, that the church may receive edification. But now, brethren, if I come to you speaking with tongues, what shall I profit you unless I speak to you either by revelation, by knowledge, by prophesying, or by teaching?

Based on this premise, we are going to highlight another passage of Scripture, and importantly, how this pertains to our future:

Daniel 2:42–43
And as the toes of the feet were part of iron, and part of clay, so the kingdom shall be partly strong, and partly broken. And whereas thou sawest iron mixed with miry clay, they shall mingle themselves with the seed of men: but they shall not cleave one to another, even as iron is not mixed with clay.

This passage is part of an overall description of the Prophet Daniel's interpretation of the vision King Nebuchadnezzar received in a dream as outlined in Daniel 2. The king sees a statue divided into four main parts: (1) head of gold, (2) chest of silver, (3) waist of bronze, and (4) legs of iron. Daniel interprets the actual meaning of the metaphoric image as, (1) head of gold—Babylonian Empire (v.38) referring to the current king of Babylon. Verse 39 refers to the successive empires that follow after Babylon. (2) Chest of silver—Medo-Persian Empire, (3) waist of bronze—Greek Empire, and (4) legs of iron—Roman Empire. This is a prophecy of the future world stemming from the vantage point of understanding at the time.

Amazingly, a fifth aspect is also described within verses 42 and 43. The two legs of iron have feet that are "…part of iron, and part of clay, so the kingdom shall be partly strong and partly broken." First of all, through human history, the Roman Empire (the two legs of iron) eventually became divided into two centres of power, Rome and Constantinople—thus the two legs that both extend and separate from the main body of the statue (historical lineage). Secondly, the once unified states of Rome eventually became separate countries of now both east and west Europe (the former empire). This is symbolized by the two feet, whose toes are "part of iron, and part of clay" fractured with strength (iron) and brittle weakness (clay). This reinforced by the phrase, "…so the kingdom shall be partly strong and partly broken." God's Word goes on to say, "And whereas thou sawest iron mixed with miry clay…" The word *miry* used here is derived from the Greek word *krima* (2917) which means condemned, condemnation and damnation. It seems this future version of the former Roman Empire will be partly strong and partly condemned, not just "partly broken" (separated).

Based on this, the next phrase comes into focus: "*they* shall mingle themselves with the *seed of men*: but they shall not cleave one to another, even as iron is not mixed with clay" (emphasis added). It seems sometime in the future from Daniel's perspective *they* (other than men, other than humans) will mingle (mix) with the *seed of men* (one seed of two seeds mentioned in Genesis 3:15). The verse goes on, "but they shall not cleave one to another, even as iron is not mixed with clay." Interesting statement here as the word *cleave*, defined in this biblical context, means strongly or emotionally attached, adhering to, abiding by, and being faithful to. This is referring to the context of marriage, between a man and a woman, as it is stated in Genesis 2:24.

The question then must be raised—who are *they* (mentioned twice in v.43)? I think, so far in this book, we have answered that question. If *they* are separate from men (other than humans), and we understand *they* are not animals, nor God, then, by deduction, *they* are the other spiritual beings, angels. More specifically, in the context of *miry*, *they* are the fallen angels. Certainly, *they* have no part in God's intended design of man, woman, and marriage (cleaving) between them.

It should be noted that there is a recent and ongoing shift in gender identity and gender assignment within society. There has been a shift towards *transhumanism*, basically defined as the reengineering of human mental and physical attributes beyond normal human capabilities. This shift is actually a concerted departure from the primary foundation of God's intended creation and procreation between man and woman.

This future version of the former Roman Empire, from *our* perspective, is most likely our present time, if not our immediate future. In addition, this future version of the former Roman Empire is not exclusive to the boundaries of eastern and western Europe. Note that most government capital buildings, especially in the United States, are built with Roman, Greek, and even Egyptian architecture, as with the Washington Monument obelisk (Egyptian) as an example. Remember, the Fourth Kingdom upon the earth will "devour the whole earth" (Daniel 7:23).

In Section One and Two, we covered the relationship between fallen angels and false gods in ancient times. In Foundational Point Seven, we covered the relationship between fallen angels and *extraterrestrials* in modern times. As presented, this is simply a shift in Satan's presentation of fallen angels to mankind from times of old (an old mindset and concept of existence) to modern times (a *new* mindset and concept of existence). While humanity may have changed somewhat over history, some things remain the same. While Satan's presentation to humanity has somewhat shifted, his ultimate goal has not changed.

Considering the fairly recent surge in alien abduction cases, over the past several decades, starting with the well-published case of Betty and Barney Hill in New Hampshire on September 19, 1961, what is at the heart of this phenomenon? Many seem to speculate that *they* are here to help us, *they* are observing us, *they* are performing experiments on animals and humans to either ensure our future, or to ensure *their* future—it is not totally clear. However, the answer at the heart of this phenomenon is definitely genetic experimentation and manipulation ("But as the days of Noah were..."). Despite the fact that thousands of reported cases worldwide describe sperm taken from men and, at times, fetuses removed from women—it is a secret. It remains a secret (relatively speaking) because, as researcher Dr. John Mack noted, that the victims of *alien* abduction are part of a club that no one wants to join. Actual abductees have a hard time coming forward and openly discussing their personal experiences of terror. It remains a secret since media-controlled information, it seems, has gone into shutdown mode lately. While eye witness reports have increased, media reports have actually dropped off in recent years. Any comprehensive information has been relegated to published books, dedicated television programs on specialty networks, and internet sites. It remains a secret also because many have a busy lifestyle between jobs, family, and self-interests. Many either don't have the time, or feel it necessary to allocate time to this topic awareness. It remains a secret since many of the popular film releases relegate this phenomenon to pure fiction and fantasy. Reality is reduced to the remotely possible and not the immediate probable. It remains a secret since hoaxes, many of them, deflect the truth. Hoaxes, for the most part, seem to get more news attention than real, spectacular events. Finally, it remains a secret since it has been asserted for decades, if not close to a hundred years, that top secret and classified departments of our militaries and scientific organizations have been directly interacting with known *alien* entities. This has been a closely guarded secret. Again, I highly recommend *Top Secret/Majic: Operation Majestic-12* and the *United States Government's UFO Cover-up* (1996) by nuclear physicist, Stanton Friedman.

Yet, worldwide overall, despite all the secrecy, millions of UFO sightings have occurred. Tens of thousands of alien abductions have been reported, and thousands of mutilated cattle have been reported in the U.S. alone. All the while, our sophisticated radio-telescopes and observatories report nothing. Still searching. Nevertheless, some aspects and clues remain, staring us all right in the face.

24.

SECRET SOCIETIES AND THE COMING ANTICHRIST

WHY ALL THE SECRECY? IF THESE *EXTRATERRESTRIALS* ARE TRULY HERE TO HELP US, and if *they* are (and have been) truly interacting with our elite and covert agencies, then why all the secrecy? Some individuals would argue the "powers that be" don't want to create mass hysteria. This explanation seems quite odd and flies in the face of reason, especially when one considers that the masses have been flocking to the movie theatres hungry for stories about aliens—the number one theme of Hollywood movie releases, as previously mentioned.

If the extraterrestrials are indeed here to help us and have been working in conjunction with official, yet secret, agencies—then why not tell us all the good news? Most, if not all, of humanity can surely understand and relate to good news. Right? Unless, of course, it isn't good news. Here the lie begins to unravel. The truth now begins to be revealed. As in the film *Wizard of Oz* (1939), the curtain is pulled back and the ugly truth reveals that, all along, it was an eccentric professor who had deceived and manipulated everyone. Humanity is being set up for the greatest and strongest delusion ever orchestrated since the Garden of Eden. Satan enticed the first man and woman, Adam and Eve, by saying:

Genesis 3:5
For God doth know that in the day ye eat thereof, then your eyes shall
be opened, and ye shall be as gods, knowing good and evil.

Today, intellectual men and women, competent within scientific disciplines and military forces, are being enticed with the same lie: the exact same offer of *knowledge* beyond one's wildest imagination. Remember, as we covered in

Section One, it is the fallen angels who are the teachers, not demons. Satan's presentation may have changed since the Garden of Eden, but the overall lie—the overall strong delusion—remains the same.

2 Thessalonians 2:11–12
And for this cause God shall send them strong delusion, that they should believe a lie: That they all might be damned who believed not the truth, but had pleasure in unrighteousness.

Send used here is derived from the Greek word *pempo* (3992), which means to dispatch (from the view or point of departure), to transmit, and thrust in. God is clearly stating that He will *dispatch* something or someone to the world. The modern day definition of *dispatch*:

1. to send off to a destination or for a purpose
2. deal with (a task, problem, or *opponent*) quickly and efficiently (emphasis added)

The second stage of the banishment of Satan and the other fallen angels (that are not in chains) permanently *from* Third and Second Heavens, exclusively to First Heaven (the confines of Earth, Revelation 12:12), is an event that takes place in our not too distant future. This event will coincide with the removal of the raptured believers in Christ from out of First Heaven, known as the Rapture ("Therefore rejoice, ye heavens, and ye that dwell in them…Revelation 12:12.) The modern day definition of *transmit*:

1. cause (something) to pass from one place or person to another
2. broadcast or send out (an electrical signal or radio or TV signal)

Satan and the fallen angels in the second stage of banishment will *pass from one place to another*. The second definition is very interesting in the context of *broadcasting signals*. As covered earlier in the chapter UFOs and Alien Abductions, the Spiritual realm is both the *seen* and the *unseen* within the Electromagnetic Light Spectrum. God is going to *broadcast* the fallen angels from out of the *unseen* Spiritual realm, into the *seen*, physical realm of Earth. Obviously, at the point of this happening, the remaining people (the left-behind unbelievers and undecided) after the Rapture clearly witness this happening:

Woe to the inhibiters of the earth and of the sea! For the devil is come down unto you, having great wrath, because he knoweth that he hath but a short time. (Revelation 12:12).

That "short time" is the Tribulation period (seven years total) between the event of the Rapture and the event of the Second Coming.

The third definition of the Greek word *pempo: thrust in* alludes to God's temperament at the time of this second stage of banishment. He is angry and He has had enough. He is essentially *hurling* or *flinging* Satan and the fallen angels down to Earth, in righteous anger.

Pertaining to all three connotations of pempo and the translated word sent, these are words that suggest coming from outside of our world to within our world. Therefore, the point is raised once more that fallen angels are not demons. Why would God dispatch, transmit, or thrust demons into our world from Second Heaven? They are already bound to the earth as terrestrial spirits.

Considering everything we have just covered regarding 2 Thessalonians 2:11–12, let us carefully consider the detail of the Scriptures that lead up to this point of no return. This is also describing a future time when the Antichrist, the devil's son and future world leader ("son of perdition"), is revealed to the world. This point in time is marked by a general *apostasy* (a falling away) from Christian values and from the general Christian church, as we covered previously concerning 1 Timothy 4:1:

2 Thessalonians 2:1–12
Now we beseech you, brethren, by the coming of our Lord Jesus Christ, and by our gathering together unto him, That ye be not soon shaken in mind, or be troubled, neither by spirit, nor by word, nor by letter as from us, as that the day of Christ is at hand. Let no man deceive you by any means: for that day shall not come, except there come a falling away first, and that man of sin be revealed, the son of perdition; Who opposeth and exalteth himself above all that is called God, or that is worshipped; so that he as God sitteth in the temple of God, shewing himself that he is God. Remember ye not, that, when I was yet with you, I told you these things? And now ye know what withholdeth that he might be revealed in his time. For the mystery of iniquity doth already work: only he who now letteth will let, until he be taken out of the way. And then shall that Wicked be revealed,

whom the Lord shall consume with the spirit of his mouth, and shall destroy with the brightness of his coming: Even him, whose coming is after the working of Satan with all power and signs and lying wonders, And with all deceivableness of unrighteousness in them that perish; because they received not the love of the truth, that they might be saved. And for this cause God shall send them strong delusion, that they should believe a lie: That they all might be damned who believed not the truth, but had pleasure in unrighteousness.

In Noah's time, the majority of the world fell away from God, and Satan and the fallen angels took control, with no opposition. It is the same here, except the Rapture removes the believers from the Earth just before this global takeover is repeated.

The term *delusion* is a very descriptive word used in 2 Thessalonians 2:11. The word means:

1) A belief held with strong conviction despite superior evidence to the contrary.
2) As a pathology (deviation), it is distinct (apparent) from a belief based on false or incomplete information, confabulation, dogma, *illusion, or other effects of perception* (emphasis added).

Satan, the great deceiver, is also a master of illusion. What appears to be a spaceship the size of a football field might not be a display of advanced technology at all—it may in fact be a complete illusion brought forth by sorcery. Especially when it has been witnessed that such a craft can suddenly appear (transform) out of a ball of light the size of a basketball—or even dematerialize into a ball of light.

Today's scientists (through pride) often comment that modern technology would have appeared like *magic* or *sorcery* to ancient man. However, what if that is exactly what it is? Technology is based on knowledge, more specifically the knowledge to use and manipulate various types of *crystals* and *electromagnetic energy* sources (invisible energy)—exactly what is utilized in sorcery and witchcraft; exactly what was taught to ancient man by the fallen angels; and perhaps, and what continues to be taught (in secrecy) to select, covert military and scientific agencies. It needs to be stated that physical "nuts and bolts" super-advanced craft are also being developed by these covert agencies as a result of this enhanced knowledge. This creates a blurring of the lines where the spiritual influence intersects with the physical and vice versa.

Once again we find profound confirmation in 1 Enoch:

1 Enoch 8:5
You have seen what Azazyel has done, how he has taught every species of iniquity upon the earth, and has disclosed to the world all the secret things which are done in the heavens.

In these last days, the world will gravitate to a three-tiered system: (1) a one-world economic system (cashless society), (2) a one-world political system (expansion of the G-7 and G-20 forums within a New World Order) and, (3) a one-world religious system (common ground sought between Christian, Islamic, Hindu, and Buddhist factions—currently being orchestrated by the Vatican).

This three-tiered system will eventually be under the direction of the coming Antichrist, the Devil's son (diametrically opposite to the Son of God, Jesus Christ). The Antichrist will come in the form of a man, fathered by Satan and born into the world by a willing, human mother. Just as unholy conception brought forth genetically altered life forms by the fallen angels and earthly women in Noah's time, this bodily form of a man will have a spirit, but he will not have a soul. He will be an unholy abomination in the eyes of God. To the rest of the world, he will appear to be a miracle worker. He will appear to have all the answers regarding economics, politics, and religion. Here are a few descriptions of this coming world leader:

Daniel 7:25
And he shall speak great words against the most High, and shall wear out the saints of the most High, and think to change times and laws: and they shall be given into his hand until a time and times and the dividing of time.

Daniel 8:23–25
And in the latter time of their kingdom, when the transgressors are come to the full, a king of fierce countenance, and understanding dark sentences, shall stand up. And his power shall be mighty, but not by his own power: and he shall destroy wonderfully, and shall prosper, and practise, and shall destroy the mighty and the holy people. And

through his policy also he shall cause craft to prosper in his hand; and he shall magnify himself in his heart, and by peace shall destroy many: he shall also stand up against the Prince of princes; but he shall be broken without hand.

Daniel 9:27
And he shall confirm the covenant with many for one week: and in the midst of the week he shall cause the sacrifice and the oblation to cease, and for the overspreading of abominations he shall make it desolate, even until the consummation, and that determined shall be poured upon the desolate

Daniel 11:21
And in his estate shall stand up a vile person, to whom they shall not give the honour of the kingdom: but he shall come in peaceably, and obtain the kingdom by flatteries.

Daniel 11:36–37
The king will do as he pleases. He will exalt and magnify himself above every god and will say unheard-of things against the God of gods. He will be successful until the time of wrath is completed, for what has been determined must take place. Neither shall he regard the God of his fathers, nor the desire of women, nor regard any god: for he shall magnify himself above all.

1 John 4:2–3
This is how you can recognize the Spirit of God: Every spirit that acknowledges that Jesus Christ has come in the flesh is from God, but every spirit that does not acknowledge Jesus is not from God. This is the spirit of the antichrist, which you have heard is coming and even now is already in the world.

Just like his father, he will deceive through pride, intellect, and logic. In fact, his presence will impact the entire world in an extremely profound way:

Revelation 13:13
And he doeth great wonders, so that he maketh fire come down from heaven on the earth in the sight of men...

I firmly believe that many have overlooked this particular Scripture. In fact, this Scripture becomes even more emphatic when one considers the Hollywood film detailing the real life story of the *alien* abduction event of Travis Walton, coincidentally entitled *Fire in the Sky* (1993). Since it is Satan who gives his son, the Antichrist, his seat and great authority over a unified conglomerate of nations (Revelation 13:4–5, confirming the fourth beast, the Fourth World Kingdom of Daniel 7:23), the Antichrist will have full authority over the remaining fallen angels. I believe the world will be thrust into an era of unparalleled manifestations of UFO and extraterrestrial visitations not seen since the days of Noah—"...he maketh fire come down from heaven on earth in the sight of men" (v.13).

Some people, after lightly considering such a scenario, have said, "If this happens, I will move to the mountains and live off the land." The reality is, with the fallen spiritual realm *thrust in* by God and fully manifested on planet Earth, there will be no place to hide. Not even prepared underground bunkers will offer refuge or safety. Nevertheless, for now, the *secrecy* continues.

For those in the know, there is a definite unbroken thread in the chain of non-disseminated, carefully guarded, information (knowledge). I believe the following Scripture has also not been understood to the fullest:

Revelation 13:4
And they worshipped the dragon which gave power unto the beast: and they worshipped the beast, saying, Who is like unto the beast? who is able to make war with him?

We know the *dragon* is Satan (Revelation 12:9). It is clear that Satan gives power to this first beast that appears, this end-time, unified conglomerate of nations as confirmed in Daniel 7:23. This first beast is *not* the Antichrist, as taught in many church circles. The first beast represents kindreds, tongues, and nations (Revelation 13:7) and rises from the sea (Revelation 13:1), just like the three previous world kingdoms that rose from the sea before it (Daniel 7:3). Land masses rise from the sea. Continents rise from the sea. Therefore, diverse nations rise from the sea, populated by peoples, kindreds, and tongues (various ethnic languages).

The second beast that appears (Revelation 13:11) is the Antichrist. This second beast is a "man" who comes out of the earth (again, land masses where nations are formed and various peoples populate—rising from the sea). Many theologians have taught, in my opinion incorrectly, that this second beast is the *false prophet* who endorses the Antichrist. Many have overlooked that Jesus Christ is the true Prophet (with a capital P, John 7:40). Just as Jesus is the King of kings, and Lord of lords (capital K and L, Revelation 19:16), He is the true Prophet (Divine) over all other prophets (mortal). Essentially, Jesus is much more than a prophet, since He is God in the flesh (John 1:1, 1:14). Therefore, the *false prophet* (Revelation 20:10) is just another name for the Antichrist and not some other religious leader. That title is reserved for the metaphoric prostitute cited in Revelation 17 and 18. God isn't being redundant by stating "…where the beast and the beast are…" (v.10), not repeating the word *beast* twice in reference to the first and second beast as described in Revelation 13, who both end up in the lake of fire, before eternity.

Perhaps the least understood aspect of Revelation 13:4 is the phrase, "And they worshipped the dragon…" Most people don't believe in the Devil, let alone worship him. Understanding this, then who are "they?" Especially, who are they that apparently *knowingly* worship Satan (the dragon)? The second phrase, "…and they worshipped the beast…" is more understandable since people, in their distracted living, tend to worship money, possessions, careers, social media, politicians, movie and music stars, sports, etc. These people worship the first beast (conglomerate of nations), which *indirectly* is worshipping Satan, "the god of this world" (2 Corinthians 4:4). However, we need to clearly define who is *knowingly* worshipping Satan.

The obvious answer would be Satanists. These individuals are clearly involved in ritualistic worship of Satan. Unfortunately, there is more to this picture than meets the eye. Researcher Gene Aven, who I quoted earlier in the chapter Stonehenge, equates this revelation of guarded knowledge, metaphorically, to the structure of an onion. The onion is structured in layers. As one peels back a layer, another layer is present, until finally, one reaches the central core of the onion. The central core represents the real existence of Satan. The inner layers represent organizations and groups directly involved with the inner core, yet somewhat shielding Satan's real existence. These are the various highly secretive Satanist groups. The next inner layers are the deeply involved secret societies. Some would point to the Illuminati, the Council of 13, and the Luciferian Society as examples. The middle layers represent organizations and groups that, on the surface, may seem rational and non-threatening, yet have undercurrent factions within. These are the mainstream secret societies. Some would point to Freemasonry (having up to 33 levels within itself), the Bilderberg Conference, and the Bohemian Grove Society as examples. The outer layers represent organizations and groups that also may seem rational and non-threatening and, being surface level, actually serve as a drawing card and/or recruitment machines for the inner layers. These are general public and private organizations well supported within mainstream society. Some would point to the Skull and Bones fraternity (Yale University), the Scroll and Key fraternity (Harvard University), and the Rhodes Scholars (Oxford University) as examples.

These examples of secret societies represent only a small glimpse of the overall landscape of layer upon layer of spiritual deception woven into our society. Overall, each progressive layer has its own set of beliefs, tenets, and rules of engagement. This is a very convoluted area of study, and can be confusing and misleading. Yet, when one does serious research and analysis of these layered factions, it all points to the *core* of the matter—Satan.

Considering the coming Antichrist, the Devil's son, there are some very astonishing symbols within established global organizations, such as the United Nations.

Considering this symbol, we are going to refer back to the book of Isaiah that we partially covered in the chapter Lucifer's Ancient Throne.

Isaiah 14:12–14
How art thou fallen from heaven, O Lucifer, son of the morning! *How* art thou cut down to the ground, which didst weaken the nations! For thou hast said in thine heart, I will ascend into heaven, I will exalt my

throne above the stars of God: I will sit also upon the mount of the congregation, in the sides of the north: I will ascend above the heights of the clouds; I will be like the most high.

We learn some important information in this passage of Scripture:

(1) Lucifer is cast out of Third Heaven (this is the Kingdom of Heaven).

(2) Lucifer states that he will ascend into Second Heaven to exalt his throne higher than God's throne in Third Heaven.

(3) Lucifer also states that he will ascend above the heights of the clouds (First Heaven) into Second Heaven (the universe) and into Third Heaven (his self-proclaimed kingdom of heaven) to become like the most high.

It is also stated here that he is "cut down to the ground, which did weaken the nations" (v.12). However, understand that Lucifer was cast down as *far* as the ground—he is not, at this point in time, *bound* by the ground (the Earth) exclusively. This is also an interesting statement in itself that his initial fall has weakened, or has adversely affected the nations of the Earth.

When we examine the symbol of the United Nations we see a few interesting aspects. All the nations of the Earth are represented in the northern hemisphere. Southern nations and continents, such as South America, Australia, and Antarctica, have been brought up to be viewed from the northern vantage point. Normally, from a viewpoint *above* the Arctic Circle, these land masses would be hidden from view by the wider Equator. The lower parts of Africa and South America would also be blocked from view.

Of course, Lucifer states in Isaiah 14:13, "I will sit also upon the mount of the congregation, in the sides of the north…" The congregation, meaning the people of the Earth and the current world political powers (centre of influence), does in fact lie in the northern hemisphere—not in the southern hemisphere.

The latitude and longitude lines of the globe when viewed from the northern vantage turn into the same configuration as the cross-hairs in a rifle scope. In other words, this is a concentrated and deliberate viewpoint.

Lucifer states in Isaiah 14:14, "I will ascend above the heights of the clouds; I will be like the most high." So this northern viewpoint of Earth is also viewed from the vantage point of space—or Second Heaven, and as alluded, can be viewed from Third Heaven as well.

Portrayed surrounding the Earth is the olive branch wreath. This is a symbol of strength with peace. This happens to be the same wreath the Caesars of the

Roman Empire wore as a symbol of authority, a crown. Of course, the Roman Empire was in power at the time of the crucifixion of Jesus Christ.

As a reminder, Lucifer and the majority of fallen angels have been banished from the Kingdom of Heaven, but they still have the ability (at this time) to travel throughout First and Second Heavens, in addition to presenting themselves before the throne room in Third Heaven.

Hence, the advent of UFOs (for real) and director Steven Spielberg's decision to portray special United Nation teams as the official contact between humans and extraterrestrials in the film *Close Encounters of the Third Kind* (1977). By the way, not only did Spielberg direct this film, he actually wrote the script, although with some advisory assistance.[156]

25.

THE 'MAN' FROM THE NORTH POLE

As we saw with the United Nations symbol, there seems to be a fixation on the north region of planet Earth. Perhaps not so coincidently, as we covered in Isaiah 14:13, Lucifer declares that he will reign over the world from the "sides of the north." Another detail worth mentioning, many of the famous pyramid structures around the world actually face due north.[157] This point also serves as a subtle, yet important, reminder of Satan's pervasive influence under assumed names such as Orion, Quetzalcoatl, Qu'qu'matz, and Virococha being the driving force behind the devoted builders of these ancient structures as we covered in Section Two. Full devotion of worship purposely aligned to the north. In addition, the military complex NORAD (North American Aerospace Defense Command), headquartered in Colorado, jointly monitors all airspace movements (in partnership with Cheyenne Mountain underground facility in Wyoming and CFB Winnipeg, Manitoba).

While the extensive monitoring of NORAD reaches globally, there is a greater focus towards the northern hemisphere in relation to Russian, Chinese, and European airspace movements. In addition, I am quite aware that NORAD monitors "unidentified" movements in world airspace daily. This source remains confidential. Various Hollywood films depict a connection between UFOs and the North Arctic region such as *The Atomic Submarine* (1959) and *The Thing* (1982). Through my discussions and research, I have learned that many appearances of UFOs tend to originate from the north, despite a recent surge of interest about anomalies discovered in Antarctica as depicted in films such as *The X-files: Fight the Future* (1998) and *Alien vs. Predator* (2004). The significance of all this will become apparent as we take a closer look at yet another fixation on the north. This particular fixation reaches and influences many individuals on a global scale. This fixation, more specifically, focuses on the North Pole.

The legend of Santa Claus has been around for centuries. However, the *true* origin of Santa Claus goes back to the beginning of civilization. Ancient Babylonians worshipped the return of the sun at the lowest point in the winter season, December 21 being the shortest day of the year, with a weeklong festival of eating and drinking. December 25 was the midpoint of their ritual celebration. This was eventually assimilated as the Roman festival *Saturnalia* as civilizations peaked and rose between the Egyptian, Median, Greek, and Roman empires. This in turn has been assimilated by our modern culture, from the early church (the Church of Rome), as the holiday (holy day) celebration of the birth of Jesus Christ, the Son of God. Prior to Christ we need to recognize that celebration of December 25 has its roots in paganism.

The first point we need to address is that December 25 is *not* the birthday of Jesus Christ. No one knows the actual birthday of Jesus. This is possibly due to the birth of Jesus occurring *after* Joseph and Mary had submitted to the Roman census, thus avoiding his detection (Luke 2:1–6). King Herod the Great heard of the prophecy of the coming King of the Jews, the Son of God, from wise men travelling in search of Him. Herod became nervously concerned of a rival king. After God warned the wise men not to report Jesus' actual location to Herod, the king ordered the death of all newborn sons in the territory of Judea (Matthew 2:1–23). Just prior to this, God warned Joseph to flee to Egypt with Mary and the newborn, Jesus (Matthew 2:13).

When Herod died, an angel instructed Joseph to return to Israel and settle in Nazareth (Matthew 2:19–23). What we do know is that Jesus was born during the fall and most likely at or near the harvest season. This is based on the mention that shepherds were tending their flocks grazing at night, obviously a high point in the crop growing season (Luke 2:8). Supporting this, all the local inns were full, possibly due to the successive Jewish Feasts in September, Rosh Hashanna (Jewish New Year), Feast of Trumpets, Yom Kippur, and the Feast of Tabernacles (Jewish harvest festival). Mary and Joseph had to resort to a possible stable, having a manger (animal feeding trough), for a place to stay (Luke 2:7). These are the basic facts. We will take a look at some more detailed facts. Here are some points to consider:

> ▸ 1 Chronicles 24:7–18 describes 24 courses, or stations, of the Jewish temple priesthood that rotate on a yearly basis.

- Luke 1:5 reveals that the priest Zacharias was on duty during the 8th course, known as Abijah.

- Shortly after his scheduled duty, the daughter of Zacharias, Elizabeth, conceived John the Baptist (Luke 1:23–24). Elizabeth is the cousin of Mary (v. 36).

- This places the conception of John the Baptist sometime in the month of June and then his birth sometime in March, nine months later.

- The angel Gabriel informed Mary of her conception of Jesus six months into Elizabeth's pregnancy (Luke 1:26–27). This places the conception of Jesus into the month of December.[158]

- This is at a time on the Jewish calendar known as Hanukkah, also known as the Festival of Lights. Interesting that Jesus Himself is referred to as the Light of the World.[159]

These points give us the month of Christ's birth, which is September (nine months after conception). Considering the actual day of the birth of Jesus, another interesting fact is Luke 2:22–28 describes Mary coming to the Temple for her own purification forty days after the birth of Jesus. This event coincided with Yom Kippur, also known as The Day of Redemption, or The Day of Atonement.[160] The Feast of Tabernacles occurs five days after Yom Kippur.

This also coincided with the month of Elul (also known as the Time of Repentance) at the beginning of her forty days of purification (Jewish law, Leviticus 12:1–4), which also coincided with the first new moon of Elul on the Hebrew lunar calendar.[161] This event was recorded by the Magi (the wise men) on stone tablets now on display in the British Museum in London.[162] This correlates with our own solar calendar date of September 11, 3 B.C.[163] This puts the birth of Jesus in mid-September.

The Church of Rome honours December 8 as the Feast of the Immaculate Conception of Mary.[164] This feast is an obligation for all Catholics to attend Mass.[165] A baby is normally born approximately nine months after conception. So, exactly nine months after this particular date, the Church of Rome also celebrates the Feast of the Nativity of Mary, which is honoured on September 8. Here, the conception of Mary (not Jesus) is apparently December 8 and *her* birth is apparently September 8. These are the two current celebrated dates focusing on Mary. As we continue, we will discover that these and other important dates have been altered.

Keeping this point in mind, and considering the development of the early church, two progressions were occurring: (1) the dissolving and fading away of the previous Roman Empire, and (2) the early development of both Christianity and the early formation of the Church of Rome (Roman Catholic Church), in which a transition was taking place to assimilate, or Christianize, former pagan traditions, customs, and rituals. In some cases, there was also acceptance, or tolerance, of some of the former pagan traditions, customs, and rituals. Just as the Roman Empire had accepted and tolerated many false religions of the world to achieve stability in governance (i.e. the creation of the Pantheon Temple in dedication to all gods), the early Church of Rome had somewhat continued in this approach as well. For further details on this subject, I highly recommend *Pagan Christianity* (2002) by Frank Viola and George Barna.

Some of the earliest records of a repositioning of important dates began with Hippolytus. The following points will put all this into perspective:

▸ Hippolytus lived during the early third century and was considered an authority in the Christian church in Rome. Hippolytus argued for March 25 as the conception date of Jesus Christ, in line with his calculation of the anniversary of the creation of the world, and simply added nine months to declare His birth date as December 25. This effectively usurped the historical pagan feast at the Spring Equinox, along with the pagan feast at the lowest point of the year, nine months later, during the Winter Solstice in December.[166]

▸ Pope Damasus I, in the early part of 380 A.D., convinced Emperor Constantine I to issue an edict to all Christians to practice the religion of Rome.[167]

▸ He continued to impress his authority over all Christians within the Roman Empire. This signaled the rise of the Roman Church authority over the faded Roman Empire.[168]

▸ During this time, the Christmas Midnight Mass became celebrated as a Catholic Holy Day on December 25. Again, this was to reinforce the replacement of the pagan worship ritual of the sun god at midnight with a higher attendance of Christians at the Midnight Mass on December 25. Although for some time both rituals were conducted on the same evening, the "Christ –Mass" slowly became accepted as the official celebration of the Nativity.[169]

▶ Eventually, the feast on September 8 celebrating the honour of Mary giving birth to Jesus was proclaimed as the day of celebration of Mary's own birth instead.[170]

▶ The previous holy day celebrating the Immaculate Conception of Jesus on December 8 also became proclaimed as the day of celebration of Mary's own conception.[171]

▶ Pope Pius IX declared the Immaculate Conception of Mary an official article of faith on December 8, 1854, which pronounced Mary as sinless.[172]

Fully understand that the Immaculate Conception of Jesus has been changed, or at least altered, to include the Immaculate Conception of Mary by the early Roman Church. This is contrary to God's Word, which states, "For all have sinned, and come short of the glory of God…" (Romans 3:23) including the human woman, Mary, and of course, with the exception of Jesus Himself, who was God in the flesh (John 1:1–2:14). To this day, two opposing factions hold to their own side of celebrating these two important days.[173]

Despite assuming and reallocating an ancient pagan ritual, and despite attributing December 25 as the birth date of Jesus, we have in recent times (over the course of only a few decades) increasingly neglected the *intended* (but false) purpose of celebrating *Christ*mas. Instead, we have exalted a rival figure to Jesus on this very same day. This rival figure is known as Santa Claus. How would you feel if all the people you knew shifted the focus and celebration of your birthday to someone else, particularly on that day? Not only that, but shifted the majority of the focus to someone considered imaginary? Now, imagine for a moment what God sees.

We are told Santa Claus originates from Saint Nicholas, a bishop who lived in medieval Turkey.[174] However, even if that were true, Saint Nicholas was a mere man—described as a good man yes, but a mere, *mortal* man. We are told throughout Scripture that all who believe in God and Christ are saints (the ancient term for a Christian believer). As the 1st and 2nd Commandments tell us, we are not to exalt ourselves (saints), nor any other god, statue, or icon above God (Exodus 20:2–3)—and we have done just that. We have exalted Saint Nicholas to the level of godhood by the immortal branding and worship of Santa Claus. We have also created various idols in the worship of Santa Claus. But what does a real life bishop from Myra, Turkey, really have to do with the North Pole?

The first thing we need to recognize is that this widespread Santa Claus fixation is especially impressionable on children. The Scriptures tell us children are a gift from God, and therefore, they are in parents' temporary care and subsequently are to be released to society in God's care upon maturity (Psalm 127:3). The worship of Santa Claus has redirected the focus of many children from the full understanding of who Jesus Christ was and is—His purpose on this Earth, and the very reasons it is important to have a personal relationship with Him. Those who believe in Jesus Christ believe He is coming back to Earth to claim his believers and establish His Kingdom on this Earth ("thy kingdom come, thy will, will be done on earth as it is in heaven"). This is the Second Coming. So if God is real, and Jesus is real—then His return is surely real. So then the question is, why would anyone, or anything, disrupt our children's learning of this?

This answer lies in the real identity of Santa Claus. There is, and always has been, a rival to Jesus Christ. We have covered that his name was Lucifer in heaven who was banished with one third of the angels and became Satan on Earth. We covered that, at the time of his banishment he arrogantly spoke five "I wills" toward God (Isaiah 14:12–14). One was, "I will exalt my throne above the stars of God" (v.13), exactly what the rival Santa has done—exalt himself above Jesus Christ (who came to Earth as God in the flesh). Another threat was, "I will look down upon the mount of the congregation from the northern parts," and this is exactly where Santa now supposedly resides—at the North Pole! It must be stressed here: St. Nicholas is from Turkey. He is *not* from the North Pole.

Let's take a closer look at Santa. Lucifer apparently sustained wounds during the heavenly war just before his first stage banishment. Many Hollywood movies depict Satan, in human form, as a cripple—using crutches or in a wheelchair, or using a *cane* with a limp. One such film was *Angel Heart* (1987). Santa is well known as the giver of *candy canes*! These candy canes have been primarily directed to children, seemingly as an enticement.

The Kingdom of Heaven, as previously covered, is Third Heaven. It is either in a spiritual dimension beyond Second Heaven (the universe), or perhaps deep within the universe itself. Either way, it is a *physical* place where spiritual beings reside, as described throughout Revelation 21 and 22. Despite the immense distances throughout the universe, in the billions of light years, Lucifer and his fallen angel followers can travel through the galaxies beyond the speed of light. They are referred to as beings of light in the Scriptures (morning stars) and there is increasing phenomena of "balls of light" displaying intelligent movements with UFO activity. The fantasy film *The Wizard of Oz* (1939) depicts the "good witch of the north," Glinda, materializing from out of a ball of light (an orb) along the yellow brick road. The name *Lucifer* translates to light bringer or light bearer (associated words: lucent/translucent, etc.) and he is referred to as the "angel of light" (2 Corinthians 11:4). Santa, apparently, also has this same ability to visit millions of homes in a single evening calculated by engineers as traveling at the *speed of light*. As we covered previously, the term Beelzebub is a reference to the "chief devil," or Satan (also known as the lord of the flies). Beel is derived from the Hebrew name Baal (a false god) and zebub is a Hebrew term referring to "one who flits from place to place" (modern translation: one who *zips* from place to place). Interesting that Santa's worldly trek coincides with the yearly ritual of NORAD tracking Santa throughout his worldwide journey to millions of homes in different countries.

As we've covered, Lucifer, or Satan, is and has been worshiped by many cultures under different names throughout history such as the feathered serpent god (Mayans, Aztecs, and Incas), or the great horned god (First Nations). Santa apparently has chosen *horned* animals to pull his sleigh (levitation) at the speed of light. Reindeer feed on poisonous mushrooms called *Amanita Muscaria,* also called *fly agaric*, which are scarlet red with white spots (the same two colours of Santa's suit) well known for LSD effects on humans.[175] Mind-altering drugs are often used in sorcery and witchcraft rituals for spiritual *journeys*, such as *Peyote* (mescaline) often used by indigenous Shamans of Mexico and bordering southern states.[176]

As a note here the colloquial term "chasing the dragon" was commonly attributed by opium and heroin addicts desperately trying to replicate the euphoric experience of a first high. Satan uses the seduction of a first high to lure people down the self-destructive path of outright addiction, while never really achieving the initial experience.[177]

The Latin word *Pharmakeia* is where we get the word pharmacy (drugs)—but many people don't realize *Pharmakeia* is the same root word for witchcraft or sorcery. The CIA experimented with LSD to enhance telepathy abilities with "psychics" in locating terrorists throughout the world (project MK-Ultra—*remote viewing*).[178] Santa Claus also seems to have this same ability to perceive who has been good or bad with telepathic precision. It should be noted that many Hollywood movies that deal with sorcery and witchcraft, such as the *Harry*

Potter and the Philosopher's Stone (2001), *The Lord of the Rings: Fellowship of the Rings* (2001), *Santa's Slay* (2005) and *Sint* (2011) are commonly released near or during the Christmas season.

Witchcraft (sorcery) and mind-altering drugs (dividing of roots) are mentioned together in the Book of Enoch, demonstrating the relationship between them as confirmed by the Latin word *Pharmakeia*. Once again, this advanced knowledge was taught to ancient humans by the direct influence of fallen angels:

1 Enoch 8:3–4
Amazarak taught all the sorcerers, and dividers of roots: Armers *taught*
the solution of sorcery;

Continuing on, we refer to Santa's *helpers* as elves. Elves, gnomes, and goblins have always been associated with demonic activity in occult circles. Santa himself is referred to as a "jolly old elf"—I would stress the word old having the connotation of *ancient*. I would also stress that Santa, as the leader of the elves, is presented in human form, therefore either the reference of a "jolly old elf" is by association, or perhaps Santa does have an alternate identity.

Many fondly refer to Santa as Saint Nick. The term Old Nick in the British Isles is a direct reference to Satan. Once again, I emphasize the word old having the connotation of ancient. Merriam Webster's Dictionary defines Old Nick as "used as a name for the devil."

We all know how Santa comes down the chimney into our homes. But I am amazed at how few people stop and think that Santa actually enters the dwelling through the *fire place*.

Perhaps the most overlooked aspect of the rival figure of Santa to Jesus Christ is simply this:

S-A-N-T-A is S-A-T-A-N

Unfortunately, the good works of the *man* Saint Nicholas have been grossly twisted into a rival figure, somehow originating from the North Pole (a place desolate of human life), who uses sorcery in every aspect of his existence and has managed to deceive "all kindreds, tongues, and nations" of the Earth into worshipping this *imaginary* figure that does not offer salvation as a free gift to all—but rather promotes receiving (not giving) material things, that in the end are finite and worthless when compared to the gift of everlasting life.

Santa is an imaginary figure overwhelmingly promoted as real. Conversely, Jesus Christ, who is real, is often labeled as imaginary.

Deception implies lies. Satan is referred to as "the father of lies" (John 8:44). We as parents have a responsibility to teach truth to our children. We are in fact lying to our children that Santa is real. To an impressionable child, the shock of the realization that Santa is not real and their parents lied to them can trigger a profound sense of mistrust, initiating the downward spiral of the breakdown of the family unit. We have a responsibility to teach our children who God is and who Jesus is. Customary and popular practices are not necessarily what God wants from us. They do not have an everlasting meaning, especially if they have their roots in deception. Consider the following Scriptures from the book of Jeremiah:

Jeremiah 10:1–5
Hear ye the word which the LORD speaketh unto you, O house of Israel: Thus saith the LORD, Learn not the way of the heathen, and be not dismayed at the signs of heaven; for the heathen are dismayed at them. For the customs of the people are vain: for one cutteth a tree out of the forest, the work of the hands of the workman, with the axe. They deck it with silver and with gold; they fasten it with nails and with hammers, that it move not. They are upright as the palm tree, but speak not: they must needs be borne, because they cannot go. Be not afraid of them; for they cannot do evil, neither also is it in them to do good.

What is truly amazing about this passage is not just that God is describing the customary fashioning of a tree cut down from the forest and adorned with silver and gold trinkets, but the fact that the prophet Jeremiah lived roughly six centuries prior to the birth of Christ (between 640 and 570 B.C.).[179] This means the *Christ*mas tree actually predates the birth of Christ by at least several centuries and, therefore, this ancient custom had nothing to do with Christ's birth. God sternly proclaims, "Learn not the way of the heathen, and be not dismayed at the signs of heaven; for heaven are dismayed at them" (v.2). Obviously, God is not pleased with this tradition. In light of this, consider the following Scripture:

Romans 1:25
Who changed the truth of God into a lie, and worshipped and served the creature more than the Creator, who is blessed for ever. Amen.

Worshipping the "creature" more than the Creator can extend to worshipping the creation more than the Creator. The cut-down tree adorned with trinkets becomes an object of idol worship (Exodus 20:4–5). In fact, considering this premise, the *Christ*mas tree becomes the symbolic representation of the creation. The garland becomes the unbroken "thread of life." The many lights (originally candles) become the stars of the universe. The trinket decorations, many in the form of coloured globes, become the celestial bodies or planets of the cosmos. Topping off this ancient custom is the placement of the pinnacle *star*, commonly regarded as the "star of Bethlehem." Yet knowing this custom predates the birth of Christ, its roots in paganism, this pinnacle *star* cannot possibly be the star of Bethlehem. Is it possible that this pinnacle *star* is the pinnacle position over all the other *stars*? Is it possible this pinnacle star is the representation of the chief *morning star*, Lucifer? Carefully consider this Scripture from Isaiah once again:

Isaiah 14:13
For thou hast said in thine heart, I will ascend into heaven, *I will exalt my throne above the stars of God*: I will sit also upon the mount of the congregation, *in the sides of the north*: (Emphasis added)

Most people recognize that the meaning of *Christ*mas is slipping away, year by year, and they feel empty about the commercialization and the materialistic focus of *Christ*mas ("the *love* of money is the root of all evil," 1 Timothy 6:10). Depression is high at this time of year and suicides are at a yearly peak. Why? Someone once told me we are spiritual beings, created by God. When our focus is off God and on something else, our inner spirit feels empty and isolated—even though we can't exactly describe why. The more we try to fill that spiritual void with something else, the emptiness increases, even though we may fool ourselves with temporary fixes. The extreme to this premise is those who profess that God is not real are, in fact, the first ones to cry out to Him when they are hanging off a cliff by their fingernails. The inner spirit (God created) cannot help but cry out when it knows it is about to be reunited with, or separated from, God—forever.

The word *Christmas* itself comes from the Church of Rome's original ceremony of Christ-mass, as we covered, which eventually replaced the pagan celebration centered on December 25. The term *mass* is a reference to the "celebration of the Eucharist" as defined by the *Merriam-Webster Dictionary*. *Eucharist* is a reference to the celebration of Communion (partaking in the wine and bread in remembrance of Christ at the Last Supper) as a tenet of the Church of Rome.

However, according to the Church of Rome, the tenet of *Transubstantiation* as defined by the *Merriam-Webster Dictionary* is:

> The miraculous change by which according to Roman Catholic and Eastern Orthodox dogma the Eucharistic elements at their consecration become the body and blood of Christ while keeping only the appearances of bread and wine.

The consecrated bread and wine are supposedly *transformed* by a priest into the actual body and blood of Christ. Communion, as derived from the Last Supper, was meant to be symbolic remembrance of what Christ did for us on the Cross (bread = body broken; wine = shed blood), not *transformed* into the actual body and blood of Christ. In speaking to His disciples, Christ meant this is a symbolic sense, not literal, although the disciples, offended, misunderstood His meaning at the time (John 6:47–56). Ingesting human flesh and blood, actual or intended, is nothing short of both cannibalism and a satanically inspired ritual (Leviticus 17:10–14). For more details on this topic, I highly recommend *Preparing for Eternity* by Mike Gendron and *Faith Undone* by Roger Oakland.

The yearly ritual of the wafer host as the body of Christ supposedly transformed by the priest into the *actual body* of Christ, especially on *Christ*mas eve, is actually a reenactment of the *death* of Christ—not in celebration of the *supposed birth* of Christ. The original Last Supper was on the eve of Christ's death. Although we are to be eternally grateful for what Jesus did for us on the cross, where Jesus Christ defeated death and took on all the sins of humanity, He is now the risen, *living* God (Romans 6:4, 10:9; Mark 16:6). He is *off* the cross (Romans 8:34). He died *once* for all (Romans 6:9, Hebrews 9:28).

Not commonly known is the fact that the round, thin wafer used in Communion and the subsequent Eucharist by the Church of Rome does not have its roots in the early church. It actually predates Christianity to the pervasive paganism of Babylon. More specifically, it was part of the false worship of the Sun god, once again. Alexander Hislop explains:

> Although the god whom Isis or Ceres brought forth, and who was offered to her under the symbol of the wafer or thin round cake, as "the bread of life," was in reality the fierce, scorching Sun, or terrible Moloch, yet in that offering all his terror was veiled, and everything repulsive was cast into the shade.[180]

This false worship extended from Babylon to many post-flood ancient cultures throughout the Middle East and was foundational to Egyptian worship of both the Sun and the Moon. Worshippers would receive the thin, round wafers from their priests in the temples and ingest them to be closer to their gods. The historical alliance of Egypt and Rome through the legendary relationship of Cleopatra and Julius Caesar ~ Mark Antony subsequently created the bridge for this wafer ritual to be assimilated into the early Church of Rome. Alexander Hislop goes on to state:

> If the sun-divinity was worshipped in Egypt as "the Seed," or in Babylon as the "Corn," precisely so is the wafer adored in Rome. "Bread-*corn* of the elect, have mercy upon us," is one of the appointed prayers of the Roman Litany, addressed to the wafer, in the celebration of the mass. And one at least of the imperative requirements as to the way in which that wafer is to be partaken of, is the very same as was enforced in the old worship of the Babylonian divinity.[181]

Jesus broke unleavened bread with His disciples at the Last Supper. He did not hand out thin, round wafers in the intended shape of the Sun or Moon.

The fact of the matter is that *Christ*mas is really not about Christ. It was never about Christ—as the celebration of December 25 predates the birth of Christ by some four thousand years. We have tried to turn a pagan/satanic ritual into a Christian holiday. The fact of the matter is that Satan wants it back. This is why the supposed meaning of *Christ*mas is slipping away. The *spirit* of *Christ*mas is not the Holy Spirit, it is not Jesus Christ—it is certainly not God. It is the false spirit, the false light, the "god of this world"—the "angel of light"—Lucifer, the fallen angel—Satan. We need to recognize that there is actually a beautiful side to evil.

I hope this information serves to enhance your understanding of the true origin of Santa Claus, the "man from the North Pole," and Satan's manipulation and influence of *Christ*mas over the people of the world. This chapter of the book is not meant to offend anyone; it is only meant to reveal the truth. Sometimes, the truth is not what we what to hear—but it is still the truth.

Many people still cling to tradition, especially when it has been the foundation of one's childhood upbringing and for many of us it has formed the basis of who we are and what we know. Yet, the Bible refers to the people of the world as being spiritually blind and deceived. As Christians we are in the world, but not to be of the world (1 John 2:15–17, Romans 12:2). For this reason, Christians will be generally hated by those who cling to the world and its traditions and forsake the Creator, God almighty (Matthew 10:22, Mark 13:13). I have to ask myself: if God is real, and Jesus is real, then how are we deceived? What are the mechanisms, or the methodology, that we are deceived by? And, more importantly, what is impairing our view that we are spiritually blind? The title of this book now comes into full focus; the people of the world are certainly under *A Strong Delusion*. Think about that carefully.

26.

A PERSONAL TESTIMONY

THE FOLLOWING IS A TESTIMONY OF A SERIES OF EVENTS I PERSONALLY experienced during one summer in the mid 1990s. Everything stated is as accurate and truthful as possible. The end result, or conclusion, to the information presented herein has profound implications to the true origin of man (as stated in God's Word), as well as serious questions as to the future of mankind (as stated in God's Word).

One Wednesday evening, I received a phone call from a complete stranger who lived several hours away from my place of residence. For the purpose of keeping the identity of this individual confidential, I will refer to him as Paul. The initial phone call went like this:

I said, "Hello."

"Hello… is this Mark?"

"Yes."

"Hi, Mark, My name is Paul. We both know a mutual friend——."

"Oh, yes."

"Yeah, he suggested that I give you a call. I understand that you investigate, or do a lot research into UFOs."

"Well, yes, I do a lot of research in that area, as well as other areas of research as well. How can I help you?"

"Well…I've got some pictures to show you. I was wondering if we could meet sometime; I would like to get your opinion on these."

"Oh yeah, what kind of pictures?"

"Well, I don't really want to discuss this over the phone, but these pictures would really be worth your while to come to (undisclosed town) and see."

"Well…I do go to (undisclosed town) occasionally to visit (friend). Maybe we could arrange a time to meet in the future."

"That would be great."

"Paul, I understand that you don't want to talk about this in detail over the phone, but could you tell where these pictures were taken?"

"Well… they were taken here, in (undisclosed town), just outside of town— in a secluded area."

"Oh yeah…is there, or do you know of, any stigma attached to this area?"

"Well…yes…it is an area where people go to have a few beers, you know… out in the woods, and…it is kinda known for occult-type activities. You know, dead animals, and that type of thing."

"Yeah, well, I will take your name and number down and I will give you a call when I can be in the area."

After I my conversation with Paul, I went about my business at home, and it wasn't more than a few hours later that it dawned on me that I would be on a business trip that coming weekend approximately 45 minutes south of where Paul was living. So I called up my friend to inform him that I would be coming to visit Sunday afternoon and asked him if he knew of this guy, Paul. He said he did and suggested we meet at his place. I then called Paul back and explained to him the good news and made arrangements.

That Sunday afternoon I met Paul at my friend's house. My friend and I had had many deep discussions on various topics before, but we hadn't seen each other for a while, so naturally the conversation became intense over a few hours. After which Paul suggested that I go over to his place so he could show me a picture in private. I accepted and we then walked a couple of blocks to his home. Paul took me downstairs to where his desk was set up.

"Before I show you this picture, I want to tell you a story. Some friends and I went out to this area outside of town, around midnight. We went out to have a few beers and gather to shoot the breeze. We weren't partying, just a casual get together. There were five of us. Then all of a sudden somebody said, 'What's that over there?'

"We were parked off the side of a dirt road, along the tree and bush line, close to an area that opened up into a glade, a grassy area. From one end of the glade this bright object came through from out of the trees and bushes. It was oval in shape and made no sound at all.

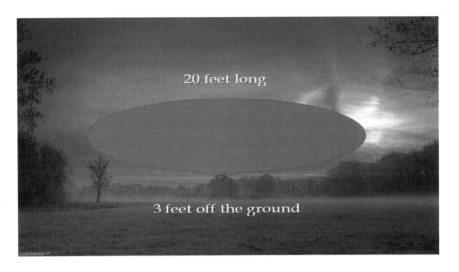

20 feet long

3 feet off the ground

"It was moving slowly, about three feet of the ground. It was about twenty feet in diameter. We were all stunned as we watched this thing. The weird thing about it is that it was so bright—very hard on the eyes to look at. And yet it didn't light up any of the bushes, or any trees nearby. It was kind of purple in colour, very similar to one of those mercury vapour lamps that you see in some industrial buildings. You have to understand that this thing was not like the proverbial UFO that one hears about. It wasn't made up of nuts and bolts, or metallic. Even though it was very bright to look at, it seemed as though you could look right through it—kinda translucent.

"One of the people with us, a girl, had a camera in the car. I didn't realize it at the time, but she had taken some pictures while we were watching this thing. Then it disappeared on the other side of the glade. We just looked at each other in disbelief and decided to get away from there. We were all freaked out. So we left.

"A couple months later, I was walking through the mall. I was kind of in a hurry when I bumped into that girl who was with us that night. She said, 'I've got some pictures of that night, do you want one?' Until then I had not talked to anyone about what had happened that night. But quickly I said sure. She handed me the picture and I just put it in my coat pocket and walked out of the mall.

"I came home and went downstairs, here to my desk, when the phone rang. As I was talking to my buddy, I pulled the picture out of my coat pocket and started glancing at it. And while I was talking on the phone, I noticed that there was nothing on the picture, except the rear part of the car that was parked that night. So, I put the picture down, thinking that there was nothing to look at—a waste of a picture.

244

"I had put the picture down, standing up against a pile of books on the desk. There was a lamp behind the books. As I was still talking on the phone, I kept glancing at the picture. And then, all of a sudden, I started seeing something in the picture. I told my buddy I would phone him back later.

"I picked up the picture, held it up to the lamp so that the light was *behind* the picture and, sure enough, I could see something appearing in the frame. Mark, I have talked to scientists, parapsychologists, and even talked to some ministers of the church—and no one can give me a straight answer. Here is the picture. I am not going to tell you what is in it; I want *you* to tell me what *you* see."

Paul handed me the picture. I must admit I was quite intrigued with his story and anxious to view what was in this picture. So, I held it up against the light with the lamp behind the picture. I stared intently at the frame. I could definitely see the car parked in the picture and after about twenty seconds Paul said, "Do you see anything?"

"No, I don't."

At this point, I am thinking to myself I had come all this way for nothing.

"Keep looking."

I focused intently on the picture and moved it slightly back and forth to get the best position against the lamp behind it. And then, suddenly, this *image* began to appear in the frame.

"I'm beginning to see something."

"What do you see?"

"I see a face, like the proverbial *alien* face."

245

"Oh yeah, what else do you see?"

I concentrated more, but I was not able to make out anything else on the picture. Paul then took a pen and pointed to the forehead of the *alien* face.

"How about here?"

Sure enough, another face began to appear in the forehead of the *alien* face. It was a sideways profile with the forehead, nose, chin, and mouth—with horns coming from the top of its head!

Paul said, "And…how about here?"

Paul pointed to another area of the face and again, another face image began to appear. This one was a straight-on profile with horns again, but with a funny, corrugated mouth. Paul showed me another face location.

According to Paul there were as many as twelve different faces incorporated inside the *alien* face, although personally I only saw three. Paul also went on to say he had taken the picture to a parapsychologist and that the woman, after viewing the picture, ran out of her office after exclaiming that the images had started to move in the picture. I personally did not witness this event, nor did I see the faces move in the picture.

Paul asked me what I made of this. And then it dawned on me. I remembered an episode of *Sightings* (a program on UFO and other paranormal occurrences in the mid-1990s, executive produced by Henry Winkler) where an amateur video was shot on a beach in Florida one evening. You could tell there were many people present on the beach by all the sounds in the background. There were many gasps and exclamations at what was being filmed out over the surf. In the video there was a luminous, oval-shaped object hovering in a still position. Again, since the video was fairly clear, you could tell this oval light was not made of steel, or material of any kind. Instead it was translucent, exactly like the oval light initially witnessed by Paul and his friends.

Florida Coastline Sighting

Suddenly, to the amazement of everyone watching, a smaller, round "ball of light" seemed to drop out from the bottom of the oval light. It hovered below for a brief time and then proceeded on its own in a horizontal direction.

Florida Coastline Sighting

I put the pieces together in my mind. I reflected that I have researched God's Word and understood that Satan was once an angel in heaven called Lucifer. He was also known as the "angel of light." He is also referred to as the "prince and power of the air." Another label, in the Hebrew language is *Beelzebub*. *Beel* is derived from *Baal* (lord of the flies/god of the underworld) and *zebub* means "one who *flits* from place to place." Or in modern language, one who *zips* from place to place.

Satan and the fallen angels were once angels in heaven. In their purest form they are beings of *light* (morning stars). As such, they travel in that mode (within the light spectrum—both 5 percent visible and 95 percent invisible). This is exactly why there were multiple faces in Paul's picture. Satanic, fallen angel faces at that. All melded together, as light, in a pack formation. As a completely separate incident in Florida, a group of people also witnessed an oval-shaped light—which they immediately assumed was a UFO. Conversely, on Paul's photo, an *alien* face emerges with other satanic faces incorporated inside it—all materializing from a similar sighting of an oval-shaped orb of light. In comparison, the oval-shaped light caught on video in Florida demonstrates that a single entity (one ball-shaped light—an orb) is "leaving the pack" (the oval light itself comprised of multiple entities—all melded together as one light) and going off on its own specific direction. As a note to Paul's sighting, what looks like an oval-shaped orb of light to the naked eye, is sometimes captured as something else on film.

Paul went on to tell me he had taken the picture to photo labs to try developing a duplicate copy of the picture. Since the type of camera used was a Kodak Instamatic camera (one where the pictures develop in front of you) and the negative is incorporated into the actual picture frame itself, no copies can be made that work the same way (to reproduce the appearing images). Whatever was caught on film is caught within the negative film portion only. This is exactly why the images were not readily seen until the light of the lamp on the Paul's desk was positioned *behind* the instamatic photograph.

Later, I learned from my friend that the area where this photograph was taken was well-known for occult activities, confirming what Paul had told me. Ritual ceremonies have occurred here and mutilated animals have been found throughout the area (including foxes, deer, and other wild animals).

This has been consistent with my research. Wherever you find UFOs, you will find the occult and wherever you find the occult, you will find UFOs. Where a lot of people, including researchers, get confused is the fact that UFOs (suggesting a seemingly evolutionary principle) and paranormal activities (suggesting a seeming spiritual principle) are actually interrelated. This is exactly the conclusion that Dr. Jacques Vallée inevitably came to, that extraterrestrials have more in common with demons (actually devils), than with advanced interstellar visitors. This is part of the overall deception Satan is presenting to mankind. What better way to separate and split society into arguing factions than to sow seeds of deception on both sides of the argument. Are we evolved beings, whereby the UFO presence is a demonstration of highly advanced, evolved beings? Or is God real, who in fact created both humans and the angels, and the UFO presence is simply a complete deception, a revised presentation to modern society, a strong delusion—one that is gaining momentum towards the end of days?

What I have stated in this personal testimony is absolutely true. This book, overall, has presented the facts. It is up to you to decide.

CONCLUSION

SOME INDIVIDUALS WOULD ARGUE, "WHAT DIFFERENCE DOES ALL THIS MAKE? I have my faith in the Lord; I go to church; I am saved and that's all that matters to me."

I have heard this very statement countless times. The information presented in this book is not just to inform the reader, it is retrievable information when talking to others, Christian or not, to help answer serious and deeper questions *others* might have. Therefore, for the person who considers himself or herself as a Christian, it is not just about self. It is about sharing the Gospel and the truth to others. This is the Great Commission. As Christians we are to go forth into the world with knowledge, the truth, and the good news:

> Matthew 28:18–20
> And Jesus came and spake unto them, saying, All power is given unto me in heaven and in earth. Go ye therefore, and teach all nations, baptizing them in the name of the Father, and of the Son, and of the Holy Ghost: teaching them to observe all things whatsoever I have commanded you: and, lo, I am with you always, *even* unto the end of the world. Amen.

A key phrase here is, "…teaching them to observe all things whatsoever I have commanded you…" Based on this, I have been led to study God's Word and to observe all things for some thirteen thousand hours over the past thirty years. I have been led by the Holy Spirit to do this. God has not brought me through all of this for nothing. There is a reason for everything.

The sad thing is, from the Lord's perspective, "Many are called, but few are chosen" (Matthew 22:14.) This is echoed in the following Scriptures:

Matthew 7:13–14
Enter ye in at the strait gate: for wide *is* the gate, and broad *is* the way, that leadeth to destruction, and many there be which go in thereat: because strait *is* the gate, and narrow *is* the way, which leadeth unto life, and few there be that find it.

When we consider the events of Noah's Flood and the destruction of Sodom and Gomorrah, very few were spared and saved. The remaining majority of society was involved beyond salvation. Even more sobering is the following statement made by Jesus Himself:

Matthew 7:21–23
Not every one that saith unto me, Lord, Lord, shall enter into the kingdom of heaven; but he that doeth the will of my Father which is in heaven. Many will say to me in that day, Lord, Lord, have we not prophesied in thy name? and in thy name have cast out devils? and in thy name done many wonderful works? And then will I profess unto them, I never knew you: depart from me, ye that work iniquity.

These individuals mentioned here are *not* non-believers; these are individuals who obviously consider themselves Christians. As such, they have no doubt gone to church, read the Bible, prayed and, as stated, even cast out devils (demons), and prophesied apparently all in the name of Jesus. Despite all of this, Jesus will reject them. Why? As He states, He never *knew* them.

There was a time when I was involved in the retail industry as a senior sales consultant. One of the key premises to success I learned, and can be applied to many areas of living, is the ability to overcome objections. In regards to the ongoing Christian life in the areas of teaching and learning, I have encountered many objections. Sadly, many of these have come from within the church itself. Here is an overview of some of these objections:

Conclusion

Objection #1: "Don't Glorify Satan!"

I would like to make it absolutely clear that the content of this book, in no shape or form, was ever intended to glorify Satan. In fact, quite the opposite. The purpose of this book is to inform and equip the saints with the knowledge of the truth so that one can avoid the wiles of the devil (Ephesians 6:11) and the pitfalls of deception, which obviously have significantly manipulated and negatively impacted ancient civilizations. Clearly, this manipulation and negative impact has continued throughout our modern civilization. Consider the following:

Ephesians 5:11–12
And have no fellowship with the unfruitful works of darkness, but rather reprove them. For it is a shame even to speak of those things which are done of them in secret.

Two things are highlighted here: (1) Christians are commanded by God not to have any association (active participation) with any area of the enemy's manipulative, offensive, and destructive crusade of false doctrine and spiritual attack. The Scripture (v.11) goes onto say, "…but rather reprove them." The word *reprove* is derived from the Greek word *elegcho* [1651], which means convict, convince, tell a fault, rebuke, and confute, which itself is defined as prove to be wrong or simply to expose. The Greek word *elegchos* [1650] is defined as proof, conviction, evidence and reproof, which itself also means reprimand and condemnation. On this basis, Christians are not to be actively involved in the "unfruitful works of darkness," but rather we are to expose them; to present evidence of them; to condemn them; and to rebuke them. (2) I believe many in the church have misinterpreted this Scripture (v.12). Here, God is *not* saying that we, as Christians, are *never* to speak about these evil works. No, He is stating it is a shame that we even *have* to speak about these things. In order to *expose* something, one has to speak about it! Plain and simple. To say otherwise is actively ignoring the facts, as 2 Peter describes:

2 Peter 3:5–6
For this *they willingly are ignorant of*, that by the word of God the heavens were of old, and the earth standing out of the water and in the water: Whereby the world that then was, being overflowed with water, perished: (Emphasis added)

Again, as Jesus described, "But as the days of Noah were…" The people of today, as with the people of Noah's time, are putting their heads in the sand, ignoring the reality of the times. Ironically, when one puts their head in the sand, their rear is exposed—open to be severely kicked!

Objection #2: "If we pay attention to what we are supposed to do as Christians, then everything will take care of itself."

This statement is actually part-truth only. Satan often deceives by part-truths and by twisting the truth. The part-truth here is revealed by the context of which this statement is actually intended. First of all, Christians are to "pay attention to what we are supposed to do." That much is true. However, this statement by its own merit is absolutely dependent upon the premise that one is, indeed, doing what they are supposed to be doing. While Christians may be called to different functions and passions within the body of Christ, doing what one is supposed to do is truly both submitting to the will of God and heeding the leading of the Holy Spirit. Anything apart from that is operating from the foundation of self, something Satan uses as a foundation to separate one from God. This is the exact lie initially told to Eve by the serpent in the Garden of Eden: "You don't need God, because you will become gods yourselves" (operating by self, paraphrase Genesis 3:4–5).

The second half of the statement is not truth at all. Nothing "takes care of itself." It is God who ultimately is in control. It is God who allows or who undertakes what does or does not happen. The second half of this objection is simply an excuse, a deflection, for the supposed Christian to do nothing at all—especially if they are *not* doing everything they are supposed to be doing. This indifference and lack of spiritual discernment is a breeding ground for deception to creep in, overwhelm, and eventually destroy. We are reminded in 1 Peter:

1 Peter 5:8
Be sober, be vigilant; because your adversary the devil, as a roaring lion, walketh about, seeking whom he may devour…

If we are not sober, vigilant, prepared, discerning, and aware, Satan will walk all over us. Not only that, he will continue to operate behind the veil of both secrecy and deception.

Objection #3: "The church leadership should not be vocal in matters of politics or social issues—our function is to attend to those who are suffering."

This sounds reasonable on the surface. Yet, when one stops to seriously consider this statement and drill down into its deeper implications, the truth becomes revealed. This statement is actually suggesting church leadership should not be pro-active in preventative measures, but instead should resign itself to dealing with the aftermath, the fallout, of the destructive seeds of deception *allowed* to take hold.

Again, this is simply an objection in an effort to avoid confrontation, to avoid offending certain groups or factions, to not get one's hands dirty with any involvement of politics or social issues. This is a defeatist attitude. This is an act of withdrawal from the front lines of the spiritual battle. One does not have to be militant or blatantly ignorant. However, one can certainly stand firmly and boldly to proclaim the truth. It is not up to Christians to change the world; for it is written that the world will reject Christianity right up to Christ's judgment at the Second Coming. However, we can certainly push back at these spiritual attacks to allow the Gospel and the truth to go forth for a season.

Following this premise to its conclusion, it seems this is suggesting that Jesus was not just and righteous when He overturned the money changers' tables, with righteous anger, within the Temple (Matthew 21:12–13). Or perhaps the various prophets in the Old Testament were not just and righteous when they actively confronted and warned the people when they were veering away from God's purpose and will, succumbing to the enemy's deception (i.e. Elijah, 1 Kings 18). This objection, in the end, is simply another act of putting one's head in the sand—and you know the rest.

Objection #4: "God is bigger" (than the issue at hand)

Yes, it is true, God is bigger than any issue or perceived insurmountable problem. God is sovereign over all things. Nothing is too big for God. God certainly plays His role in our lives; after all, He created us and all things. Yet this statement is often misused and abused as an objection to do nothing once again. God does His part, but we have a role to play as well. Whether that may be in prayer—and I don't mean thinking to pray or stating "I will pray for you" and not actually following through, or whether that means to actively get involved in any given situation (by the prompting of the Holy Spirit), we have a role to play. Consider the following passage of Scripture:

James 4:3–7
Ye ask, and receive not, because ye ask amiss, that ye may consume it upon your lusts. Ye adulterers and adulteresses, know ye not that the friendship of the world is enmity with God? whosoever therefore will be a friend of the world is the enemy of God. Do ye think that the scripture saith in vain, The spirit that dwelleth in us lusteth to envy? But he giveth more grace. Wherefore he saith, God resisteth the proud, but giveth grace unto the humble. Submit yourselves therefore to God. Resist the devil, and he will flee from you.

The word *resist* is derived from the Greek word *anthistemi,* which means to stand against, oppose, withstand. These are words of action. These words do not suggest we simply do nothing and expect God to do it all.

We have a role to play. We, as disciples in Christ, are encouraged to be Christ-like (1 John 2:6, Romans 12:1–2, Philippians 4:13). Jesus also told us that we, as disciples, would be capable of doing great tasks and accomplishments in His Name:

John 14:12
Verily, verily, I say unto you, He that believeth on me, the works that I do shall he do also; and greater works than these shall he do; because I go unto my Father.

Those who are raised up as disciples in Christ will press forward and execute "greater works than these…" Again, these are words of action. Our role will also extend beyond this plane of physical existence:

1 Corinthians 6:3
Know ye not that we shall judge angels? how much more things that pertain to this life?

There is much more than to just simply believe in God, or believe in Jesus. Even the fallen angels and demons are beyond mere belief and *know* exactly who God and Jesus are. We as Christians are to become disciples in the faith. We are to go beyond mere belief and go beyond being just mere followers—we are to become disciples in Christ.

What difference does this make? This information is extremely important for three main reasons:

1) We are to witness to the lost. Many people have questions, serious questions, about what is going on in the world. The church in general has failed to answer many pertinent questions and by this, has failed to lead many people to the truth and to a real relationship with Jesus Christ. This failure, overall, is directly due to a very narrow and limited understanding of spiritual matters. As we have covered in the beginning of this book, "My people are destroyed for a lack of knowledge" (Hosea 4:6).

2) We, as Christians and as disciples, are engaged in spiritual warfare. To be successful in this battle we need to put on the full armour of God. We need to be led by the Holy Spirit. I encourage you to read 1 Corinthians 2 as an overview of being led by the Holy Spirit. We need to be informed and equipped with the knowledge of the truth. We need to be discerning in all things pertaining to spiritual matters. We need to pray effectively.

3) When we shine the Light of Truth (Christ in us) in to the darkness, the darkness has to scatter. It cannot remain darkness. By shining the Light of Truth into the darkness Satan's ability to maneuver is reduced; his ability to deceive is exposed and his ability to destroy is rendered inept.

These three important and foundational reasons are my main purpose for writing this book. One of the greatest deceptions ever sown in to this world is the notion that Satan does not exist. Amazingly, this notion is absolutely far from reality. Reflecting on everything covered in this book, it is absolutely apparent that Satan and the fallen realm have drastically impacted human history, right from the dawn of time to present day. Why would the overall majority of ancient cultures be so preoccupied in worshipping the dragon, the feathered serpent, or the feathered snake god 24/7 and dedicating massive structures to him, if Satan did not exist?

However, God is indeed bigger. It is because of Christ in us that we have victory over the evil one. We do not have to fear the enemy. Fear is leverage used by Satan to prevent one from doing something—preventing action. Therefore, the question needs to be raised, how strong and deep is your faith, if you are in fear? For that matter, are you truly born again, or do you just profess to be a Christian? From the words of Franklin D. Roosevelt, at his first Inaugural Address, "The only thing we have to fear is fear itself." For the born-again Christian, these words ring true in the everyday spiritual battle we are engaged in. This book is meant to provide vital knowledge, not to invoke fear.

Many professing Christians today are going through the motions. They may attend a church regularly, but they are not growing spiritually. Many are also oblivious to the fact that we are engaged in a *real* war with a *real* enemy. I fully understand one should not place all their attention on Satan, placing too much emphasis on his power—but at the same time, one should not be indifferent (in some cases, willingly ignorant) to his tactics of deception either. There should be a balance, based on discernment, to the Christian walk.

I have eventually come to the conclusion that there are many, many individuals who are simply sleep walking through life.

1 Thessalonians 5:6
Therefore let us not sleep, as *do* others; but let us watch and be sober.

Again, considering everything that has been addressed in this book, think carefully about where we are as a society in the overall progression leading to the return of our Lord and Saviour. As mentioned at the beginning of this book, Jesus described the people of Noah's time as "eating, drinking and marrying," carrying on with day-to-day living, as if nothing was wrong. They had accepted each gradual level of the overall progression of degradation as being normal— even when their lives had reached an ultimate stage of absolute wickedness, degradation, and chaos.

It is time to wake up.

I pray that this book has been a source of enhanced spiritual knowledge and has been thought-provoking regarding the bigger picture.

I also pray that this book has brought a sense of importance to the use of words and definitions. Lately, I have noticed a great departure in many church circles regarding the validity and necessity of sound doctrine. It is the Holy Spirit that leads us to all truth (John 16:13, 1 John 5:6.) It is the Holy Spirit that reveals this truth through the Word of God—the sound doctrine of Scripture (1 John 5:7.)

It is the Word of God that divides truth from error. It is the Word of God that divides truth from deception. It is the Word of God that divides soul and spirit, and discerns between thoughts and intents of the heart (Hebrews 4:12). It is the Word of God that is the sword that divides the righteous from the unrighteous. In the end, it is the Word of God, the sword, which proceeds from the mouth of Christ who casts judgment on the nations of the Earth at His Second Coming (Revelation 19:11–15.) Just as God spoke everything into existence when He created everything, "and God said..." (Genesis 1), He, in the form of Jesus Christ, will speak specific elements into destruction at His future arrival. Regarding His return, consider His own words regarding the purpose of His first coming:

Matthew 10:34
Think not that I am come to send peace on earth: I came not to send peace, but a sword.

True peace, true victory, and true unity can only come from aligning our spirit with His Spirit. The Word of God is fully revealed through His Spirit. This will be fulfilled at His Second Coming. Therefore, until then, through His Spirit, we must adhere to sound doctrine. Anything else, apart from His Spirit, can only bring chaos and discord, can only bring defeat and can only foster a false unity. This is usually brought about by a departure from His Spirit leading to a discounting of sound doctrine.

Contend for the faith.

May the Lord lead you and bless you as you grow in your walk, and grow in your discipleship!

In Christ's Service,
Mark G. Toop

A NOTE ABOUT THE AUTHORIZED KING JAMES VERSION

There are many versions of the Bible available on the open market in bookstores throughout the world. Newer and revised versions are continually being published and offered. However, how do we know which versions have retained the purity and integrity of God's Word and which versions have deviated from it?

I, for one, maintain that all of the Scripture quotes and references within all of my writings are quoted from the authorized King James Version (KJV). I do this for several reasons.

First of all, I would like to state that the simple gospel, the message of salvation of Christ, can be found and received in various versions other than the KJV. Some examples are the English Standard Version (ESV); the New International Version (NIV); the American Standard Version (ASV); etc., despite various errors of doctrine found in these versions as well. Based on this, I am not *dogmatically* opposed to other versions of the Bible (a so-called King James *only* theology). Having said that, there are various versions that have blatantly deviated from the integrity of the Word (corrupt) and, considering certain other versions, these are found to be absolutely blasphemous. These are versions where the integrity of the Word has been twisted and changed, where the character of the Almighty God has been altered and maligned, and where the simple gospel, a pathway to a real relationship with the savior, Jesus Christ, has been blasphemed and compromised.

As one grows in their relationship with the Lord through their spiritual walk, the Holy Spirit will reveal what is truth and what is not.

Prior to the publishing of the KJV, there was a time when the general population was forbidden to have a Bible, much less able to read one. Imagine, God's people prevented from having and reading His Word. The office of the institutional church was in control, even above the level of power of the ruling kings themselves. The kings were considered in a position of divine rule under God, although subservient to the church leaders who were the proclaimed authority stemming from the *office* of God. The Word was kept behind closed doors and stone walls and used as leverage against both the rulers and the common people of the land. It was the church that became wealthier than royalty by way of the collection of taxes (the institutional church being tax -exempt).

Various men of the Spirit began to challenge this status quo in order to bring the Word to the common people. Men such as John Wycliffe, Martin Luther, William Tyndale, Myles Coverdale and John Calvin pushed for a refined translation of the original tongues into common English. It would be King James I (soon after his crowning) who would meet with the bishops at the Hampton Court Conference in 1604, summon 47 scholars to work within six separate committees, and encourage the careful consideration of the ancient texts and former translations to arrive at a mutual consensus of the resulting translation into English. The King James Version was completed in 1611.

I believe this endeavor came about through Divine intervention. I believe this was a major turning point in human history where the Word would eventually be preached unto all nations. This reaching to all four corners of the earth is one of the final signs of prophecy before the Second Coming of Christ.

My first Bible was a copy of the authorized King James Version. It was given to me by close friends who knew I was becoming interested in studying the Word. It wasn't until much later that it was pointed out to me by another friend that serious studiers and scholars of the Word tend to use the KJV as their main reference, whereas many false teachers tend to use any other version but the KJV—and if they do quote from the KJV, it is done quite sparingly.

There are those who claim that the old English is hard to grasp in today's world of simple, slang and, at times, profane language. I would put to those proclaiming this that the old English is in fact more colourful, more descriptive, and reveals far more depth in understanding in its broad scope of communication. We are losing the roots and essence of our own English language as it is gradually being replaced with 'texts' and 'tweets' that offer singular thought statements, and even worse, sterile, cryptic abbreviations. While our TV sets have gone from black and white, to colour, to high definition and even to ultra-high definition, our own spoken language has been going in the opposite direction.

This is precisely one of the reasons why some of the new and latest translations are corrupt and void of the Spirit. If it is true that the KJV was a result of Divine intervention, then how is it possible that man, and more specifically any singular man, can improve on it? Despite the fact that the KJV has its own inherent errors of translation, these are merely incidental errors and do not detract from the simple gospel of the salvation message. We have to understand that the original translators (although diligent in their work) were also directly influenced by the mindset of the 16th century. Besides, today, in a modern information age, we have the instant ability to access and reference the original Hebrew and Greek language texts and source of translation ourselves. Recent discoveries of ancient sites, artifacts, and manuscripts have also contributed to bringing more clarity and confirmation to an overall understanding of the Word.

On this basis, overall, I hold to and maintain all quotes and references of Scripture from the authorized King James Version of the Bible.

A NOTE ABOUT THE
BOOK OF ENOCH

There are those who say that the "First Book of Enoch" is not included in the Bible because it is not the inspired Word of God. However, despite this opinion, this text (more specifically the segment of the Book of the Watchers) was widely read between 400 B.C and 300 A.D. and was considered Holy Scripture by some of the early scholars of the Middle East. It wasn't until the Council of Laodicea, starting in 363 A.D., that the text was banned from the official canonization along with a large group of other 'lost books' (some of which may *not* be inspired texts). This banishment was executed by the Church of Rome. But despite this fact, the Ethiopic text has maintained Enoch as part of its official canonization.

Also, the Book of Jude (Jude 14–15) quotes a passage from Enoch (1 Enoch 1:9), nearly word for word and precedes this with a paraphrase of 1 Enoch 1:1. Ask yourself, how does *any* passage of Enoch (supposedly an uninspired text) end up included within the official canon of the inspired Word? Why did Jesus quote the Book of Enoch on several occasions? Why did God allow this to happen?

The Book of Enoch was considered lost until renewed interest in the text surfaced during the time of the Reformation (rebellion of the doctrines of the Church of Rome by the people holding to the actual Word of God) in the 1400s. The official rediscovery was attributed to the famous explorer James Bruce in 1773 returning from Abyssinia with three copies of the Ethiopic text. It was retained and read by Beta Israel (Ethiopian Jewish communities who had settled in the northern horn of Africa spoken in the Ge'ez language).

In the early 1900s, portions of the Greek text surfaced, and later, seven fragments of the Aramaic text were discovered in Cave 4 (part of the dead Sea

Scrolls). However, it is portrayed in the text that it was Enoch himself who wrote the text prior to the Great Flood.

The bottom line is that perhaps it is Satan who doesn't want the truths revealed in this text to be known, such as (a) the total genetic manipulation of human and animal kind through a falling away from God's plan and laws; (b) the reality of genetic abominations in our past history, such as Giants, Minotaurs, Centaurs, Cyclops, Pegasus, etc.; (c) the truth of the origin of demonic, terrestrial spirits (which has been perpetuated through the ancient customs of Samhain—now known as Halloween); (d) the truth of the origin of Astrology, Cosmetics, Jewelry, Fabrication of Metal Alloys, Fabrication of Weaponry, the Disciplines of Witchcraft, etc. These are only but a few of some *very* serious questions and points for consideration.

On a personal note, I was introduced to the Book of Enoch in the mid-1990s. I was engaged in a serious study of the Word and related research, growing in my faith and a deeper understanding of spiritual matters. However, after my initial reading of Enoch, I thought the text was really nonsensical and plain gibberish. It would be several years later, after considering other related research, that the text began to make sense—bringing clarity to controversial areas of study, and, surprisingly, actually confirming various elements of the Scriptures of the Bible that many teachers and persons in leadership have simply overlooked—even flat-out dismissed.

Looking back on things, I now realize my initial lack of understanding of the passages of Enoch was not unlike my initial inability to understand the Scriptures of the Bible as an unsaved, secular human being. It is through the Holy Spirit where understanding of spiritual matters is brought into clear focus. So, there was a time when I had dismissed the Book of Enoch. Now, its revelations have continued to surprise me and have actually strengthened my faith in the Lord and His Word.

As a final note here, there is great prophetic and symbolic significance regarding lives and relationship of both Enoch and Noah. Enoch was Noah's great grandfather. They were four generations apart. The Bible cites that many of the pre-flood men lived much longer lives than post-flood men, due to a massive shift in environmental change, such as Noah who lived 950 years: 600 years pre-flood (Genesis 7:11) and 350 years post-flood (Genesis 9:28–29). The post-flood lifespans were reduced to a maximum of 120 years (Genesis 6:3). This is exactly what we are experiencing today where the oldest humans on record are between 114 to 119 years old. However, pre-flood, Enoch only lived 365 years due to the fact that God "took him" (Genesis 5:23–24). Enoch was the very first person to be raptured. Enoch did not die a natural death. This is reinforced in Hebrews 11:5 where it is stated that Enoch "should not see death" and that "God had *translated* him" (emphasis added). The word *translated* is derived from the Greek word *metatithemi* [3346] which means, transport, change, and remove.

The profound revelation to this is the fact that Enoch was raptured before the great tribulation, the Great Flood, of his time. Enoch symbolically represents the future *raptured saints* to be taken (transported and removed) before the future Great Tribulation. Noah, on the other hand, built the Ark and physically went through the great tribulation, the Great Flood, of his time. Noah symbolically represents the *tribulation saints*—those who are left behind after the Rapture and go through Great Tribulation just before the Second Coming of Christ. As God remembered Noah, through his tribulation (Genesis 8:1), so shall Jesus remember those who call on His name during the Great Tribulation (Revelation 20:4–6).

There is a reason for everything.

JESUS QUOTES ENOCH

Matthew 5:5
Blessed *are* the meek: for they shall inherit the earth.

Enoch 5:7
The elect shall possess light, joy and peace, and they shall inherit the earth

John 5:22
For the Father judgeth no man, but hath committed all judgment unto the Son:

Enoch 69:27
…the principal part of the judgment was assigned to him, the Son of man.

Luke 6:24
But woe unto you that are rich! for ye have received your consolation.

Enoch 94:8
Woe to you who are rich, for in your riches have you trusted; but from your riches you shall be removed.

Matthew 19:28
…ye also shall sit upon twelve thrones, judging the twelve tribes of Israel.

Enoch 108:12
I will place each of them on a throne of glory.

Matthew 26:24
The Son of man goeth as it is written of him: but woe unto that man by whom the Son of man is betrayed! it had been good for that man if he had not been born.

Enoch 38:2
Where will the habitation of sinners be . . . who have rejected the Lord of spirits. It would have been better for them, had they never been born.

HIDDEN ENCODED SCRIPTURE IN GENESIS

All names have a meaning associated with them (the Book of Names). When we look at the lineage of individuals in the Book of Genesis and translate their individual meanings we find this:

Adam	translated means 'man'
Seth	translated means 'appointed'
Enosh	translated means 'mortal'
Kenan	translated means 'sorrow'
Mahalalel	translated means 'the blessed God'
Jared	translated means 'shall come down'
Enoch	translated means 'teaching'
Methuselah	translated means 'His death shall bring'
Lamech	translated means 'the despairing'
Noah	translated means 'rest, or comfort'

We then see a revealing of a Scripture that describes the coming of the Lord, Jesus Christ to a future world (no mortal men could have planned this out):

"Man appointed mortal sorrow, the blessed God shall come down teaching {and/that} His death shall bring {to} the despairing rest, or comfort."

In Genesis 5 that describes this ancient lineage of man, we find that Enoch was the first person on earth to be Raptured (taken up into Third Heaven—Genesis 5:22–24). This is confirmed in Hebrews 11:5 where God 'translated' Enoch (*translated* from the Greek means "to transport" or "remove" or "carry away").

Also, very interesting is that Enoch was the very first human being to see Jesus Christ in Third Heaven—referred to as the "Son of man" in 1 Enoch (before coming to earth to be born as a baby and dying on the cross at Calvary).

BIBLICAL HISTORY OF HUMANITY

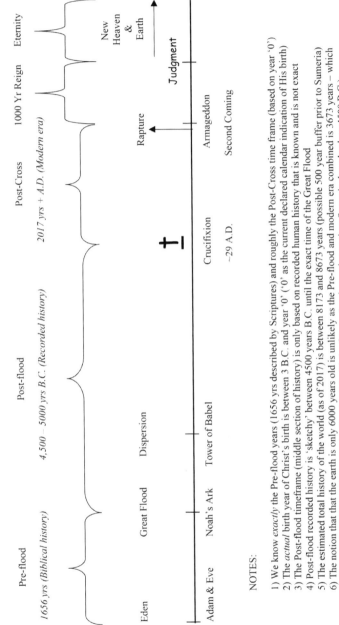

Pre-flood	Post-flood	Post-Cross	1000 Yr Reign	Eternity
1656 yrs (Biblical history)	*4,500 – 5000 yrs B.C. (Recorded history)*	*2017 yrs + A.D. (Modern era)*		

New
Heaven
&
Earth

Judgment

Rapture

Eden	Great Flood	Dispersion		Crucifixion		Armageddon

Adam & Eve · Noah's Ark · Tower of Babel · ~29 A.D. · Second Coming

NOTES:

1) We know *exactly* the Pre-flood years (1656 yrs described by Scriptures) and roughly the Post-Cross time frame (based on year '0')
2) The *actual* birth year of Christ's birth is between 3 B.C. and year '0' ('0' as the current declared calendar indication of His birth)
3) The Post-flood timeframe (middle section of history) is only based on recorded human history that is known and is not exact
4) Post-flood recorded history is 'sketchy' between 4500 years B.C. until the exact time of the Great Flood
5) The estimated total history of the world (as of 2017) is between 8173 and 8673 years (possible 500 year buffer prior to Sumeria)
6) The notion that that the earth is only 6000 years old is unlikely as the Pre-flood and modern era combined is 3673 years – which leaves only 2327 years between the flood and the birth of Jesus (we know that ancient Sumeria dates back to 4500 B.C.)
7) Based on the information above, our world is less than 10,000 years old

*Illustration purpose only – not displayed to exact scale

© 2017 Search Light Presentation Ministry

SECTION III ENDNOTES

85   Article, *The Breastplate of Precious Stones*, excerpt from *From Egypt to Canaan*, Jonathan Bayley, 1867, posted on The Science of Corespondances, website: http://www.scienceofcorrespondences.com/breastplate-of-precious-stones.htm

86   Article, *Stones of Fire*, Dr. Daniel K. Olukoya, Nairaland Forum, April 16th, 2006, website: http://www.nairaland.com/10704/stones-fire-courtesy-dr-daniel

87   Article, *Space Volcanoes*, NASA Space Place, October 2, 2013, website: http://spaceplace.nasa.gov/volcanoes/en/

88   Article, *Astrocrystals*, segment, *The Planets and their Crystals*, website: http://www.astrocrystals.com/crystal-zodiac?chapter=2

89   Article, *Christian Angelology*, Wikipedia, website: https://en.wikipedia.org/wiki/Christian_angelology

90   Article, *Kuiper Belt Objects: Facts About the Kuiper Belt & KBOs*, Nola Taylor Redd, Space.com contributor, January 22, 2016, website: http://www.space.com/16144-kuiper-belt-objects.html

91   Article, *Asteroid Belt: Facts & Formation*, Nola Taylor Redd, Space.com contributor, June 11, 2012, website: http://www.space.com/16105-asteroid-belt.html

92   Article, Ibid.

93   Article, Ibid.

94   Article, Ibid.

95   Quote, *Dawn Discovers Evidence for Organic Material on Ceres*, Jet Propulsion Laboratory, California Institute of Technology, February 16th, 2017, website: https://www.jpl.nasa.gov/news/news.php?release=2017-042

96   Quote, Weathering, Geology, Encyclopedia Britannica, Jan 21, 2011, website: https://www.britannica.com/science/weathering-geology

97   Quote, *Comments on Velikovsky*, Harry Hess, The Velikovsky Encyclopedia, website: http://www.velikovsky.info/Harry_H._Hess

98   Quote, *Gods, Demons and Symbols of Ancient Mesopotamia: An Illustrated Dictionary*, page 34, Jeremy Black and Anthony Green, University of Texas Press, August 1992

99   Article, *Tiamat*, Wikipedia, website: https://en.wikipedia.org/wiki/Tiamat

100 Article, Ibid.

101 Article, *The Worship of Jupiter*, Immanuel Velikovsky, website: http://www.varchive.org/itb/jupiter.htm

102 Article, *Tiamat*, Micha F. Lindermans, Encyclopedia Mythica, March 3rd, 1997, website: http://www.pantheon.org/articles/t/tiamat.html

103 Article, *Tiamat Planet theory*, Token Rock, website: http://www.tokenrock.com/explain-tiamat-planetary-theory-144.html

104 Article, Ibid.

105 Article, *Nibiru (Babylonian Astronomy)*, Wikipedia, website: https://en.wikipedia.org/wiki/Nibiru_%28Babylonian_astronomy%29

106 Article, *Tiamat*, Forgotten Realms Wiki, website: http://forgottenrealms.wikia.com/wiki/Tiamat

107 Article, *Jewish History*, Joshua (1355-1245 BCE), website: http://www.chabad.org/library/article_cdo/aid/129625/jewish/Joshua.htm

108 Article, *The Name Rahab in the Bible*, Abarim Publications, website: http://www.abarim-publications.com/Meaning/Rahab.html#.WLb6sIWcGUk

109 Article, *Dragons and Sea Monsters*, Hebrew Bible, Word Press, website: https://dragonsandseamonsters.wordpress.com/enuma-elish/

110 Article, *What is the Typical Temperature on Mars?*, The Astronomy Café, Questions and Answers, Solar System, website: http://www.astronomycafe.net/FAQs/q2681x.html

111 Article, *Valless Marineri: Facts About the Grand Canyon of Mars*, Nola Taylor Reid, Space.com contributor, March 29th, 2013, website: http://www.space.com/20446-valles-marineris.html

112 Article, *Ocean Trench*, National Geographic Society, website: http://www.nationalgeographic.org/encyclopedia/ocean-trench/

113 Article, *Mount St. Helens: Evidence in Support of Biblical Catastrophism*, NW Creation Network, 2016, website: http://nwcreation.net/mtsthelens.html

114 Article, *Footprints of a Martian Flood*, Mars Express, European Space Agency, Feb 18th, 2016, website: http://www.esa.int/Our_Activities/Space_Science/Mars_Express/Footprints_of_a_martian_flood

115 Quote, *Cydonia, Mars, "The Stones of Fire" and Pre-Adamic Civilizations*, submitted by Simon Gerrard, Hidden Mysteries The Magazine, website: http://www.hiddenmysteries.org/themagazine/vol11/research/cydonia.shtml

116 Article, *Astera, What Does Astera Mean?* Think Baby Names, 2017, website: http://www.thinkbabynames.com/meaning/0/Astera

117 Article, *Hellas Basin: Mars Deep Down*, SpaceRef: Mars Today, August 18th, 2014. Source: European Space Agency, website: http://spaceref.com/mars/hellas-basin-mars-deep-down.html

118 Article, *Tharsis Montes*, NASA's Mars Exploration Program, website: http://mars.jpl.nasa.gov/gallery/atlas/tharsis-montes.html

119 Article, *The Tallest Mountains in the Solar System*, Sarah Zielinski, Smithsonian.com, January 12th, 2012, website: http://mars.jpl.nasa.gov/gallery/atlas/tharsis-montes.html

120 Article, *Mars' Moons: Facts About Phobos and Deimos*, Nola Taylor Reid, June 27th, 2016, Space.com Contributor, website: http://www.space.com/20413-phobos-deimos-mars-moons.html

121 Article, *Deimos and Phobos*, Aaron J. Atsma, Theoi Project, 2000, website: http://www.theoi.com/Daimon/Deimos.html

122 Article, *Cell-Like Structures Found in Martian Meteorite*, The Red Planet, JPL NASA, Janet Fang, September 15th, 2014, Website: http://www.iflscience.com/space/cell-structure-found-martian-meteorite/

123 Article, *Cydonia (region of Mars)*, *"Face on Mars"*, Wikipedia, The Free Encyclopedia, website: https://en.wikipedia.org/wiki/Cydonia_(region_of_Mars)

124 Article, *The 20 Highest-Grossing Movies of All Time*, Metal Floss, Austin Thompson and Haley Harding, July 18th, 2015, website: http://mental-floss.com/article/64952/20-highest-grossing-movies-all-time

125 Article, *10 Official Government Agencies That Studied UFOs*, Listverse, David Tormsen, March 23, 2015, website: http://listverse.com/2015/03/23/10-official-government-programs-that-studied-ufos/

126 Article, CDB Evolution Inc., Gary Tahlmore, President, website: http://www.cdb.li/cdb-evolution-staff.html

127 Article, *May 16, 1960, Researcher Shines A Laser Light*, Wired, Randy Alfred, May 16th, 2011, website: https://www.wired.com/2011/05/0516maiman-creates-first-laser-ruby-crystal/

128 Article, *Alien Implants*, Alien-UFO Research, website: http://alien-ufo-research.com/alien-implants/

129 Segment, *Film Appearance*, Jacques Vallée, Wikipedia, website: https://en.wikipedia.org/wiki/Jacques_Vall%C3%A9e

130 Quote, *Five Arguments Against the Extraterrestrial Origin of Unidentified Flying Objects*, Jacques F. Vallée, Journal of Scientific Exploration, page 105, Vol 4, No 1, Pergamon Press, 1990, website: http://www.jacquesvallee.net/bookdocs/arguments.pdf

131 Quote, *Jacques Vallée Quotes*, AZ Quotes, website: http://www.azquotes. com/author/33226-Jacques_Vallee

132 Quote, Ibid.

133 Quote, Ibid.

134 *From Here to Armageddon: I Am Ashtar*, Second Edition, Phoenix Source Publishers Inc., 1995, website: http://www.phoenixsourcedistributors.com/ Phoenix_Journal_005.pdf

135 Article, *Heaven's Gate (Religious Group)*, Wikipedia, website: https://en.wikipedia.org/wiki/Heaven%27s_Gate_%28religious_group%29

136 Article, Ibid.

137 Article, Ibid.

138 Article, Ibid.

139 Article, Ibid.

140 Article, Ibid.

141 Article, Ibid.

142 Article, Ibid.

143 Article, Ibid.

144 Article, Ibid.

145 Article, *The Ankh*, Definition, Ancient History Encyclopedia, Joshua J, Mark, September 19th, 2016, website: http://www.ancient.eu/Ankh/

146 Article, *L.U.C.I.F.E.R. Project*, Truth for the Coming Deception, Time to Believe, January 29th, 2013, website: http://www.timetobelieve. com/2013/01/l-u-c-i-f-e-r-project/

147 Article, Ibid.

148 Article, *Tom Horn—The Vatican, Pope and UFOs: How Are They Linked?*, Tom Horn, Koinonia House Resource Center, 2013, website: https://resources.khouse.org/individual_sessions/dlkidvd27d/

149 Article, *Pope Contradicts Genesis Account of Creation, Argues 'God and Evolution' Are Compatible*, Heather Clark, Christian News Network, October 27th, 2014, website: http://christiannews.net/2014/10/27/pope-refutes-genesis-account-of-creation-argues-god-and-evolution-are-compatible/

150 Article, *Genetically Modified Sweet Corn Can Reduce Insecticide Use*, Science Daily, Entomological Society of America, October 7th, 2013, website: https://www.sciencedaily.com/releases/2013/10/131007094508.htm

151 Article, *What is Fructose?*, Norma Devault, Livestrong, September 25th, 2015, website: http://www.livestrong.com/article/128948-fructose/

152 Article, *Genetically Modified Organism*, History, Wikipedia, website: https://en.wikipedia.org/wiki/Genetically_modified_organism

153 Article, *In Cloning, Failure Far Exceeds Success*, Science, Gina Kolata, New York Times, December 11th, 2001, website: http://www.nytimes.com/2001/12/11/science/in-cloning-failure-far-exceeds-success.html

154 Article, *The Pros and Cons of Cloning*, Natasha Quinonez, Udemy Blog, May 26th, 2014, website: http://www.nytimes.com/2001/12/11/science/in-cloning-failure-far-exceeds-success.html

155 Article, T. Rex Soft Tissues Found Preserved, Hillary Mayell, National Geographic, March 24th, 2005, website: http://news.nationalgeographic.com/news/2005/03/0324_050324_trexsofttissue.html

156 Article, *Steven Spielberg*, Wikipedia, website: https://en.wikipedia.org/wiki/Steven_Spielberg

157 Article, *Alignment of the Pyramids to True North*, website: http://www.math.nus.edu.sg/aslaksen/gem-projects/hm/0102-1-pyramids/page1002.htm

158 Chart, *The Course of Abijah Points To The Birth of Christ*, Mary Casale, 2001, website: http://www.marieslibrary.com/PDF_Articles/JesusBornCourseOfAbijah.pdf

159 Article, *The Jewish Calendar*, Bible Truth Website, Cooper P Abrams III, 1996, website: http://bible-truth.org/Feasts-Jewishcalendar.html

160 Article, *When Exactly was Jesus Born?* Chapel Perilous, 1998, website: http://petragrail.tripod.com/page5.html

161 Article, Ibid.

162 Article, Ibid.

163 Article, Ibid.

164 Article, *Feast of the Immaculate Conception*, Wikipedia, website: https://en.wikipedia.org/wiki/Feast_of_the_Immaculate_Conception

165 Article, Ibid.

166 Article, *Calculating December 25th as the Birth of Jesus in Hippolytus' Canon and Chronicon*, Thomas C. Schmidt, Yale Religious Studies, Vigiliae Christianae, 2015, website: https://tcschmidtblog.files.wordpress.com/2015/11/schmidt-calculating-december-25-as-the-birth-of-jesus-in-hippolytus1.pdf

167 Article, *When Exactly was Jesus Born?* Chapel Perilous, 1998, website: http://petragrail.tripod.com/page5.html

168 Article, Ibid.

169 Article, Ibid.

170 Article, Ibid.

171 Article, Ibid.

172 Article, *Immaculate Conception Became Catholic Doctrine*, Church History Timeline, Dianna Severance, PhD, edited by Dan Graves MSL, July 2007, website: http://www.christianity.com/church/church-history/timeline/1801-1900/immaculate-conception-became-catholic-doctrine-11630497.html

173 Article, Ibid.

174 Article, *St. Nicholas, Bishop of Myra*, Editors of Encyclopedia Briannica, March 28, 2017, website, https://www.britannica.com/biography/Saint-Nicholas

175 Article, Magic *Mushrooms May Explain Santa & His Flying Reindeer*, Douglas Main, Live Science, December 20th , 2012, website: https://www.livescience.com/25731-magic-mushrooms-santa-claus.html

176 Article, *Peyote*, Hallucinogens, website: http://hallucinogens.com/peyote/

177 Article, *Chasing the Dragon*, Woody, Urban Dictionary, December 29th, 2004, website: http://www.urbandictionary.com/define.php?term=Chasing%20the%20dragon

178 Article, Project MK-Ultra, Wikipedia, website: https://en.wikipedia.org/wiki/Project_MKUltra

179 Article, *Jeremiah and Jesus: Warning, Lament and Comfort*, Hebrew for Christians, John J. Parsons, website: http://www.hebrew4christians.com/Holidays/Summer_Holidays/Tishah_B_Av/Jeremiah/jeremiah.html

180 Article, *The Sacrifice of the Mass*, The Two Babylons, Chapter IV, Section III, The Alexander Hislop, website: http://www.biblebelievers.com/babylon/sect43.htm

181 Article, Ibid.

RECOMMENDED INFO

BOOKS

Alien Encounters	Dr. Chuck Missler / Dr. Mark Eastman
Something's Going On Out There	David Wimbish
UFOs: Operation Trojan Horse	John A. Keel
Messengers of Deception	Dr. Jacques Vallée
Alien Agenda	Jim Marrs
Top Secret/Majic	Stanton Friedman
UFOs: Generals, Pilots and Government	Leslie Kean
Crop Circles: Harbingers of World Change	Alick Bartholomew
Circular Evidence	Colin Andrews / Pat Delgado
The Watchers	Raymond E. Fowler
Intruders	Budd Hopkins
Abduction: Human Encounters with Aliens	Dr. John E. Mack
Alien Rapture: The Chosen	Brad Steiger / Edgar Rothschild Fouche
The Omega Conspiracy	I.D.E. Thomas
Fallen Angels and Aliens	Steve Quayle
Genetic Armageddon	Steve Quayle
Fingerprints of the Gods	Graham Hancock
The Monuments of Mars	Richard C. Hoagland
Dark Mission: Secret History of NASA	Richard C. Hoagland
Cydonia: The Secret Chronicles of Mars	David Flynn
Temple at the Center of Time	David Flynn

Conversations with Ogotemmeli:	Marcel Griaule
An Introduction to Dogon Religious Ideas	
The Canadian UFO Report	Chris Rutkowski
America B.C	Barry Fell
Mysteries of the Mexican Pyramids	Peter Tompkins
Dragons or Dinosaurs?	Darek Isaacs
Pagan Christianity	Frank Viola / George Barna
The Vatican's Holocaust	Avro Manhattan
Faith Undone	Roger Oakland
The Evidence for Creation	Roger Oakland / Dr. G.S. McLean
The Design and Complexity of the Cell	Dr. Jeffrey Tomkins
The Signature of God	Grant R. Jeffrey
Preparing For Eternity	Mike Gendron
Me & Lee	Judith Vary Baker
Dr. Mary's Monkey	Edward T. Haslam

VIDEOS

Return of the Nephilim	Dr. Chuck Missler
The Watchman Chronicles	L.A. Marzulli
The UFO Conspiracy	Brian Barkley
Aliens & UFOs: The Secret Agenda	Alchemy Werks
Dark Mission: The Secret History of NASA	Mike Bara / Richard C. Hoagland
Loose Change 9/11	Jason Bermas / Dylan Avery
Invisible Empire:	
A New World Order Defined	Jason Bermas / Alex Jones
Freemasonry: From Darkness to Light?	Jeremiah Films
Secret Mysteries of America	Christian J. Pinto
Searching For the Truth on Origins	Roger Oakland
Food Matters	James Colquhoun / Carlo Ledesma
Genetic Roulette	Jeffrey Smith

FILMS PRODUCED BY HOLLYWOOD (Now seen in a new light)

Close Encounters of the Third Kind
Fire in the Sky
Kpax
The Astronaut's Wife
The Arrival

Dark City
Contact
The Forgotten
The Invasion
Taken (Steven Spielberg 10 part series)
The Fourth Kind
Area 51
5 Million Years to Earth (1967)
Skyline
Prometheus
The Host
Oblivion

WEBSITES
Website on Alien Abduction Overview:
http://www.crystalinks.com/abduction.html

Dr. John Mack & Budd Hopkins Exchange:
http://hiddenexperience.blogspot.ca/2011/10/hopkins-and-mack-side-by-side.html

UFO Sighting Archives:
www.anomymousFO.com

ABOUT THE AUTHOR

Mark always had an interest in writing throughout his early school years. However, after pursuing a career in music in the United States and eventually returning back to Canada, he moved from a small city in British Columbia to a small city in Saskatchewan. Rebuilding his life, Mark experienced various lines of work, from major construction projects to becoming a financial advisor in the Credit Union system to being a Senior Sales Consultant in retail to working with a national courier service. All through this time, Mark began to receive revelations from God—starting in 1986, but with a major revelation in May of 1988.

Since those early years, Mark recognized that he was a sinner. He has declared and has received Jesus Christ as Lord and Savior of his life. He married and started a family and continued to pursue research and study of God's Word in the areas of Eschatology and Creation research during the early 1990s. For over twenty-eight years, some thirteen thousand hours of research and study have been logged in.

After attending various conferences, Mark was inspired to develop multiple presentations (based on both his own research and the collective research of others). Mark has presented these at speaking seminars to the general public over a period of four years. Plans are currently being made to develop these presentations into DVD format in the near future.

It was at this point that Mark was led by the Holy Spirit to write his first book, *What Happens at the Rapture?* as a first step. This second book, *A Strong Delusion: Fallen Angels and Demons Revealed* was a four-year project derived from one of his live presentations of the same title.

All of this will be collectively presented and offered through a ministry website under Search Light Presentation Ministry. The desired goal is to share the validity of the Word of God, demonstrating the Spiritual nature of man and the validity of the coming event of the Rapture fulfilling the redeemed church under Christ for all eternity.

Check out Mark Toop's best selling first book,
What Happens at the Rapture?

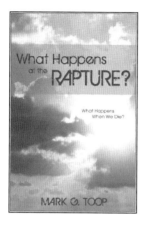

There are varied opinions regarding death, the after-life and the much-debated event of the Rapture. This book probes deep into the Word of God to reveal what is actually stated within these Scriptures.

It is Mark's prayer that you will find increased spiritual revelation and deeper understanding, as led by the Holy Spirit, after carefully and prayerfully considering *What Happens at the Rapture?*

You are encouraged to open your Bible and read along as you embark on this journey of spiritual understanding.

"I highly encourage you to read this inspirational book and allow yourself the opportunity of unraveling a mystery like no other. It will set you on a path to fully comprehend that death itself has been conquered and will shift your focus now for a transition into wonders that God has reserved for you. You will find treasures that will remain in you and will move you to seek more. This is a wonderful gift that comes to us by a divinely inspired and spiritually guided writer."

—Dristin J. Suarez

"A well written book about a complicated subject. A great read for the believer and a great read for a non-believer or a person searching about salvation. The book is written with all the content being applicable to the subject, that is, not a lot of filler text to just take up volume. It gives the reader a written disposition on the subject as well as graphs and a point form summary. It points the reader to Salvation texts from the Bible as well as plenty of references to support his writings. I appreciate the matter of fact approach the author has taken to express the content subject."

—Wally Groot